Social Justice in
World Cinema and Theatre

Recent Titles in
Civic Discourse for the Third Millennium
Michael H. Prosser, Series Editor

Civic Discourse: Multiculturalism, Cultural Diversity, and Global
Communication, Volume 1
K. S. Sitaram and Michael H. Prosser, editors

Civic Discourse: Intercultural, International, and Global Media,
Volume 2
Michael H. Prosser and K. S. Sitaram, editors

The Double Helix: Technology and Democracy in the American Future
Edward Wenk, Jr.

Civic Discourse, Civil Society, and Chinese Communities
Randy Kluver and John H. Powers, editors

Human Rights in the International Public Sphere: Civic Discourse
for the 21st Century
William Over

Civic Discourse and Digital Age Communications in the Middle East
Leo A. Gehr and Hussein Y. Amin, editors

Culture and Technology in the New Europe: Civic Discourse in
Transformation in Post-Communist Nations
Laura Lengel, editor

Civic Discourse: Communication, Technology, and Cultural Values,
Volume 3
K. S. Sitaram and Michael H. Prosser, editors

In Search of Greatness: Russia's Communications with Africa and the
World
Festus Eribo

The Remaking of the Chinese Character and Identity in the 21st
Century: The Chinese Face Practices
Wenshan Jia

Social Justice in World Cinema and Theatre

William Over

Civic Discourse for the Third Millennium
Michael H. Prosser, Series Editor

ABLEX PUBLISHING
Westport, Connecticut • London

Library of Congress Cataloging-in-Publication Data

Over, William.
 Social justice in world cinema and theatre / William Over.
  p. cm.—(Civic discourse for the third millennium)
 Includes bibliographical references and index.
 ISBN 1–56750–522–X (alk. paper)—ISBN 1–56750–553–8 (pbk. : alk. paper)
  1. Theater—Political aspects—Developing countries. 2. Political plays—
History and criticism. 3. Theater and society—Developing countries.
 4. Motion pictures—Political aspects—Developing countries. I. Title.
 II. Series.
 PN2049.O95 2001
 809.2′9358—dc21   00–049577

British Library Cataloguing in Publication Data is available.

Library of Congress Catalog Card Number: 00–049577
ISBN: 1–56750–552–X
       1–56750–553–8 (pbk.)

First published in 2001

Ablex Publishing, 88 Post Road West, Westport, CT 06881
An imprint of Greenwood Publishing Group, Inc.
www.ablexbooks.com

Printed in the United States of America

The paper used in this book complies with the
Permanent Paper Standard issued by the National
Information Standards Organization (Z39.48–1984).

10 9 8 7 6 5 4 3 2 1

For Terry,
supporter and best critic

CONTENTS

PREFACE

One of George Bernard Shaw's characters once quipped that the upper classes need the lower classes to keep them in line. This is perhaps more true in a different way than even Shaw in his typical understatement meant. The drama of social justice reveals lives at the bottom in vivid detail, an endeavor that can inform the most advanced progressive thought, clarifying democratic agendas for the future. Just how the changing idioms of human dignity, justice, identity, and commonality will shape the trajectories of history remains uncertain. Still, drama has within its varied expressions capacities yet undiscovered, for peoples and locations unrealized. Shaw's remark recognizes that the communities of the least power and freedom in a culture often possess the greatest ability to uncover new social truths and awaken political commitment. Extending Shaw's comment beyond its class basis, other marginalized identities need to be included in drama's brief chronicles of the times. Social justice and human rights issues are rarely studied as subject matter in dramatic forms, despite the drama's lengthy history of social and political involvement. Advocacy and dramatic performance, as often as not undertaken by relatively powerless minorities, continue to inspire mainstream as well as minority audiences.

This study attempts to include many disempowered and oppressed communities represented by world drama, in both the first and third worlds. It is, by admission, in no way comprehensive. Rather, it offers selected instances of cinematic and theatrical production, together with their official and unofficial movements, for the purpose of appreciating unique social and political discourses. While I have given some consideration to geographical, cultural, and demographic variety, this volume has ignored some significant dramatic traditions that operate from a political perspective. Some of these cultures are easily recognized by their absence: the Arab world, India—always a dynamic and manifold source for social commentary—and the exciting nascent forms inspired by the new South African state. My reasons for exclusion are primarily practical— each of these traditions demands its own full-length work and so awaits more study.

The relation of the arts in general to concrete social agendas for change has a long and not fully satisfactory history. The debate— perhaps ultimately unanswerable—as to whether or to what extent aesthetic structures can influence the direction of local and global history seems more inevitable than conclusive. The Romantics reintroduced the debate two centuries ago, but soon fell into a morass of absolute statements and parochial concerns. Poets such as Wordsworth, Burns, and Shelley recognized the dehumanizing possibilities of early industrial capitalism. Thus, Shelley's lament in *A Defense of Poetry*: "we want the poetry of life: our calculations have outrun conception; we have eaten more than we can digest," found a solution in "Poetry," which would counter "the Principle of Self," identified as "Money" (1965, p. 42). However, as Raymond Williams (1963) observed of Shelley's elevation of poetry as the particular antidote to the greed of industrialism, such a "specialization" became too narrow a focus, making poetry by itself ineffectual as a critical alternative to comprehensive social forces. For Williams, the Romantics failed to distinguish culture as art from culture as a way of life (pp. 59–60). Moreover, citing Wordsworth, Williams found that "a more active relationship" is needed to allow artistic expression to engage social change (pp. 57–58). Culture as a way of life rather than a narrow (elitist) specialty meant grounding artistic conventions, such as the drama, in social movements and settings. It is from within today's particular movements and settings that this study attempts to comprehend the drama of social justice.

Michael Prosser has encouraged and supported my decision to explore the relation of contemporary dramatic forms to social justice and human rights issues. His interdisciplinary approach to scholarship and his personal understanding of cross-cultural complexities has been an inspiration to me during this study. I would also like to thank K.S. Sitaram for his long-term recognition, as well as the many scholars and friends from the annual July intercultural communications conferences at Rochester Institute of Technology, developed and maintained by Michael Prosser and K.S. Sitaram,

This book is appropriate as a textbook for a variety of undergraduate and graduate courses, including areas of social science, cultural studies, area studies, intercultural communication, modern drama, and thematic courses in the humanities.

INTRODUCTION: LOCATING SOCIAL JUSTICE DRAMA

WITHIN AND BEYOND GLOBALIZATION

Social justice drama at the end of the twentieth century was decidedly heterogeneous in both content and form. Perhaps the one overriding characteristic, however, is its relatively slight productivity. While mainstream "boulevard" theatre as well as international corporate filmmaking (Hollywood foremost in the world, Bollywood the most prolific) have aimed at the inevitable formula for the sake of blockbuster sales and long-run predictability, human rights subject matter has remained largely neglected. The lack of social commitment extends as well to the U.S. independent film tradition, now a few decades old, which for the most part has remained content to produce somewhat more insightful or artistically ambitious versions of major studio subject matter. Moreover, New York and regional theatre playwrights have largely shunned "political plays," despite their somewhat more advantageous position as writers not for the broad public of the movies but for more homogeneous, selective urban audiences. There are, of course, notable exceptions among First World dramatists and film directors. My study explores the artistic styles, goals, and thematic interests of these positive exceptions. My use of the term "drama" throughout these chapters is wide and includes stage plays, street theatre, screenplays, videodramas, and their respective traditions.

Taking the notion of "the location of culture" from the postcolonial critic Homi Bhabha, I will explore the view that Third World cultures are at once part of the globalized world of transnational corporate power and technological development—the so-called global village of advanced communication—and also representative of their own local cultural traditions that to a great extent remain distinct from Western influence. The notion of cultural hybridity, the commensurability of cultures and human identities in a shrinking world, is manifest in the various drama and film movements worldwide that reflect social and political concerns. Certainly, non-Western playwrights and filmmakers of social protest have relied on the appeal of universal notions of human rights that have largely been articulated in the West. Yet, at the same time, these practitioners seek critical perspectives on the culture and thought traditions coming from the West. This potentially contradictory circumstance has nevertheless motivated many creative and effectual forms of politically based drama. The divided perspective of many postcolonial dramatists, film and videoplay writers has influenced both the form and content of their work. This study will also explore the ambivalences of postcolonial cultures as they enable or hinder the presentation of social justice issues within artistic and social contexts that have come to be interpreted in terms of the universalistic "human story."

In the twentieth century, the most significant social justice drama and films were produced in the Third World venue. Some countries, most notably Nigeria, have been blessed with a conscious national tradition of cultural development, particularly in drama, in their postcolonial periods. At the same time, many of these nations, including Nigeria, are cursed with recent histories of economic exploitation and political tyranny. Other countries, such as China and Taiwan, have recently rediscovered their largely oppressed traditions of drama and film and have undertaken the training of new generations of screenwriters and filmmakers in order to develop new national and international audiences. These traditions have decidedly progressive agendas that sit uneasily with official governmental policy. In Latin America, certain arts have flourished in some countries, such as poetry in Nicaragua during the Sandinista years and subsequently (Rushdie, 1987). However, drama and filmmaking remain tenuous traditions, largely because of a general lack of national focus, erratic economic and governmental support, and technical capacity. Nevertheless, as in the case of the U.S. film industry, there remain the notable exceptions. The *cinema novo* tradition of Brazil, for example, while offering a decidedly critical approach to the status quo in favor of social justice, has experienced alternating periods of governmental support and censorship since its emergence in the 1960s.

The following chapters focus on international social justice drama in its current local, national, and international manifestations. These three contexts developed from the historical particularities of colonial and postcolonial economic structures and educational institutions. The overwhelming majority of Third World playwrights and filmmakers received much of their general education and technical training in Western secondary schools and universities, a circumstance that has influenced their connection with international audiences as well as their relation—not always close—to their first cultures. Cultural hybridity can in this context hinder authentic dramatic expression, but it can also give that expression a cogency and perspective that challenges the existing order. Since the development of cultural hybridity within an increasingly globalized world is a major consideration in the assessment of the effectiveness of social issue drama, this study will consider the current state of international civil society and the conflictual nature of cultural allegiance experienced by many Third World dramatists and filmmakers.

Authenticity and International Recognition: Are They Incompatible?

To become recognized, Third World writers have commonly returned to the Western cultural forms acquired during their colonial and postcolonial schooling. While this may seem an obvious point, it is also a relative point—recognition by whom, for whom? Writers of "drama" are already writing in a Western form, which they learned not only in their formal education but through the cultural osmosis of television, radio, novels, and Western performing arts traditions. It is here that the major dilemma of social justice drama emerges. While these voices mainly seek to promote indigenous culture and to expose the negativities of Western civilization, particularly colonialism and neocolonialism, the cultural channels chosen for such criticism are often Western by default. This contradiction has by no means been insurmountable—as the many examples in the following chapters demonstrate—nonetheless, it has been a major concern of Third World stage- and screenwriters, who find their forms of drama prescribed or heavily influenced by European artistic conventions and their audiences often international rather than local. Writing about African theatre forms in the early 1980s, Michael Etherton (1982) painted a more pessimistic view than perhaps applies to the world situation at the beginning of the twenty-first century:

Taken together, these two observations—namely (1) an intellectual drama which barely touches the mass of the people though it professes to be concerned with them, and (2) a theatre of the people which in every instant seems quickly to become debased—raises the crucial problem of African drama and theatre in an acute form. (p. 318)

Another problem identified by Etherton deserving further examination is the tendency of postcolonial governments to exploit the "drama of the people" for its own ends—"The people's culture, and in particular those arts of the rural masses which have actually managed to survive colonialism, are used to reinforce the dominance of the new elites" (p. 316). Such co-optation has been documented in the films of Ousmane Sembene and has created a long-standing tension between artists and the state when controlled by indigenous political elites. The following chapters consider the implications of such dangers within particular settings. Despite these negatives, human rights and social justice groups, by utilizing the expanded global telecommunications systems during the 1990s, have greatly enhanced the international public sphere, just as the rapidly increasing number of nongovernmental organizations (NGOs) devoted to such issues have increased international awareness of conditions in local communities. These circumstances have given outwardly directed—as opposed to locally based—drama and film movements a positive rather than a negative value. However, the problem of cultural authenticity in drama of and for "the people" may remain as Etherton found it. The following chapters attempt to reconsider this dilemma, a project that must include an appraisement of cultural relativism as well as postcolonial hybridity, since the necessary conditions that make political drama culturally authentic cannot remain an unexamined given.

Associated with the problem of artistic allegiance is a further concern, the ability of social justice drama to foster real social change, given the nature of civil society in a world divided by nation states, ethnic and religious exclusivity, and the globalization of culture by transnational corporate power. When Third World playwrights and screenwriters seek to expose issues of social injustice, ecological spoliation, and obstacles to cultural identity on the national level, to some degree, they must universalize their messages in order to become internationally—and thus politically—viable. As Michael Clough (1999) has commented,

NGOs [nongovernmental organizations], ethnic groups, private associations and corporations alike must recognize that society can no longer afford for them to operate according to the narrow, self-interested, rights-oriented calculus of classical liberalism. Instead, they need to join in creating a new global ethic of responsibility. . . . The only reliable option for the poor and disempowered is self-reliance. (p. 18)

Fortunately, the need to create unifying social action movements that transcend national, religious, and ethnic boundaries is commensurate with the development of the international public sphere, where telecommunications, world publishing and performing arts traditions, and, most importantly, the recent rapid growth of nongovernmental organizations accommodate such artistic trajectories. Certainly, the incipient development of a vital international civil society can have its negative, retrogressive side, as David Rieff (1999) has cautioned (pp. 11–16). Still, the sheer abundance of progressive NGOs in the first and third worlds—along with a few socially responsible national governments—have created the possibility of a viable international audience for social justice theatre and "new film" movements of great variety.

In the post-Cold War era, where multilateral geopolitical movements seek to replace the unilateralist mandates of the older binary opposition, East and West, there is the possibility that a renewed investment in international cooperation and understanding will enhance social justice drama, particularly in Third World venues but also among subaltern groups within the First World. Emergent regional movements that clarify socially responsible agendas are beginning to call for such solidarity across continents. Nelson Mandela's unifying efforts among the postcolonial and post-apartheid states of southern Africa also envision the development of ideological forms of expression that include drama and film. At present, South Africa's traditional regional influence is expanding to all of sub-Saharan Africa, as the attempts in 1998 to solve the political strife in Congo demonstrate (Over, 1999, pp. 115–125). In Latin America, where the European colonial presence has been the longest and most profound, the *cinema novo* movements of various countries consciously influence each other by virtue of a common leftist political commitment and through the cultural integrity of a common language tradition (Spanish and Portuguese). In Asia, Taiwanese theatre forms and film traditions are beginning to question the past political repression of the Nationalist government, particularly as it has affected native Taiwanese culture (Wang, 1999).

Michael Etherton's assessment of the effectiveness of political drama for social and political change has generally been negative: "The theatre, and even its 'revolutionary' drama, remains inaccessible to the mass of people. The socially committed theatre contributes to the process of social change only insofar as the intellectuals themselves acquire political consciousness" (1982, p. 318). He leaves open the possibility, however, for more effective social action drama and performance activism in Africa, but only if playwrights and directors take a more direct interest in developing social consciousness among their less privileged citizens. This was the very concern of Bertolt Brecht's Epic Theatre theory, especially as it developed during the 1930s, in the face of Stalinist repression and the rise of European fascism.

DISTANCE AND EMPATHY IN POLITICAL DRAMA

Brecht's (1964) rejection of the "literarization" of European drama was grounded in his central thesis that theatre should speak to the great majority about their social condition. On this point his essays are clear and forceful: "There is only one ally against the growth of barbarism: the people on whom it imposes these sufferings. Only the people offer any prospects. Thus it is natural to turn to them, and more necessary than ever to speak their language" (p. 107). Confronted with the regrettable choice between the certain, though compromised, recognition afforded by the boulevard theatre and his own standards for social justice, Brecht by the mid-1930s decidedly opted for a theatre of social change. His polemic joined the intense debate in Europe between expressionism (Ernst Bloch) and "realism" (Georg Lukacs). Brecht's insights are perhaps more relevant to Third World drama today than they were to prewar Europe, since the commercialism of the boulevard theatre has been overtaken by the centripetal force of the globalized telecommunications industry during the 1980s and 1990s. His words, from a 1958 article, merit quoting at length.

As we have in mind a fighting people that is changing the real world, we must not cling to "well-tried" rules for telling a story, worthy models set up by literary history, eternal aesthetic laws. We must not abstract the one and only realism from certain given works, but shall make a lively use of all means, old and new, tried and untried, deriving from art and deriving from other sources, in order to put living reality in the hands of living people in such a way that it can be mastered. . . . Our conception of *realism* needs to be broad and political, free from aesthetic restrictions and independent of convention. (p. 109)

Certainly, the rejection of Western "worthy models" in favor of indigenous theatre forms and effective hybrid creations has been conscious, and often successful, in many African, Asian, and Latin American settings. Still, the ubiquity of global capital in the form of telecommunications programming, but also other Western models of culture—epitomized by the universal wearing of clothing with American-style logos advertising Western goods and pastimes—has made attempts at viable progressive drama in Third World settings difficult to sustain and even more difficult to distribute (Sanders, 1998).

Brecht's definition of realism, influenced in part by Lukacs' rebuttals, offers a confrontational approach to commercial art forms: "*Realist* means: laying bare society's causal network/showing up the dominant viewpoint of the dominators/writing from the standpoint of the class which has prepared the broadest solutions for the most pressing problems afflicting human society/emphasizing the dynamics of development/concrete and so as to encourage abstraction" (1964, p. 109). He understood that the exposition of concrete and local social issues and problems must be followed by the development of a capacity among the exploited to abstract from such particularities. This is necessary in order to comprehend the underlying causal connections between social inequality and economic power structures. Such abstraction is often missed by present-day activists in both the First and Third Worlds. For example, in a recent interview, the U.S. filmmaker and actor Tim Robbins prefers to forego ideology in his progressive films (referring specifically to *The Cradle Will Rock*, 1999):

The larger theme—you can't really humanize those kinds of things on film. I have to find something that I can key into that's very simple, very emotional and very personal. For me that's much more compelling than the grand statement. . . . if you're talking about a strike, for example, you don't need a hell of a lot of ideology or belief in any kind of socialism, communism, unionism, whatever. I would say eight out of ten workers don't have that. What they had was hunger. Hunger and fear of losing jobs and not being protected. You're approaching it from a personal point of view. . . . That's one of the traps that some period movies fall into—the fallacy that you have to express the philosophy in order to understand the time. I think what you have to do is express the hunger to understand the time. (Biskind, p. 17)

Brecht and many Third World advocates today would respond that the representation of hunger does not automatically suggest its solutions. What is needed is a realism, in Brecht's words, that is "broad and political," offering a dialectic that, while not necessarily presenting verbatim tracts from sociology, nonetheless comments on the social forces that influence the characters' individual desires and struggles. Brecht's character Mother Courage does this when she steps out of the play's dramatic action to explain to the audience why she did a particular stage action. Robbins, perhaps influenced in part by the pragmatism of traditional U.S. culture, in part by the Disney Corporation funding of *The Cradle Will Rock*, becomes ideological in his avoidance of ideology. Disputing this thinking, Brecht's "abstraction" has affinity with elements of Alan Monroe's "Motivated Sequence."

Monroe, a U.S. rhetorician at Purdue University, developed his method in the 1930s to motivate an audience—or "public"—for immediate action. While his strategy was primarily intended for speeches and was ultimately used widely in the advertising industry, its relevance to didactic and activist drama remains. He developed five steps that follow what he regarded as the psychology of persuasion: (1) Attention; (2) Need; (3) Satisfaction; (4) Visualization; (5) Action. Most relevant here is the last step, Action. "Once the audience is convinced your policy is beneficial, you are ready to call for action. Say exactly what you want the audience to do—and how to do it. . . . Then conclude with a final stirring appeal that reinforces their commitment to act" (Lucas, 1998, p. 389).

A basic rubric of advertising today, Monroe's Motivated Sequence emphasizes Step 3, Satisfaction, which presents a solution to the problem, and ends with Step 5, the "call to action." The pervasiveness of this strategy today in U.S. and transnational advertising calls into question the view of Robbins and other film activists who stop short of ideological solutions in their screenplays. Typically restricted by market-sensitive corporate financing rather than official censorship policy, most politically motivated drama in the U.S. must present the heart without the head, leaving audiences to interpret implied conclusions only. However, Monroe's theory was expressly devised to overcome the insufficiency of such discourse, which brings the spectator or listener to new perceptions without identifying underlying causes and—from there—offering possible solutions. For Robbins and any other Hollywood filmmaker to suggest boycotts, civil demonstrations, local networking, and so on, in their films would be unprecedented, and perhaps result initially in little or no distribution, at least through mainstream industry channels. However, ways of circumventing such corporate practices remain possible.

Mainstream dramatic criticism has commonly devalued political statement in drama, arguing that the ideas expressed by the characters are less important than the characters' interactions within particular social settings. Thus Susanne Langer (1968) distinguished between "environment" and "setting": "Where 'environment' enters into drama at all, it enters as an idea entertained by persons in the play, such as slum visitors and reformers of the 'radical' problem play. They themselves, however, do not appear in an environment, because that sociological abstraction has no meaning for the theater." For Langer, environment is an "invisible constant," which does not immediately affect the characters, in contrast to setting (p. 257). Such distinctions, however, may apply only to plays of popular realism, where the *mise-en-scène* attempts photographic reality, the plots are illusionistic and linear, and the performance style representational. On the other hand, in the Epic Theatre tradition of Brecht and Erwin Piscator, characters step out of the action to comment on their actions, choruses present running commentary, and multimedia effects, such as projections of news photographs and quotations, can give Langer's "environment" a place within the dramatic/theatrical performance.

That Brecht's own plays have typically stopped short of offering Monroe's Steps 3 and 5—Satisfaction and Action in the form of articulated solutions—derives from Brecht's stagecraft, which usually avoids ideological formulation in favor of articulating the social and political forces influencing the characters' individual and group actions. Thus Brechtian "abstraction" comments on the dramatic action without becoming prescriptive or overly committed ideologically. Epic Theatre's "Visualization," Step 3 of Monroe, shows the connection between the action of individuals in the drama and broader structures of power. Step 5, Call to Action, remains only implicit in Brecht's most famous plays. By contrast, in much of contemporary political drama and performance theatre of the Third World—the California-based Teatro Camposino, for example, solutions are often explicit and overtly hortatory. Aesthetic distance—the actors' ignoring the audience—is frequently broken in favor of direct discourse with the audience, and audience participation in the dramatic action is encouraged to varying degrees. Since the 1960s, theatre performance styles for political activism—from "street theatre" to discreet productions at national religious shrines—have demonstrated great variability and effectiveness. Hence, the legacy of Brecht has transcended the particular stage interpretations of his own theory. Before considering particular dramas and films in their political and social settings, it is necessary to look more closely at the elements of performed drama that most concern plays of social justice worldwide.

What Works Best for Social Justice?

Brecht considered "the technique of sympathetic understanding" endemic to the commercial theatre the main hindrance to the development of a viable and efficacious political drama. Audiences typically are guided to empathize with the protagonist, feeling and thinking what he or she feels and thinks, in order to gain the vicarious pleasure of a night out at the theatre. His solution was the famous *Verfremdungseffekt* (alienation effect), which allows the audience to view characters beyond their individual conflicts by focusing on the social context of their struggle. "The process of alienation . . . is the process of historifying, of presenting events and persons as historical, and therefore as ephemeral" (Calderwood & Toliver, 1968, p. 273). More is involved in the Epic Theatre technique, however, than bringing to center stage the broader historical matter. The audience, according to Brecht, must also be "surprised" by what they experience. They must come to see the characters and action in a new, strange way. This is required not only to allow theatregoers to break loose from the centripetal force of the commercial drama's pathos of individualism, but also to bring in a new kind of didactic drama—one that educates through shock and surprise to propel the audience into a critical perspective.

Brecht was not alone among twentieth-century dramatists in demanding radically new responses from his audiences, but his structurally innovative performance techniques have a straightforward goal—the exposure of the underlying structures of power within contemporary society. Epic Theatre's distancing effect avoided what he called "the illusionary, passive, resigned-to-fate attitude" of the commercial drama" (1964, p. 272). To what extent his famous distancing effect (alienation effect; A-effect) can be attributed to a presentational acting style, multimedia commentary, and narrative techniques, on the one hand, and, on the other, an overtly political message that undermines conventional dramatic resolutions, remains unsettled. Certainly, in the 1990s, Hollywood films typically avoided issue-based plots that challenged the status quo. John Clark (1999) observes, "The public will accept a political film if it's driven by story and character, and has an element of wish-fulfillment in it—in other words, if the politics depicted are as Americans would like them to be, driven by idealism, rather than as they are, partisan and opportunistic" (p. 33). Here the "idealism" is overly determined by stereotypes of national myth, such as the altruistic Founding Fathers, best-intentioned international police actions, heroic freedom fighters—all products of U.S. foreign policy exceptionalism. Brecht would immediately have dismissed such dramatic fare as overtly nationalistic and retrogressive. Happily, Third World political playwrights and filmmakers have been quite conscious of the pitfalls created by First World film and theatre industries, which depend upon profit from a few apolitical—but inevitably supportive of the status quo—blockbuster hits to carry their industry (Schatz, 1999, pp. 26–31; Cooper, 1999, pp. 21–26).

Socially conscious international New Cinema directors and political theatre practitioners have proven Brecht's contention that the theatre of social justice is so easily exportable because it is so highly adaptable. Writing in 1961, Brecht envisioned not one political thea-

tre but innumerable, all of which must face the challenge of a socially unequal and unjust world: "How can the shackled, ignorant,
freedom- and knowledge-seeking human being of our century, the
tormented and heroic, abused and ingenious, the changeable and
the world-changing human being of this frightful and important
century achieve his own theatre which will help him to master not
only himself but also the world?" (Calderwood & Toliver, 1968,
p. 275). Forty years later, democratic movements within postcolonial
societies, under threat from the pervasive effects of global capital
and political elites at home, have created a more responsive Third
World tradition of political drama. Issues of distance in the theatre
have been overshadowed by the challenge of creating a performance
approach that reaches out to the disenfranchised. This project has
proven formidable, since the globalization of business and the effects of telecommunications technology can only further endanger
particular cultural traditions and identities. What activist drama in
these societies has discovered is that Brecht's binary opposition of
empathic boulevard theatre and a distanced political theatre no longer applies—perhaps never applied—to many audience situations.
Rather than performance distance for audiences of the disenfranchised, political drama for social justice can offer immediacy and direct social commentary without excluding empathic response. Despite
the individualistic-based literary traditions of the European-derived
commercial theatre in their countries, these audiences are prepared
to connect—without distancing devices—actions and characters
with social themes. Aware of the contradictions between official
words and actions, the Third World poor are often already alienated
from the values propagated by the institutions of power within their
own countries. For these audiences, whose sense of irony is highly
developed, a special alienation effect would be gratuitous, since they
have been estranged from the dominant values of their globalized
societies for some time. Regrettably, much of this type of grassroots
theatre loses its authenticity when it is "discovered" and packaged
as a commodity for First and Third World elite audiences.

Clearly, other views of politically based drama need to be explored, as Brecht himself urged during his later, less dogmatic period. The philosopher Martha Nussbaum finds the educational value
of politically based drama in the imagination, which allows, in her
example, a young man to experience how it must feel to face concerns particular to women in most societies. Imagination, as a general human faculty, was assumed by Brecht, but never became a
critical term in his theory. On the other hand, to Nussbaum imagination through drama explicitly serves the exploration of human
similarities and differences. This kind of vicarious experience is valu-

able only if particularities, rather than generalities, remain the focus. Approaching theatre as a socially oriented artistic medium, Nussbaum is more confident than Brecht that the spectator can escape the drama's individualistic bias to make strange the dominant values of her or his society. Thus, Nussbaum finds the social value of drama not by escaping the complacency of commercial theatre and film fare, but by making universal connections through the concrete and particular. For her, Greek tragedy was supreme in the cogency of its universal messages, but it lacked the necessary knowledge applied to the particular: "The tragic form asks its spectators to cross cultural and national boundaries. On the other hand, in its universality and abstractness it omits much of the fabric of daily civic life, with its concrete distinctions of rank and power and wealth and the associated ways of thinking and speaking" (1997, p. 94). In Greek comedy Nussbaum locates the necessary local venue that allowed its Greek audiences to see how universal ideas such as justice and social well-being can be applied to the particularities of power structures. Although Nussbaum does not explore the discourse of social justice drama beyond her project of comparing Greek dramatic forms with contemporary needs to affirm the value of the other, she recognizes the unique value of political drama:

Literature does not transform society single-handed. . . . Certain ideas about others may be grasped for a time and yet not be acted upon, so powerful are the forces of habit and the entrenched structures of privilege and convention. Nonetheless, the artistic form makes its spectator perceive, for a time, the invisible people of their world—at least a beginning of social justice. (1997, p. 94)

Brecht might respond that the examples of her students' abilities to cross boundaries in order to appreciate other life experiences can succeed only in the comparatively special learning situation of a university classroom or among graduate students of a research center. There the alienation effect has already been carefully imbued by thoughtful teachers and focused study programs. In rebuttal, Nussbaum could state that her U.S. university students nevertheless need first to be shocked and surprised out of their passive acceptance of the mainstream media's version of reality, and so on, before they can begin to understand the plight of the Third World masses. In that case, First World political drama must take a different approach for more privileged audiences than for audiences in the Third World. With respect to disenfranchised and subaltern audiences in the First and Third Worlds, insight beyond the dominant version of reality may occur more readily, given the particular awareness of people who live under economic and social oppression. These chapters offer many examples of drama that is understood by audiences who have no special learning beyond their own collective experience of social injustice.

Brecht and Nussbaum agree that minds can be changed when their presuppositions are challenged. Other progressive voices have reaffirmed this basic optimism. For example, the U.S. activist and historian Howard Zinn (1999) notes that art, particularly the protest songs of folk music, has influenced both the labor movement of the 1930s and the civil rights movement of the 1960s (pp. 47–52). On the question of art and social transformation, he cautions that activists look too quickly for such change, when in fact progress may take much longer than anticipated (pp. 66–67). Zinn's *The Future of History* (1999) is intended as a positive rebuttal to the current body of political writing that presumes the end of history has arrived because the advent of worldwide democracy—in the form of neoliberal international capitalism—has brought the long history of class struggle to an end. While Zinn knows the struggle for social justice is not yet over, he remains confident that grassroots movements can prevent the abandonment of democratic practice, which he does not associate with global capitalism.

The Nigerian playwright, activist, Nobel laureate, and political theorist Wole Soyinka, now teaching at a U.S. university, values the power of literature, particularly drama, in the struggle for real democracy. He is by no means unschooled in the difficulty of the challenge ahead, particularly in Africa. Soyinka (1999) recently questioned the ultimate value of the current South Africa government's Truth and Reconciliation Program, intended to offer the former apartheid regime members amnesty (pp. 33–35). The hearings, proposed by Nelson Mandela and others, exonerated the perpetrators of crimes against humanity, a situation Soyinka finds compromising at best. Nigeria, which began its postcolonial period with a buoyant program of national cultural development—not the least of which was a grand vision of a national theatre and drama tradition—has nevertheless suffered from factions of economic self-interest and ethnic divisionism (Adedeji, 1993; Cohen, 1998c). Soyinka's worthy successor as national dramatist, Ken Saro-Wiwa, was murdered in the 1990s attempting to protest the corruption of oil money and military dictatorship. For Soyinka, only a conscientious program of clear national goals for political equality can overcome the penchant in colonial and postcolonial Africa to surrender democracy to local political elites and transnational corporate interests. However, in situations where human rights are denied and social equality is discouraged, the production of political drama, though difficult to establish, remains vital for maintaining political awareness. Countries such as

Taiwan, which has loosened its political restrictions in recent years, has begun to produce theatre forms critical of the status quo. In such political climates, the effectiveness of social drama, satire, and other performance pieces can often be measured and evaluated by the extent to which their voices are heard and understood by the general populace.

Brecht's Rejection of Empathy: Does It Have a Place in the Third World?

Brecht's attempt at "distanciation" in Epic Theatre was intended to place the audience in a critical position towards the social values underlying the lives of the characters. As a young dramatist, he apparently dismissed altogether the value of feelings in the actor-audience relationship: "[The play's characters] are not a matter of empathy; they are there to be understood. Feelings are private and limited. Against that the reason is fairly comprehensive and to be relied on" (Brecht 1964, p. 15). Later, Brecht accepts emotions in the theatre, but not empathy, which he continues to consider obstructive of an appropriate critical perspective: "The crude aesthetic thesis that emotions can only be stimulated by means of empathy is wrong. None the less a non-aristotelian dramaturgy has to apply a cautious criticism to the emotions which it aims at and incorporates" (p. 85). Suspicious of emotion as a didactic tool, the audience of Epic Theatre must find alternatives to the events on stage. There must be different options open to the characters, different outcomes in the plotline, alternative social systems and frames of references set forth or implied (Chaim, 1984, p. 27). Enlisted to this end, his actors must show the character but not "become" them—"[h]e achieves this by looking strangely at himself and his work. As a result everything put forward by him has a touch of the amazing. Everyday things are thereby raised above the level of the obvious and automatic" (Brecht, 1964, p. 92). However, Brecht admitted that his actors often used too little, when the commercial theatre performers often used too much. "We make no attempt to share the emotions of the characters we portray, but these emotions must none the less be fully and movingly represented" (p. 248). Thus Epic Theatre theory—leaving aside the actual productions, which may have been another matter—regarded emotional response as problematic, something to be carefully finessed; it intended to reject any form of audience empathy with the characters, which would, for Brecht, be "sharing" the emotions instead of confronting their social implications. Nevertheless, the question remains whether the discarding of all forms of empathy is relevant to the setting of world drama, where class, ethnic,

gender, and other forms of social and political disparity are so bla-
tantly obvious to subaltern audiences.

Brecht's rejection of empathy was a justified reaction to the commercial success of an overly determined European social institution, the theatre, where audience response was carefully controlled
to validate existing relations of power. In that service empathy becomes retrogressive, supporting the underlying values—usually assumed and unspoken—of the protagonist, who remains in many
ways a representative ideal of dominant ideologies. It must be observed, however, that there is no reason to associate empathy *per se*
with one political system or another. Because it is a response of the
audience, not a creation of a dramatist, director, or actor, the consequences of empathy are influenced by the social/political circumstances and cultural dispositions of the spectators. Certainly, if an
audience of mixed social classes were to watch a play wherein a
monarch or aristocrat dies in a cause that perpetuates hereditary
rule and the divine right of kings, empathy may be less evident
among the disenfranchised than among the privileged spectators.
On the other hand, in a play about the degradations of factory workers, wherein an organizer dies in the cause of labor rights, empathy
will be strong among working-class spectators and weak or nonexistent among upper-middle class spectators. In such situations, a
carefully prepared distancing effect from the emotional life of the
characters through Brechtian or another stagecraft is less significant than are the particular assumptions and social perspectives of
the audience attending that particular performance. Accordingly,
Brecht's premise that a critical perspective in the drama cannot be
attained with empathy denies the ability of some audience members
to respond with a critical—even antagonistic—view of the presentation of their society's dominant value system. Drama *for* the disenfranchised will evoke empathy for those characters who associate
most closely with that political consciousness, and this empathy
does not stand in the way of that audience's critical perspective on
the power structures of its society. In other words, empathy and
critical perspective are not exclusive of one another in drama.

The question of representation and class consciousness leads
many cultural critics to question the efforts and presuppositions of
Brecht's Epic Theatre. Citing Brecht and Walter Benjamin's failure
to develop a viable theatre of class consciousness and class struggle
in 1930s Europe, Fredric Jameson (1990) finds the market of capitalism too problematic for genuine political theatre in the First
World—"art becomes one more branch of commodity production"
(pp. 18, 23). Instead, Jameson believes that authentic cultural production exists only when it "can draw on the collective experience of

marginal pockets of the social life of the world system" (p. 23). From these pockets he instances black literature and blues, British working-class rock, women's literature, gay literature, and Third World literature. Mindful of the overpowering presence of the transnational market, however, he cautions that these forms of solidarity have remained efficacious by keeping independent of the market and commodity system (p. 24). Moreover, authentic political art does not emerge merely by infusing the art work with political slogans and class-identifying signals. Rather, "class struggle, and the slow and intermittent development of genuine class consciousness, are themselves the process whereby a new and organic group constitutes itself, whereby the collective breaks through the reified atomization . . . of capitalist social life" (p. 24). In other words, genuine art expressive of social justice arises only through the developing political consciousness of its audience. Such circumstances may occur within small groups, certain subcultures of dominant cultures, and among those directly disenfranchised. These grassroots movements manage to elude the mainstream market, providing, at least for their immediate audiences, solidarity and the class awareness Jameson finds lacking in the general culture. While most of the social groups Jameson mentions would fall under the category of "identity politics," left open is the possibility that such groups could come together to form broad social coalitions. These circumstances exist today within Third World countries such as Nigeria, Indonesia, and Brazil.

Jameson dismisses First World attempts to produce "compensatory structures"—alternatives to the injustices of the dominant social structure—by recognizing the ability of mass culture to co-opt such structures through the substitution of its own "imaginary resolutions" and the "projection of an optical illusion of social harmony" (p. 26). On the other hand, he does not address the positive dynamic of grassroots efforts to expose oppressive systems. Earlier in the twentieth century, the U.S. philosopher John Dewey held a more affirming view of the capacity of art to both raise general social consciousness and reflect new levels of awareness among the working classes. According to Dewey's *Art as Experience* (1958), a vital working-class art movement must be both varied in form and expansive in social reach. Art would reflect the egalitarian nature of progressive society and, in turn, influence the working class towards a greater sensibility and a broadened understanding. Much more than Jameson today, Dewey invested faith in the capacity of the masses to comprehend their circumstances through art, and also through art to express the various levels of awareness that comprise the social whole. Although he had in mind a First World, highly industrialized society—post-World War I United States—his vision remains relevant to Third World societies that struggle under the restraints of globalized labor.

Dewey's openness to change may seem closer to the optimism of postcolonial societies than it does to First World consumer-oriented societies with highly indoctrinated citizenry. His authentic art for the broad base of people is predicated on a total social transformation of society. Such a comprehensive understanding of artistic expression seldom has been contemplated, and never attempted, in the First World commercial theatre, television, and corporate film industry that have increasingly dominated public discourse since World War II.

What is true is that art itself is not secure under modern conditions until the mass of men and women who do the useful work of the world have the opportunity to be free in conducting the processes of production and are richly endowed in capacity for enjoying the fruits of collective work. That the material for art should be drawn from all sources whatever and that the products of art should be accessible to all is a demand by the side of which the personal political intent of the artist is insignificant. (1958, p. 344)

That artistic expression can contribute to the democratic transformation of society and at the same time be a (necessary) reflection of that democratic transformation is a viewpoint that is not appreciated by most students of drama today. Certainly, there has been recognition of the occasional "political drama" produced as commercial fare within New York's off-Broadway theatre and the various U.S. regional theatres. One such widely acknowledged "political play" is Naomi Wallace's *One Flea Spare* (1996), which begins with the forced quarantining of different classes in a wealthy townhouse during the Great Plague of seventeenth-century London. The U.S. playwright justified her decision to set the play at an historical distance from the inequities of the late twentieth century by claiming the difficulty of presenting class-based analyses of post-Cold War society to commercial audiences wary of ideological themes. Jameson would not be surprised at such fecklessness among contemporary First World playwrights, but Dewey would have been decidedly perplexed, since he viewed the impulse to progressive democratic change and the development of a viable political art form as one and the same.

Views from the Third World: Beyond Identity Politics

In the past few decades, Dewey's social optimism has reappeared in Third World political movements. Grassroots-based "popular education" programs in Latin America and democratically based government initiatives in South Africa, for example, have envisioned the sort of comprehensive social transformation Dewey proposed. The popular education movement throughout much of Latin America has included theatre performances at the local level, often in the simple but powerful form of political satire and skits against oppressive government practices and economic power interests (Hammond, 1999). In its draft of the new South African Constitution of the early 1990s, the African National Congress (ANC) extended a view of education that proposed a comprehensive transformation of its own society and included an international outlook: "Education shall be directed towards the development of the human personality and a sense of personal dignity, and shall aim at strengthening respect for human rights and fundamental freedoms and promoting understanding, tolerance and friendship amongst South Africans and between nations" (in Nussbaum, 1997, p. 66). The ANC deliberators avoided the particularities of identity politics in favor of a more inclusive understanding of human rights and dignity. Their term "dignity" in fact was informed by its prominent use in the Universal Declaration of Human Rights (1948), in the subsequent covenants of the United Nations Bill of Rights adopted in the 1960s, and in most seminal human rights agreements and conventions since then (Levin, 1981; Over, 1999).

The ANC's rights-affirming universalism may be part of the answer to the problem raised earlier in this chapter: How can an authentic grassroots drama movement manage to remain viable and its political message clear once it achieves national or global recognition and promotion, whereby it may become commodified as a commercial package? Put another way, is it always true that "the truth will out" in all social and political circumstances? So long as the political theatre's message is universalized as a human rights message, as expressive of the dignity of humankind, "promoting understanding, tolerance and friendship amongst South Africans and between nations," then its transposition to First World metropolitan centers has a chance of preserving at least a portion of its local authenticity and, perhaps more importantly, allows for the intercultural appreciation of social justice issues. Given globalization and the telecommunications revolution, First World populations receptive to human rights issues in the Third World remain a potentially growing audience for such drama.

Relativistic positions have often questioned the commensurability of social justice drama, doubting whether characters, settings, and themes can be meaningfully understood out of local cultural contexts. While Jameson doubts meaningful cultural transference on the grounds that dominant global culture remains too strong a force, relativists attribute this impossibility to fundamental cultural differences. As Aijaz Ahmad (1996) remarks, "Postfoundational history" has repudiated all cultural essence, including that of "the third world" (pp. 298, 303). In rebuttal, Ahmad offers a more balanced view of the particularity/universality binary. Taking exception to radical relativism, he questions the view that "all historical moments are *sui generis*" (p. 288), arguing that "differentialism" is counterproductive to freedom and equality for both the individual and the group (p. 289). On the other hand, Ahmad does not uncritically accept postcolonial notions of the "hybridization" of contemporary cultures, finding that "commodified cultures are equal only to the extent of their commodification" (p. 290). Instead, he finds that both tendencies—to see the world as an increasing homogenization of culture and to see worldwide cultural incommensurability—are antihistorical. The world is not becoming all the same, and yet the world is shrinking in many ways. Boundaries between cultures remain complex and elude simple expositions.

Perhaps the best articulation of this complexity comes from Homi Bhabha, with the assistance of the Guyanese writer Wilson Harris. Pointing out Harris' goal of the "assimilation of contraries," Bhabha (1994) calls for a "Third Space," which

may open the way to conceptualizing an *inter*national culture, based not on the exoticism of multiculturalism or the *diversity* of cultures, but on the inscription and articulation of culture's *hybridity*. To that end we should remember that it is the 'inter'—the cutting edge of translation and negotiation, the *in-between* space—that carries the burden of the meaning of culture. (p. 38)

Certainly, Bhabha cautions against the co-optation of "an 'other' culture" by the grand theories of the First World, "however antiethnocentrically it is represented." This co-optation is "the demand that, in analytical terms, [the 'other' culture] be always the good object of knowledge, the docile body of difference, that reproduces a relation of domination and is the most serious indictment of the institutional powers of critical theory" (p. 31). Accordingly, Bhabha sees cultural hybridity as a positive state, becoming "the cutting edge of translation and negotiation" that successfully eludes the politics of polarity. Less suspicious even than Ahmad of cultural hybridity in the international public sphere, Bhabha views the First World translation of Third World social justice drama as a potential cosmopolitan good, creating the necessary "*in-between* space" for social progress. Although Ahmad remains wary of the commodification of culture in a globalized world of transnational corporate power, he is also suspicious of radical relativism's tendency to stop human rights discourse through notions of cultural exceptionalism of one form or another. From that perspective, he would welcome cross-cultural art forms that expose the underlying hegemonic motivations of geopolitical forces as well as the "differentialism" of repugnant creeds and ethnic exclusivity.

Third World views of political drama's cultural commensurability cannot be easily summarized, since they vary perhaps to the extent of the number of individuals articulating such positions. Nonetheless, Bhabha and Ahmad represent two well-informed, tolerant, and cutting-edge voices that raise significant issues of local integrity and international organization. While this study will often refer to Brecht's influential Epic Theatre tradition as a source for comparison, and also as a means of critiquing Brecht's own artistic conventions and political standards, my ultimate goal is the search for alternative forms of social justice drama within Third World settings and subaltern settings in the First World. The aim is to arrive at a greater understanding of the particular artistic conventions, audience-development techniques, and discourse methods that have been most effective in conveying, locally and internationally, the exposition of social inequities and, in some cases, the articulation of pragmatic formulas for change.

This study assumes a "world-citizen" approach to the analysis of social justice drama, a view that affirms the need for all citizens of the world to explore differences and commonalities. Accordingly, it regards the world's peoples as striving to understand and deliberate across cultural and political boundaries. It also attempts to avoid the pitfalls of the more unthinking forms of identity politics, which often prioritize cultural difference in such a way as to acknowledge it without understanding it. Absolute notions of difference under various guises discourage international cooperation. The claim of cultural exceptionalism is only one strategy commonly used by diplomats of countries intent on maintaining particular forms of social repression. In fact, the recognition of radical relativism's potential social indifference began before the appearance of postmodernist identity politics. Writing in 1961, the philosopher H. P. Rickman cautioned his generation,

if every religion, every philosophy, every moral system is tainted with relativity, merely the product of the strains and stresses, the hopes and intentions of an age, how is decisive action, based on independent moral conviction, possible? Are we not condemned to skeptical inactivity, or worse still, are we not tempted into a type of higher opportunism, into bowing down before the forces which seem to be carried vigorously by the tendencies of history? (p. 57)

If organized and sustained political action is the only pathway to meaningful progressive change, then the "skeptical inactivity" that results from the abandonment of universal standards of justice, equality, and other democratic virtues can lead only to a self-centered opportunism, as evident in today's global marketplace. Rickman was more of a prophet than perhaps he would care to know. Politically based drama remains a potentially important method of discourse in the struggle to overcome minimalist interpretations that dismiss universal standards of social justice and thus inhibit political action. In fact, the arts have functioned at pivotal moments in human rights history as motivational discourse. For instance, the social protest convention within the U.S. folk music tradition helped drive the civil rights movement of the 1950s and 1960s. It remains for the twenty-first century to discover forms—wholly new or inspired revisions—of political activism in the performing arts.

Part I

THE DRAMA OF NATIONHOOD

Chapter 1

"MINISTERING TO HISTORY:"
THE FORMATION OF NIGERIAN DRAMA

With the recent exception of post-apartheid South Africa, no other African state in the postcolonial era has sought to shape a new culture to the same extent as Nigeria. Its incipient attempt to build institutions of art, literature, and the performing arts demonstrated an exceptional vision of self-identity, all the more remarkable for appearing so soon after independence from Britain in 1960. Actually, the idea of a national theatre began as far back as the 1880s (Alston, 1989). These early efforts anticipated in many important ways the vocabulary of self-determination that would not reach the international ear until decades later. For Nigeria, the need for a postcolonial identity was understood immediately and comprehensively. For example, the effort to found a national theatre movement was coeval with similar European and North American goals, and indigenous arts and crafts, already recognized by First World curators, were soon encouraged as conscious national treasures. The fact that the colonial borders that formed Nigeria never contained a homogeneous culture, either before or after independence, makes Nigeria's early postcolonial cultural achievements even more impressive.

Nevertheless, subsequent economic and political events at first overshadowed and then inhibited cultural production that focused on identity formation and self-determination. Nigeria's continued economic distress since the 1960s has been well documented as part of a continental trend. By the 1980s, African economic growth rates were negative. Adding to the economic disappointment were deteriorating social conditions, armed conflict between traditional and colonial-defined groups, civil unrest, drought, and refugee movements on a large scale. In 1992, the overall GNP growth rate of Africa was only 1.9 percent. When placed in context of a rapid population increase of 3.1 percent in 1992, the effect on per capita income was negative (Adedeji, 1993, p. 4). As Africa's share of world GNP fell in the three decades following independence, its share of the total global population and official development assistance from the first and second worlds has increased. In fact, the threat of external dependence has only deepened in recent decades, creating a quasi-colonial—sometimes called a neocolonial—state of existence wherein political independence is undermined by the actions of international lending and aid institutions.

The new investment-oriented Nigerian elites were seduced by notions of individual aggrandizement based on global market investment. Thus, the hybridity of the postcolonial subject, to use a central term of Homi Bhabha (1994) and other recent postcolonial scholars, is most evident in groups at the top of Nigerian society. The significance of the investment class for social justice discourse in Nigeria cannot be exaggerated. "Riding the restless wave" of venture capital, they are primarily Western-oriented but often hold dominant political and economic positions in their home countries (Cohen, 1998b). The state of alienation within its ruling population is a cultural handicap for Nigeria, as it gropes to overcome mounting debt obligations and confronts major hindrances to success, such as failed infrastructures, overburdened educational institutions, highly corrupt government structures, and inadequate public health programs. Moreover, the very groups that assume direction of national planning programs, aid distribution, and contact with First World aid and human rights organizations are often the ones least able to identify with the Nigerians most in need.

In the 1970s Nigerians proudly proclaimed their country "the largest Black nation in the world." Then it ranked 33rd among all countries of the world in per capita income. By the late 1990s it became the 13th poorest state. Its infant mortality rate is more than 10 times that of the United States and its life expectancy average is 54 years. More than half of Nigerian women are illiterate, and the 1996 inflation rate is 57 percent. The death in 1998 of Nigeria's best hope for positive change, Moshood K. O. Abiola, has left the country once more bereft of effective elected leadership, a crisis that will continue after the 1999 elections unless group unity can overcome the formidable influences of foreign aid policy and the conditionalities of international business. Nigeria seemed once again firmly in the hands of the military elite after Abiola's mysterious death. Moreover, intergovernmental organizations and unilateral diplomacy have offered the Nigerian people little hope for progressive change. Nigerians are aware that Washington's foreign policy is more concerned with Nigeria's oil, which the U.S. invests heavily in, than with democracy (French, 1998; Reuters, 1998). Neither the UK nor the U.S. has pressed the Nigerian government for an investigation into the 1993 election scandal. Moreover, the 1995 execution of Ken Saro-Wiwa, punished for exposing the relationship between Shell Oil Corporation and the Nigerian regime, and the alleged involvement of Chevron, the giant U.S. oil corporation, in the killing of two activists in the Nigerian delta area in 1998 demonstrated to Nigerian villagers that the Nigerian military performs convenient executions for transnational oil in the country (Drilling and Killing, 1998).

During the 1990s, Sani Abacha pillaged Nigeria for personal riches during a five-year regime and was as responsible as any other Nigerian dictator in violating human rights standards. He imprisoned or forced into exile journalists and advocates across the board, including Nigeria's Nobel laureate, the novelist, poet, and playwright Wole Soyinka. The most publicized instance of such abuse was his execution of Ken Saro-Wiwa, community activist and playwright, who had achieved sufficient international reputation to gain the attention of the First World media in 1996. Saro-Wiwa's death directly followed his advocacy of social equality, one plan of which would distribute Nigeria's oil profits to people in local communities. Under these circumstances of social crisis, Nigerian drama has been varied and responsive over the decades. Saro-Wiwa's direct activist stance followed a postcolonial tradition undertaken most notably by Wole Soyinka.

SOYINKA'S SOCIAL VISION

Soyinka began his political commitment early. In the late 1950s and early 1960s, his first plays focused directly on social issues in a newly independent but heterogeneous country. The arbitrary boundaries established in the nineteenth century by British colonialism left Nigeria a nation state with hundreds of ethnic groups, one preeminent political group, a few dominant cultural groups, and a powerful transnational petroleum presence. Soyinka's involvement in the tumultuous civil war of 1966–1967 decidedly changed his perspectives but did not end his commitment to a democratic political struggle. Always at issue for him were the nature and efficacy of Nigerian identity, given the tremendous colonial and neocolonial influence on a people whose land contained abundant natural resources. However, the promise of national self-determination has been predicated on the ideal of social equality, a goal that has appeared just as vital as cultural identity and, for Soyinka, inevitably at some point converges with the latter.

Complicating the writer's political focus has been a third circumstance, manifest in the issue of cultural hybridity. One implication of this hybridity has been the necessity of fashioning an entirely new identity rather than resurrecting a previously established identity. Unlike other postcolonial nations such as India and Mexico, most of Nigeria's precolonial cultures were not similar and were often unrelated. While India and Mexico possessed numerous cultures before the Europeans, they were related by local empires and/or predominant cultures. Soyinka and other Western-educated intellectuals undertook the building of a new culture based on elements from Nigeria's own past(s), but they incorporated Western concepts of education, equality, individualism, democratic government, and aesthetics.

For Soyinka, certain contradictions needed to be confronted as his new nation formed after independence. Nigeria needed to distance itself from Britain as the former colonial power, but it remained dependent upon it culturally. Especially affected by this dilemma were artists, intellectuals, and political leaders who would guide the new nation. For example, Soyinka's chosen literary genres, the novel, modern poetry, and drama, were derivative of European forms. To what extent could he or any other Nigerian writer undertake the creation of a new culture when the fashioners of that endeavor were already significantly invested not only in their own particular tribal culture—in Soyinka's case, Yoruban—but also in the culture of the former colonizer? For Soyinka the solution was obvious—take from both local and colonial cultures to forge a new identity. Moreover, by using Western concepts of equality and political solidarity, Soyinka sought to develop a viably long-lasting political culture for his country.

Soyinka's awareness of problems endemic to First World cultures has motivated his search for empowering elements from within Yoruban and West African cultures. The threat from the globalized culture industry, which particularly affects Western-trained writers such as Soyinka, derives primarily from its capacity for co-optation. As Stephen Eric Bronner (1994) observes, "the sole concern of the culture industry is to turn every cultural object into a commodity for sale. . . . Such developments undermine the power of reflection and the commitment to emancipatory concerns. . . . [E]ven the most radical and bohemian works are condemned by the culture industry" (p. 239). Or, as Herbert Marcuse (1964) wrote during the years Soyinka was writing his first important plays, "the avant-garde . . . entertain without endangering the conscience of the men of good will" (p. 70). This is because of the ability of advanced capitalism to absorb critical political thought and render it innocuous through the commodification of its products. Both Chinua Achebe and Soyinka found that the solution to this threat to their critical works was to emphasize social solidarity. Soyinka's plays were performed in public institutions—state university theatre departments—and his themes concerned cultural appropriation, the clash of cultures, the tension between Western individualism and indigenous consensual culture and, most of all, the persistence of radical evils brought by political corruption, ethnic hatred, and class divisionism. For Soyinka, these circumstances associate with negative effects of Western assimilation, but even more, with the inhumanity of modern institutions of power. The only remedy for a society that has given way to mass evil is a return to social consciousness and a tolerant pluralism that nonetheless retains a vital cultural rootedness.

The "vacillation between subjectivity and solidarity" that mired the thinking of the Frankfort School during the 1950s and 1960s was understood by Nigerian writers, who sought to ground individual liberation upon social liberation. In the same period, Erich Fromm also discerned the personal and the political as mutually supportive, often quoting Hillel's saying, "If I do not stand up for myself, who will; but if I stand up only for myself, what am I then?" (in Bronner, 1994, p. 225). More than any other Nigerian writer of the first two decades after independence, Soyinka possessed a first-hand knowledge of institutional malignancy.

"Ministering to History": Soyinka and Social Justice

Comparing the situation of blacks in apartheid South Africa and Nigeria, Soyinka identified the South African position in positive, almost envious terms: "For the South African still has the right to hope; and this prospect of a future yet uncompromised by failure on his own part, in his own right, is something which has lately ceased to exist for other African writers" (in First, 1970, p. 12). For Soyinka, the problems of postcolonial Nigeria confuse any clear ethical distinction of black and white history. The social failures of his own country after independence, while to a significant degree brought on by the divisive policies of the former European colonizer, replaced clarity with complication. However, Soyinka's perplexity did not preclude a strong political awareness, a quality of his writing that has often been ignored by critics who have overstressed the contradictions and complexities of his dramatic works. In *Ogun Abibiman* (1976), a poetic essay celebrating the eventual liberation of Africans in South Africa, Soyinka's discourse approaches a heroic optimism rare in twentieth-century literature. Responding to William Butler

Yeats' famous rejection of the modern predicament, "Mere anarchy is loosed upon the world," Soyinka responds, "Remember too, the awesome beauty at the door of birth. Labour is holy—behold our midwives with The dark wine and black wafers of communion, Ministering to history, delivering the missing Chapter of the text" (*Ogun Abibiman*, p. 21).

In an era when intellectuals have been confined to university settings, dismissed as "tenured radicals," or compromised by corporate business grants and governmental agencies, Soyinka has retained a critical perspective in literature and political analysis. His involvement in activism, though varying in degrees of danger, has remained consistent over the decades. Today, although he may fit into Yeats' category that he contests in *Ogun Abibiman*—"When, safely distanced, throned in saintly Censure, the prophet's voice possesses you"—Soyinka has not rejected his commitment to Nigeria's liberation by turning to a categorical pessimism, like Yeats, but instead has used his secure university position in the U.S. to strike all the more firmly against the brutalities of his homeland. Of Soyinka it can be said that rarely in history—let alone in the twentieth century—has a major literary figure invested so much of his life and personal security for political justice.

Criticism of Soyinka's stagecraft has often juxtaposed his absorption of the ritual and myth of Yoruban culture—the study of which was financed by a Rockefeller research fellowship in 1960, the year of Nigeria's independence—with political themes from the postcolonial struggle. Western critics in particular have tended to consider the ritualized theatre and incorporation of the Yoruban pantheon as thematically problematic and in many cases gratuitous, although nuanced and often compelling (see, for example, Wright, 1993; Wilkinson, 1978; and Lindfors, 1976). Wright has even suggested that many of Soyinka's plays are more about "religious salvation" than revolutionary social transformation (p. 33). Often ignored in the critical tradition from the 1970s on has been discussion of the radio and stage dramas as political discourse *per se*. Critics have habitually begun with the assumption that Soyinka's dramaturgy is highly ritualized and mythologized interpretations of contemporary problems and issues, and therefore either ineffective because unfocused or ambiguous because overwritten. In an attempt to clarify the playwright's social justice themes, I will discuss a major play, focusing on its methods of human rights discourse.

Madmen and Specialists: The Triumph of Ideology

Written in the wake of Soyinka's imprisonment in the late 1960s for actions against the Biafra War, *Madmen and Specialists* (1971) is characteristically overburdened with symbolism/allegory, satirical allusions, and parodic language to be readily appreciated by First World commercial theatre audiences, yet its political voice is timely, powerful, and in part indebted to a European literary tradition that extends from Greek tragedy to Jonathan Swift ("A Modest Proposal") to Samuel Beckett. During a violent civil war, Bero, an army doctor turned intelligence specialist, has detained his father, Old Man, in his laboratory until he reveals the secrets of the theology of As, which promises great powers to those possessed of its knowledge. The Old Man, in an act of mad wisdom, had served human flesh to his son and fellow officers to point out the absurdity and inhumanity of the war. But Bero has become power hungry and returns home to train a group of disabled mendicants, themselves victims of war violence, to service his power-mad schemes. Bero envisions a particularly vicious scientism where labels, anatomy, and drugs represent a facile substitute for the humanistic impulses of his father and sister, Si Bero, who controls a supply of traditional African herbal medicines that Bero seeks to control. The mendicants have been taught "to think" by Old Man, but their articulate speech is a confused parody of Christian ritual and totalitarian ideology. In the end, Old Man destroys the herb house where Si Bero and her women have stored the health-giving drugs so that his son cannot use them for his diabolical scheme to control society and introduce cannibalism as an ultimate form of social control. While the inhuman and sadistic Bero is, at least temporarily, denied his grab for power, Old Man has not overcome his country's wartime madness and greed because he has also destroyed the women's life-giving medicines.

Madmen's social commentary is deeply embedded in the dramatic form. For example, the mendicants, representing a tragic (and comic) Greek chorus of common citizens spiritually and physically impaired by war, at times relish their captivity and controlled devotion to As. Aafaa, the leader, proudly declares that they are "Creatures of As in the timeless parade" (*Madmen and Specialists*, 1971, p. 5). The willingness of the mendicants to blindly follow leaders, first Old Man and then Bero, who have seduced them with a theology they do not understand, associates with the willingness of citizens in the contemporary nation state to be indoctrinated by hegemonic rule. Moreover, the mindless devotion of the mendicants extends to spying for Bero, "clean[ing] up [his] mess," and identifying with his heartless institutional specialty (pp. 10, 16). Although aware of their subservient status—"You are an underdog"—they still revel in the vicious radical relativism of their master Bero by scorning truth and boasting of their ability to manipulate it (pp. 16, 26, 78). It appears that Aafaa was once in army intelligence himself, and he and the others are quick to act out bureaucratic roles with fierce glee (p. 34). In fact, at the play's opening, the mendicants as disabled war veterans are involved in wagering their replaced body parts in a dice game. This powerful theatrical image underscores the susceptibility of modern citizenry to their own appropriation in the name of ideology, but also to the crude materialism operative throughout the play, most centrally in Bero, whose reductive scientism equates material life with human value. Such references clearly characterize the particularities of Nigerian politics under Lt. Col. Yakubu Gowon in the late 1960s and early 1970s, when vaulting greed and ambition among political elites perpetuated unnecessary war and civil violence.

The play's women represent positive public forces. But Si Bero, Iya Agba, and Iya Mate are at the mercy of Bero's diabolism and their life-affirming natural medicines are finally destroyed. The women herbalists allegorize traditional culture, which, like the humanism of the Old Man, is superseded by the pseudo-science of Bero's will to power. Overshadowing the drama's affirmative discourse, represented by Old Man's incisive criticism of the regime and the women's curative and familial relationality, is the all-consuming seductiveness of Bero and his ideology of control, which seeks to enlist the As theology in its cause. The chorus of disabled mendicants embody the insufficiency of the modern public, which knows its powerlessness but strives to identify with the elites who would control it through totalizing ideologies. In fact, the mendicants are postmodern subjects in that they are keenly aware of their role-playing, are able to assume and abandon belief systems quite readily, and at times retain a distant perspective of their own and their leaders' follies. Moreover, their submissiveness to the ideology that has indentured them is often exhibited in acts of gratuitous cruelty toward one another. In a passage from Soyinka's autobiography of his two-year imprisonment just before the play was written, *The Man Died* (1972), prisoners of the regime cheer as two bragging soldiers are released after murdering civilians. The prisoners' gesture of loyalty to the regime that victimized them disheartened Soyinka (p. 44).

Madmen expresses Soyinka's profound disillusionment with public humanity, which, like the mendicants, understand their victimhood but are nonetheless seduced by the forces that control them. In a critical essay, Soyinka (1988) lamented the "total collapse of ideals and the collapse of humanity" during the 1966 Biafra war. However, this disillusionment would be replaced by a renewed faith in the "strong breed" of grassroots movements that can overcome repression and the cultural seductions of power (The writer in a modern African state, 1988, p. 19; Gates, 1975, p. 41). Still, his wariness of the ability of the populace to support their best interests prevented him from ascribing to left ideologies during this period.

While the mendicants are lured by Bero's ideology of control and charismatic power, Bero remains obsessed by his own image. His pseudo-science has subverted his own critical faculties such that he has become bound by his own desire to control not only his social environment but nature itself. He tells his sister that "Power comes from bending nature to your will;" accordingly his relation to others has become clinical and inhuman: "You analyse, you diagnose, you prescribe" (p. 43). Bero's Swiftian solution, to legalize cannibalism, is wildly absurd, but his mad fanaticism has become a compelling desire that is not faked: "I give you my personal words as a scientist. Human flesh is delicious" (p. 47). The master of seduction and indoctrination is himself seduced by his own dogma. Soyinka implies that public culture in the modern state becomes self-perpetuating by seducing itself. Hegemony comes to believe its big lies, just as its victims are driven to internalize the values that oppress them. Following the same illusions, the madmen and the specialists become the same. Much to the displeasure of critics, the play's nihilism is not palliated by final affirmations of grassroots activism or the triumph of nature, familial, and feminine forces.

Sharpening the play's satirical edge is the parody of religious language, which associates the theology of As with a cannibalistic interpretation of the Christian eucharist and a political triumphalism. Bero's understanding of Old Man's parodic formula for eating human flesh makes this connection, an act that places him in defiance of his father's humanistic criticism of the civil war. "As Was the Beginning, As is, As Ever shall be . . . world without. . . . " Bero's first exposure to this unholy communion instigates his lust for political control, as he explains to his sister: "It was the first step to power you understand. Power in its purest sense. The end of inhibitions. The conquest of the weakness of your too-human flesh with all its sentiment. So again, all to myself I said Amen to his grace" (p. 50). Bero's interpolation of the liturgy has Nietzschean overtones— "too-human flesh"—but his subsequent description of his retraining program for the mendicants now under his control reveals a will-to-power more associated with modern (and postmodern) consumerism than with Nietzsche's vision of a higher, more critical perception of humankind. Bero is confounded by his father's goal to teach the mendicants to think for themselves—"Can you picture a more treacherous deed than to place a working mind in a mangled body?"—Bero's scheme is to have them learn skills that would allow them to fit into the meritocratic and consumerist culture that has hindered real independent political development throughout postcolonial Africa—"Teach them to amuse themselves, make something of themselves" (p. 51).

Soyinka's characterization prevents his drama from becoming a simple exposition of the capacity of capitalism—in the case of West Africa, transnational corporate capitalism and local political elites—to endoctrinate and discipline its populace. Far from being the class upon which the future of social development depends, the mendicants are a proletariat that gleefully parrots the theology of As taught to them by rote (for examples, see pp. 52–57 and throughout). With little conscious understanding of Old Man's thought system, even less of its importance as a critical standard to implicate the false values of nationalism, tribalism, and consumerism, the mendicants dream of Bero performing his specialty upon their bodies to make them born anew (pp. 65–66). Their wholly materialistic understanding of individual and social salvation makes Bero into a Christ figure capable of resurrecting them from the degradation of their lives as dependent victims of social oppression. If Old Man as the father represents a creator god, his only son Bero becomes the Christ of a holy trinity, a configuration the mendicants understand unconsciously. For example, after hearing Cripple's dream, Aafaa responds by quoting the Jesus of the Gospels, "Arise, throw off thy crutches and follow me" (p. 66). Bero as divine healer is only self-promotion, not reality; still, his indoctrination of the mendicants remains complete. This is perhaps the bleakest message of *Madmen*. Soyinka deliberately challenges the optimism of orthodox Marxism, which posited the hope of history within the working classes. It is a position that perhaps proved too bleak even for Soyinka during these years, as his ambivalence towards grassroots solidarity for political action reveals.

While Bero attempts to change Old Man's mendicants from underdogs into watchdogs of his ideology of control (p. 78), Old Man retains hope that the chorus of physically impaired veterans will realize their humanity in the face of the degradations and false values that validate the civil war and power struggle. He regrets that they have "lost the gift of self-disgust," remarking that "[d]isgust is cheap. I asked for self-disgust" (p. 83). As Bero presses his father to reveal the secrets of As, Old Man reflects on his son's illusion that social power will grant him greater strength. Bero insists, "I do not need illusions. I control lives" (p. 96). But Old Man reminds him that social control does not automatically create superior human beings, nor even a just world: "Control—lives? What does that mean? Tell me what is the experience of it. Is it a taste? A smell? A feel? Do you have a testament that vindicates?" (p. 96. Old Man's platonistic queries remind Bero that human happiness involves the body as well as the mind and is for that reason a simple matter of individual and social integrity. Bero's discernment, however, is clouded by his institutional categories, and he can only dismiss his father by reminding him that he has been certified insane. Old Man then laments that ideology has replaced human commonality and connection with nature. His final words reject political systems in favor of a resigned pessimism. "The pious pronouncements. Manifestos. Charades. At the bottom of it all humanity choking in silence." He sees nothing but "these midgets" who would tamper with God and nature to reconstruct the world in their own self-image (p. 98).

The mendicants occupy positions in the play more center stage than do their Greek chorus predecessors. Unlike the choral members of Western tragedy, however, they remain incomplete in spirit as well as body. Their ineffectual bodies become a trope of the fecklessness of the populace enthralled by the institutions of post-colonial—and postmodern—culture. Perhaps somewhat to their credit, they are self-aware moral midgets, as the sarcastic *stichomythia* reveals throughout the play in Greek comic style:

> We're more decent than most.
> Hidden under pension schemes you are.
> Tail-of-the-parade outings.
> Behind the big drum.
> Under royalty visits.
> Imperial commendations.
> Unveiling of the plaque.
> Commemoration occasion.
> Certificates of merit.
> Long-service medals.

Baubles of the meritocracy—pseudo because distributed in support of political elites—substitute for true decency, as a facile respectability replaces individual and social integrity. The mendicants mark their lives by such honorifics and ceremonies, despite their distance from middle-class culture. Soyinka is aware of recent Marxist rethinking of the inadequacies of the working class to overcome the culture of international corporate capitalism (see, for example, Bronner, 1994; Jameson, 1991). Although he places responsibility for the inequities and oppression of so many postcolonial African societies upon all classes, Soyinka is also clear about which end of the class spectrum has profited and which has suffered.

In the final moments of *Madmen*, the set speeches, delivered towards the real audience across the fourth wall, are rambling parodies of political and social discourse in the sub-Saharan context. While some point to the particular rhetoric of politicians—"What though the wind of change is blowing over the entire continent, our principles and traditions—yes, must be maintained"—others are ironic commentary on the nature of twentieth-century mass evil—"excuse me, please, but we are entitled to match you history for history to the nearest half-million souls" (p. 107). The mock political rhetoric spouted by Blindman and later Old Man not only reflect the self-serving exceptionalism of African elites, but also European colonizers: "The black menace is no figment of my father's imagination. . . . have you had the experience of watching them—breed?" (p. 108). This comprehensive parodic approach allows Soyinka to uncover the particularities of Nigerian plutocracy while connecting the society of Bero, Old Man, and the mendicants to the plight of (post)modern humankind. Old Man's final speech becomes a literary allusion to T. S. Eliot's poetic voice, an association that underscores the spiritual vacuity of systems based solely on class divisionism and cultural commodification.

And even if you say unto them, do I not know you, did I not know you in rompers, with leaky noses and smutty face? Did I not know you thereafter, know you in the haunt of cat-houses, did I not know you rifling the poor-boxes in the local church, did I not know you dissolving the night in fumes of human self-indulgence simply simply did I not know you, do you not defecate, fornicate, prevaricate when heaven and earth implore you to abdicate and are you not prey to headaches, indigestion, colds . . . corns and chilblains? Simply simply, do I not know you Man like me? (p. 110)

But if the speeches are destitute glances off the spiritual vacuity of Eliot's middle-class conventionality ("The Love Song of J. Alfred Prufrock"), a postcolonial restatement of First World secular nihilism, the last few moments of the play resummon Christian liturgy and New Testament passages. These reveal Soyinka's general distrust of twentieth-century belief systems—whether Christianity in its colonizing form or political ideology in its misguided tendentiousness: "As Was the Beginning, As Is Now, As Ever Shall Be, World Without. . . . In the Beginning was the Priesthood, and the Priesthood was one. Then came schism after schism . . . look at the dog in dogma raising his hindquarters to cast the scent of his individuality on the mappost of Destiny!" (pp. 111–112). Old Man's theology of As and Bero's control of nature, represent the totality of ideologies that begin with idealism and end—like Bero and finally Old Man himself—with labels in place of human relationships, social engineering and careerism instead of moral vision, and cannibalism to replace the food of knowledge.

In *Madmen*, the gods have departed, leaving not Ogun's double nature of suffering and redemption, but instead a denouement of moral entropy. With no moral vision at the end, the women, representing the only hope of redemption through nature, destroy their craft of herbal healing, thereby eliminating the possibility of traditional culture as a support for social change. Soyinka has remarked that "Cripple represents the mental cripple, the war cripple, the really dissociated personality in modern contemporary terms" (Morell, 1975, p. 119). Madmen and specialists in the play's postcolonial regime have become dissociated not only from their cultural roots—as the Negritude movement had affirmed—but also from any understanding of the human dimension of the new culture of the colonizer. Thus science is misapplied, and modern institutional structures become bureaucracies of brutal force. In what seems an entirely negative resolution, Soyinka has abandoned his earlier commitment to develop a new Yoruban tragic form that would move beyond the Western tragic form. The latter is " 'event-ended': the circumstances constitute the end of the tragic act. Man overreaches himself, displays a flaw, he is destroyed, and that is the end. . . . " By contrast, Soyinka's vision of Yoruban tragedy had within it "the experience of disintegration and reassemblage of the human personality for the sake of, for the benefit of the community" (in Katrak, 1986, p. 19).

Soyinka has been influenced by Bertolt Brecht's Epic Theatre program, which seeks to overcome the Western tragic form. Brecht felt that modern Western tragedy, as presented in the commercial theatre, offered a magnified fate or destiny as a hollow answer to human striving. Following Brecht, Soyinka called for a theatre of commitment wherein answers to social conditions are presented, or at least inferred, after the catastrophe has destroyed or humbled the tragic characters. Although *Madmen* offers the climax, it withholds the social vision. Moreover, it does not extend the traditional theological consolation of hubris, fate, justice, and the power of the gods. In fact, the resolutions of Soyinka's main plays have been questioned by many social-minded critics, not all of whom write from a Marxist perspective. How can such theatre hope to present a positive social theme, let alone function as affirmative activism at the grassroots level, as Soyinka at first envisioned?

Lewis Nkosi (1981) points to the extreme negativity and nihilism of Soyinka's dramatic works as evidence of a lack of commitment to social change and democratic agendas. Put simply, Nkosi charges the playwright with a preoccupation with form over content and a striving for "metaphysical formulas" designed for only a select African audience (p. 191). To this may be added the charge that Soyinka has principally aimed for First World recognition through a heavy reliance on Western dramatic structure and literary movements—including elements not only from Epic Theatre but also from Theatre of the Absurd and even politically conservative poets such as Eliot. In that respect, Soyinka may be considered among the most eclectic writers of the twentieth century.

Transgressive Commentary: Soyinka's Critical Approach

What may be said in his favor? Undoubtedly, Obi Maduakor's (1986) summary description of the theology of As in *Madmen*, "the end result of cynicism and nihilism, the final retreat of the ego into an obscure corner," is accurate (p. 232). The women characters, representing the superego consciousness in the play, are effective only in preventing the id forces of Bero from acquiring their herbal medicines, not in using their natural powers for positive purposes. While Bero demonstrates a lack of humanity and an addictive reliance upon his own ideology of control, he alone represents the dominant position at the play's end. Hence, if it is to be effective in promoting positive social change, *Madmen* and Soyinka's other major plays must affect wide audiences through their uncompromising negativity alone. At this point it needs to be pointed out that Brecht had problems offering clear social prescriptions in his dramas. Perhaps only one or two of them suggested specific social aims and focused futuristically at some point in the drama. His major plays depended much more upon inference rather than prescription and pragmatic ideologies. How does one approach Soyinka's major dramas as contributors to social change other than through affective levels?

Although Soyinka's drama evokes powerful and sustained emotional responses to what seem uncompromisingly negative themes, alternative viewpoints are expressed, less overt but more discerning than the dissociative language of the play's hegemonic voices. Soyinka's answer to Brecht's prescription for a socially responsive theatre is to expose the inhumanity of oppression. Brecht's own definition of realism, more fully quoted in the introduction to this volume, involves not only "laying bare society's causal network" and "showing up the dominant viewpoint of the dominators," but also "emphasizing the dynamics of development/concrete and so as to encourage abstraction" (Brecht, 1964, p. 109). Rather than presenting the dynamic means of social development, Soyinka uncovers the interpersonal flaws within the oppressors that motivate their lust for power. In *Madmen*, the task of uncovering is carried out by Old Man and the women. Their approach is rhetorical and often concise—intrusive remarks and sideline shots at the controlling action, much like Greek choral commentary, but perhaps more incisive.

Selected examples of this *stichomythia* reveal Soyinka's penetrating attack on the system of oppression throughout Nigeria. To Bero's warning that army intelligence is still looking for him, Old Man's response is succinct: "They should be looking for themselves. I robbed them of salvation" (p. 76). To the mendicants who show disgust for one another, Old Man replies, "Disgust is cheap. I asked for self-disgust." The old women represent an older moral impulse than Old Man's humanist decency. Their traditional village community life has enlisted nature, which in the play associates with deep interpersonal bonds and respect for the natural environment. At the beginning of the play, Iya Agba, the leader of the herbalists, reveals that Bero had been her chief prospect for continuing the earth cult, but she senses his unnatural turn and refuses to give him her secrets— "I haven't burrowed so deep to cast good earth on worthless seeds" (p. 39). In Part Two she admonishes Bero that he and his military government cannot destroy the women's cult. "We move as the Earth moves, nothing more. We age as Earth ages" (p. 86).

Iya Agba's advice to Bero establishes her, along with Old Man, as the play's *raisonneuse/raisonneur,* who gives the running commentary on the dominant regime's system of values. Bero's "mind has run farther than the truth. I see it searching, going round and round in darkness. Truth is always too simple for a desperate mind" (p. 87). Here her counseling is as humanistic and as psychologically based as Old Man's, who makes similar pronouncements to Bero and the mendicants formerly under his control. Iya's moral reasoning reflects both the Yoruban regard for balance in nature and the classical Greek understanding of *dike,* divine justice that rights the imbalances of nature. Of Bero's scheme to gain all power from the villagers, Iya remarks, "We put back what we take, in one form or another. Or more than we take. It's the only law. What laws do you obey?" (p. 88). Her discourse of rebuttal, like Old Man's, moves the play towards an adversarial level, where the oppressive impulses of Bero and the mendicants in his service are placed on trial. Instead of expressing wonderment, like the choral members in Sophoclean tragedy, Soyinka's rhetorical method has closer affinity with the one-line asides and commentary of Aristophanean and Roman comedy, where sarcasm, rephrasing of words, and caustic advice establish alternative responses to the foibles of the main characters. At times these rebuttals seem indistinguishable from the exuberant repartee of traditional Western farce. Iya shouts to Bero, "What will you step on, young fool? Even on the road to damnation a man must rest his foot somewhere" (p. 88). Though Bero derides Old Man's "piffling battering ram" of criticism, in fact, the critical discourse of Iya and Old Man together lays bare the tragic failures of Bero's ascendancy.

Iya tells Si Bero that "hope is dead" because of Bero's dominance, and then destroys her own creation (p. 103). The balance of nature she believes in as a Yoruban spiritual leader now requires her to "pay our dues to earth in time" (p. 104). Her dues are not the dues of Aafaa, who seeks only the thrown bones of the postcolonial meritocracy, "hidden under pension schemes" (p. 106). Soyinka's pessimism overwhelms, for the time being, the critical opposition in the play. Iya reluctantly scuttles what she dare not surrender to the enemies of nature, but her haunting aphorism to Si Bero and Iya Mate leaves a glimmer of hope for future restitution. Although "evil hands soon find a use for the best of things," still, "What is used for evil is also put to use." The double nature of Ogun will turn the seasons again in favor of wholeness and nature—"Rains fall and seasons turn. Night comes and goes" (p. 114). Lewis Nkosi considers such statements examples of Soyinka's "metaphysical formulas" that present a facile redirection of the social message, a mystification of the particularities of postcolonial oppression. However, Soyinka's dramaturgy is never purely mythical and ritualized. His *raisonneuse* always returns to the immediate and psychological. To Si Bero's promise that she will repay all that was lost by Bero's ambition and greed, Iya counsels, "I said this gift is not one you gather in one hand. If your other hand is fouled the first withers also" (p. 114). As both specialist and madman, Bero labels and dissects, just as he dismembers the lives of the mendicants and anyone who stands in his way. But Iya understands that life cannot be so dissected and categorized. Rather, it must be taken whole and in balance.

Despite the common critical view that Soyinka substitutes myth and ritual for the particular solutions of Brechtian theatre, in fact, Soyinka combines myth and ritual, psychological insight and humanistic argument to establish alternatives to modern tyranny's determinism. Though Bero stands alone on the stage at the end, his brutal methods are placed in critical perspective throughout the drama. Derek Wright has commented that the "linguistic anarchy" throughout the play, evidenced by the mendicants' parody of imperialistic apologetics, shows that political injustice "has so debased language . . . that all that is left to the writer is to anatomize it, to take it apart and see what it is made of" (p. 100). We have seen, however, that Soyinka's dramatic vision is not thus reduced. His own bitterness after the civil war and renewed repression has not led him to abandon critical response. If Soyinka's political solutions—as in most of Brecht's dramas—are left unstated in *Madmen* and other of his plays, they offer in their place penetrating criticism of the ongoing inhumanity and point to new possibilities in the future.

Chapter 2

NIGERIAN DRAMA II:
A NEW DIALECTIC

Herbert Marcuse's reluctant observation that the proletariat no longer was the "revolutionary subject" of history compelled his search for new sources of political action. Believing that advanced capitalist society was quickly confirming a "closure of the political universe," Marcuse (1970) enlisted a dialectical method that would "risk defining freedom in such a way that people become conscious of and recognize it as something that is nowhere already in existence" (pp. 68–69). Dialectics for Marcuse involves foremost the presentation of "negative thinking," which counteracts the tendency of the culture industry to represent social conditions and individual life positively, much as preindustrial hegemony had attempted to reinforce a "happy consciousness" among its citizenry.

The problem that Marcuse foresaw is the practice of the present culture industry to turn every cultural endeavor into a commodity for sale, an undertaking that is its chief concern. New views, art products, and even dialectical literary works become merely additional opportunities to maximize profits. Hence, negative thinking, the dialectic that Marcuse considered the only viable source of creativity, can be rendered ineffective by a simple process of economic cooptation. Even the most radical and alternative aesthetic productions

suffer the fate of being absorbed by what they refute. As modern classics, the avant-garde and the beatniks share the function of entertaining without endangering the conscience of the men of good will. This absorption is justified by technical progress; the refusal is refuted by the alleviation of misery in the advanced industrial society. (Marcuse, 1964, p. 70)

Marcuse's fear that the industrial culture will assimilate its own criticism has become even more justified at the beginning of the twentieth-first century. Postmodernism is, after all, marked by its ability to turn upon itself, create its own restatement or caricature, and thus subvert its own message. For example, even a highly sarcastic statement against the commodification of culture, Janis Joplin's famous song, "Oh Lord, Please Buy Me a Mercedes Benz," was in the 1990s used by Daimler-Benz to sell its automobile in a television commercial that may have consciously intended to rebut Joplin's critical irony.

Within the context of contemporary Nigerian culture, and postcolonial culture more widely, to what extent is Marcuse's threat from the culture industry of advanced capitalism relevant? Globalized capital has left profound effects on Third World culture, particularly in oil-rich Nigeria. However, the postmodern sensibility, as it has been developed by subaltern groups, groups representing ex-centric perspectives, may manifest particular resistances to the appropriations of transnational capital. Graham Clarke (1980) has observed that black fiction in general embodies the postmodern desire to "make and unmake meaning, effect a simultaneous creative surge and destructive will" that answer the cooptations of the culture industry (p. 201). Nigerian playwrights such as Wole Soyinka and his student, Femi Osofisan, easily move from realism to social ritual to literary allusion and parody, where the self-reflexive nature of their discourse seems to resist the usual cultural commodification and appropriation by the corporate mainstream. Certainly, both playwrights produce plays for university communities, which in Nigeria especially means highly conscious national and political settings that are relatively open to drama's rhetorical efforts. Soyinka's favorite divine character, Ogun, is a Yoruban god of revolutions. However, global capital may be as effective as the First World culture industry in neutralizing even the most anti-establishment formations. The question remains whether alternative art and cultural products, even the most revolutionary, can escape eventual commodification and elimination by the dominant culture.

Chapter 1 explored Soyinka's capacity to offer incisive criticism of the powerful forces within and outside Nigeria that have hindered democratic development. But can "[q]uietist wisdom, resignation, and acceptance of one's fate," as Andrew Gurr (1980) has described Soyinka's use of the Ogun mysteries in the play *The Strong Breed*, ever be a substitute for the political drama of commitment as Brecht envisioned? The dramas of Osofisan address questions of hegemony and oppression more directly than do Soyinka's works. A member of the "second generation" of Nigerian intellectuals, Osofisan suddenly ended his collaboration with Soyinka when the latter was arrested for anti-war activism in 1967 (Richards, 1987). Rather than obstructing political awareness in Nigeria, the termination of their artistic relationship signaled a new beginning in Nigerian drama and intellectual life.

FEMI OSOFISAN

Younger than Soyinka and more sensitive to the globalizing channels of Westernization, Osofisan's political thought confronted Marcuse's dilemma of the co-optation of "negative thinking" more directly and clearly than his former mentor. His university dissertation, never published, addressed the social and political efficacy of drama and literature. Particularly aware of the hegemonic formations of universities, Osofisan took a highly critical approach to education in its class service to ruling elites. Although censured at times, he gained success within the Nigerian university community, holding prominent theatre positions at three major universities during the 1980s. Defying the categorizations of power, Osofisan also succeeded in breaching the ivory tower by maintaining widely read political columns in leading national newspapers. His prominent membership in the student group known as "The Ibadan-Ife axis" proclaimed a commitment to the socialist reordering of Nigerian society, a stance that his mentor Soyinka took only problematically (Irele, 1995). The adversarial strategy undertaken by this post-1970 movement hoped to prevent Marcuse's prognosis of cultural assimilation by retaining a highly critical and self-conscious attitude towards capitalist absorption. Herein lay the paradox, and strength, of Osofisan's drama. By strategizing a distance from hegemonic culture, his plays, in fact, remained preoccupied with a cluster of issues centering on the seductions of the politically aware.

The rhetorical effect of *The Oriki of a Grasshopper* (1995), originally written for a convocation of university scholars, is to question the moral underpinnings of political advocacy by the Nigerian middle class. Its intense self-scrutiny—many Marxists would say self-centeredness—enriches its social analysis, since Osofisan raises the issue of self-scrutiny in the play, turning it into a more complex dialectical exercise than it may at first seem. Its Shavian structural approach—"purpose, passion, discussion"—follows in the tradition of Soyinka and other Nigerian writers. Osofisan's three characters elicit—still at the beginning of the new century—strong polemical

feelings, perhaps because they each represent polarized viewpoints
that transcend First World–Third World boundaries, although not
Nigerian class boundaries. The restrictive middle-class orientation
of the characters becomes an issue in the characters' political discourse. In this respect, the charge that Osofisan has restricted his
play to a middle-class perspective is beside the point. The question
of middle-class lifestyle as a formidable obstacle to significant political action remains the main theme and motivating force of the dramatic action.

Paralleling Soyinka's common ascription of the enabling social
force of nature to women, Osofisan casts Moni, a young student socialist, as the uncompromising voice of egalitarianism and community action. Conscientious and idealistic, she scolds her boyfriend,
Imaro, a university faculty member and fellow socialist who has begun to waiver under the strain of student protests and violent government reaction. Claudius, friend of Imaro and one-time political
ally, has become a successful businessman who bribes government
officials for contracts. Retreating to his faculty office, Imaro laments
his disillusionment with the popular cause, calling his participation
a "masquerade." "We're intellectuals, whatever labels we give ourselves. We're just as privileged as the rest" (Oriki, 1995, p. 5). The his-
trionic sensibility shared by Imaro and Claudius is conscious and
ironically reenacts the daily role-playing of the postcolonial intellectual, who is situated between Western culture, with its cultural and
economic privileges, and subaltern obligations. The stage characters both men name themselves after in their role-playing are from
Samuel Beckett's Absurdist play *Waiting for Godot*, wherein two
men, Vladimir and Estragon, calling themselves Gogo and Didi, wait
for an employer who never appears. The futility of the Third World
privileged classes becomes a self-reflexive Theatre of the Absurd,
where false hopes are extended into lifelong pursuits of First World
material goods and local institutional status. The false hopes Imaro
and Claudius act out mirror the false values of the privileged elites,
whose ideals have become co-opted or undermined by globalizing
economic and political forces.

Osofisan extends the allegorical drama of postcolonial Africa by
casting Pozzo, the pompous slave driver in *Godot*, as the politically
powerful; and Lucky, the slave with a rope around his neck, as the
poor majority. If Imaro and Claudius represent "professional waiters,"
Pozzo, in the successful burger's suit and habit of poetic speechifying, represents the class holding the strings—in his case a thick
rope attached to the neck of Lucky. In Beckett's play, Pozzo's florid
language and panache suggest the self-absorption of the wealthy
classes, who have become preoccupied with their own self-serving

ideologies. His position of power is made possible by Lucky, who labors under harsh and disdainful treatment. Lucky has internalized his servitude to the point that he makes no attempt to escape his subjection. He only breaks his silent labor at the command of Pozzo in a long set speech that is a pastiche of vivid and nostalgic memories of people and places. Osofisan associates Lucky with the long-suffering underclasses of Africa, who remain perplexed by new cultural enticements and old tribal allegiances. Imaro becomes the mouthpiece of the playwright when he describes the predicament of the poor majorities, "[w]ho suffer and continue to suffer mainly because they are incapable of shedding their burden. Because, absurdly, they have been persuaded to accept patiently the lavish whips of their oppressors" (p. 7).

Imaro and Claudius classify their society into three groups: intellectuals, business and political elites, and the poor. However, the play demonstrates that this three-tiered structure of neocolonialism is malleable. Osofisan uses theatrical devices to underscore the universal complicity, and victimhood, of colonial and postcolonial history. The intellectuals, Imaro and Claudius as Gogo and Didi, stand as the African benefactors of this history; Pozzo represents the business interests—both black and white—who have ravaged the continent while pontificating their own reason for being; and Lucky embodies the exploited African majorities. However, these identities overlap and confuse, a circumstance theatrically depicted by Lucky's hat in the original theatre production, which is taken from Lucky and passed between Imaro and Claudius. They each try it on for size, passing it back and forth to one another. When Claudius tries on Lucky's hat, he gives his own to Imaro, who tries it on for size. This bit of stage business becomes a dramatic allusion to the stage business in Beckett's play, where Vladimir and Estragon, Gogo and Didi, try on the same hats and pass them back and forth. Osofisan's imitation of Beckett's characters suggests that the average person, whose commonality is represented by Beckett's two vagrants and Imaro and Claudius, is both exploited and implicated in the power structure of society, no matter what the social configuration is.

Imaro is tired of risking his career for good but socially unacceptable causes. Claudius has traded his principles years before for a business career dependent upon bribery and other socially irresponsible actions. Both men have played roles to avoid rocking the boat and to advance their own careers. During their conversation it is revealed that Claudius has saved Imaro from arrest by deliberately misleading the police manhunt, an action made possible by his social power and status. While Beckett's *Godot* deliberately lacks explicit political reference, *Oriki*'s Nigerian context registers the exchange of hats as the political culpability of both intellectuals and business leaders, who are aware of the self-serving roles they perform. While alternately wearing Lucky's and Claudius' hats, Imaro recites a history of colonial exploitation, an account that includes the chief image of "white ships" (pp. 13–14).

And they continue to sell our people. Once it was for mirrors, for cheap jewelry, for cowries. The rich men raided the poor, captured them, and sold them off to the slave ships. Then came the age of palm oil, of cocoa, timber, and cotton. The rich men made slaves work on their plantations, carting off the products of their labor into the white ships. Always into the white ships. Then came the age of mineral ore, of tin, marble, and gold dust. And the rich now have policemen. They have soldiers, with numbers and uniforms. They make their numerous Luckys go down into the mines and bring out the ore. And then straight into the white ships. Always, always into the white ships. Into the insatible white ships. While they send us their second-rate experts, their second-rate machines, their mind-destroying music, their corrupting culture, their consoling bible. Put all our best products into the white ships. And now, it is the age of oil, of uranium. And we still pass the hat . . . hoping that one day, perhaps, Godot will come, and we will be saved. (pp.13–14)

Imaro's history moves from human cargo, the most precious commodity of all, to less lucrative products, then to very profitable investments—oil and uranium. In the theatricalization of Imaro's account of European exploitation, dominated by the commerical and racial image of white ships, Africans continue to "pass the hat," that is, continue to assume the roles of neocolonial domination while waiting for an uncertain delivery. In the same way, Beckett's two vagrants remain unaware of the nature of their own salvation but nevertheless live in hope by consciously assuming various identities. Osofisan has brilliantly politicized Beckett's existentialist message, but his political types, like Beckett's apolitical tramps, remain highly conscious of the meaninglessness of their lives within an oppressive social order.

Although Imaro and Claudius lament the real-life role-playing they have fallen into, it is Moni who articulates the interpersonal implications of their self-interest, a perception that neither Imaro nor Claudius fully achieves in their overly generalized understanding of their own complicity. As in Soyinka's *Madmen and Specialists*, women possess the voice of conscience and community well-being. Imaro's hypocrisy results from his habit of running "with the hare, in the morning, and then at noon, to change skins and hunt with the hounds" (p. 17). As for Claudius, Moni is resigned to his hegemonic complicity: "You're a business man. You live by sucking on others. You cheat and extort and ruin others, and you call it making profits" (p. 17). For Moni, Imaro's dissimulation is worse than Claudius,' since Imaro has pretended to possess a social conscience, has based his career and fame on it, but in fact has led a double life. Moni's keen sense of the difference between respectability and integrity forces Imaro at first into vehement denial, then acceptance of her judgment. To Claudius' charge that she has followed her cause blindly at the expense of her closest friends, Moni responds by pointing out that Claudius is concerned only about losing his wealth and status. Preferring not to speculate on the Godot who will come to redeem their country, Moni instead places faith in the rightness of the cause and the appropriateness of its methods. She wisely understands that social movements are self-evident democratic developments rather than the redemptive machinations of great leaders: "When the day comes, it will have enough words to describe itself" (p. 18). To Imaro's rebuttal that not all the wealthy are bad, Moni comments that he is merely "making exceptions for his friends" (p. 18). This Shavian dialectic ends with Moni's victory, when Imaro admits the shallowness of his turnabout and rejoins the radical cause.

Before Imaro returns to the cause, he and Claudius play-act once more, this time under Claudius' stage direction. They recreate a scene between a business executive and a government official in which bribery becomes the main channel of commerce. Claudius intends to demonstrate to Imaro the nature of his business, an enterprise so morally degrading that he knows his idealistic friend will not want to leave the university for its sake. Imaro role-plays again when he recites from Vladimir's lament in *Godot:* "Astride of a grave and a difficult birth. Down in the hole, lingeringly, the grave-digger puts on the forceps. We have time to grow old. The air is full of our cries. But habit is a great deadener" (p. 29). Beckett's lyricism registers the nature of human life as meaningless repetition, of a world of existential dread under continual threat of meaninglessness and cultural decay. Osofisan recontextualizes the passage to postcolonial Nigeria, where the repetitiveness of cultural repression and class complicity—"the grave-digger puts on the forceps"—creates a social and political angst. Imaro's troubled consciousness despairs from the repeated deferment of democratic objectives in his country. The play thus reinterprets Beckett in political terms while retaining a highly personal and intimate context. *Oriki* is not about the struggle for democracy but rather about the struggler's despair, a fact that has left it open to misinterpretation. Osofisan has been accused of narcissism and a kind of class complacency, a political position he would strongly deny. Attention to the spiritual health of the politically conscious has never been a popular subject. Since activists on the left especially are notoriously callous about their own psychological health, Osofisan's venture into this realm shows courage and independence.

The general movement of the play, however, goes beyond the documentation of activist burnout. Moni finally turns Imaro's self-pity into affirmation when she sings ballads about the struggle for social justice. The ongoing nature of this struggle counters Beckett's recurring pessimism through a straightforward belief in the revolution's linear progress: "And I shall sing my love/Of a shield called Freedom/Against which the talons of eagles break" (p. 30). As Moni rescues Imaro from his recent fatalistic resignation, hope is revived in a social arrangement where top-heavy local power and foreign economic dominion have long prevailed. When Imaro and Moni become reconciled lovers, their union in love confirms a solidarity that defeats the cynical materialism of Claudius, whose name suggests the reluctant republican emperor who came to rule Rome with an iron hand.

Oriki imparts a level of political optimism lacking in Soyinka's more complex and circumspect plays. In this work, Osofisan documents something close to the positive and utopian attributes of Jurgen Habermas' humanistic "life world," which is capable of overcoming its "colonization" by postmodern commodification and bureaucratic rationality (Habermas, 1992, p. 266). According to Habermas, systems "colonize" the life-world of the human community by rendering its citizens incapable of resisting institutional structures. For Habermas, human spontaneity and ingenuousness—represented in Osofisan's play by the reconciliation of Moni and Imaro—repulse the reification of power and conventionality—embodied in Claudius and Pozzo, who proclaim the self-perpetuating wisdom of the status quo. However, Moni and Imaro's utopian humanism that is conveyed most strikingly in their presentational songs would not succeed in their defeat of hegemony if they were not also rededicating themselves to the cause of a grassroots solidarity movement. Osofisan thus has clearly chosen the pathway of political activism, though he has argued the difficulty of such an undertaking, which is by no means inevitable, despite the optimism of Moni's song of social militancy.

Overcoming the self-serving philosophy of conventionality, the "go with the flow" approach to social development expressed by Claudius, Moni, followed by Imaro, invests in what Nancy S. Love (1986) attributes to the historical orientation of both Marx and Nietzsche, who "understand life's activity as a creative [future oriented] process which requires constant striving to destroy what has gone before" (p. 52). Osofisan's activists, however, avoid Nietzsche's poetic turn towards a new elitism of the superman. They do not view humankind in any way derisively nor categorically compare the popular value systems of human beings in negative terms. They reject the idea of a superior leader who will lead a select remnant of individuals to a higher plain. Instead, they take an egalitarian approach to liberation and human dignity, which emphasizes commonality, not guidance associated with the local political elites of their society. Nor do they regard the present populace as incapable of participation in a better society, as held by Nietzsche, who thought humankind's redemption possible only in a distant utopian fulfillment. Zarathustra's "appeals to live and die for a future a long way off" assume redemption by a vaguely historical superman (see Lampert, 1996, p. 79). Moni's vituperative objection to the status quo is confined to the formations of power within Nigerian culture. Her faith in the commonality of citizenry becomes the only hope of redemption, as she and Imaro express a wariness towards outside programs of development (the First World "white ships"). Their political orientation within Nigeria depends upon a transcendence of traditional tribal divisionism and a solidarity based on defeating social inequality, not on recreating superior individuals.

Birthdays Are Not for Dying

Oriki's depiction of dedicated political idealists and sympathetic business executives contrasts with the portrayal of more sullied social practitioners in the one-act play *Birthdays Are Not for Dying* (1990). Kunle, scion of a large family business, has decided to fire the old cronies of his recently deceased father because of their general prodigality and collusion with the government. Unlike Moni and Imaro, however, Kunle's iconoclastic motives are far from altruistic. He exhibits an Oedipal pathology that subjects him to his unconscious drives at the expense of a rational commitment to social progress. Lacking the political consciousness and individuation of the activists in *Oriki*, Kunle behaves with an impulsiveness that turns family and friends against him. He rashly calls a meeting of the board of directors where he summarily dismisses men at his father's age after exposing their duplicity. Osofisan enjoys the exposure of these members of his country's political and economic elite, as they clumsily bluster their outrage at the sudden change of fortune. However, this moment of *peripeteia* ends as quickly as it began when Kunle's wife, Bosede, announces the death of their son, who died on the way to the hospital after Kunle in his rage refused to drive him to the emergency room himself. Just before the board meeting, Kunle had harshly accused his wife of infidelity and refused to listen to her justifications. Out of anger, she poisons him. Thus, Kunle's plans to

begin a new corporation based on honesty and moral integrity found-
ers before it can begin because of his self-righteous disregard for
others and his refusal to discern his own corrupted motivations.

Birthdays presents a profile of a Dostoyevskian character who fails
to discern the shadow side of his own soul. Like Raskolnikov, the
young student protagonist of Dostoyevski's novel *Crime and Punishment,* Kunle's accurate perception of the social evils of his day is not
enough to make him an agent of positive reform. Intelligent and sensitive, he nonetheless fails to consider the destructive elements of
his own psyche, contradictions that lead him to universal judgment
against all around him, including the majority of people who walk a
middle course between integrity and hypocrisy. Like Raskolnikov,
his conceit leads him down pathways of social isolation, where he is
soon vanquished by his own fears and isolation. In the most dramatic moment of the play, the Councillor, whom Kunle has just de-
nounced for tolerating the corruption around him, shows Kunle an
object that the audience never sees. The sight of this mysterious "gift"
horrifies Kunle so much that he easily accepts Bosede's poisonous
drink. Osofisan implies that fear of the unknown—especially of the objects and images from our own psychological pasts—will defeat the
individual unwise enough to divorce himself from family, friends, and
the wider community. *Crime and Punishment* documents the gradual
deterioration of a lone individual who feels he is above ordinary, self-
serving morality. His murder of a heartless landlady in the name of
social justice leads to an unanticipated remorse, an emotion he
thought he could dispense with in the service of a higher cause.

Like Raskolnikov, Kunle ignores the ultimate goal of his convictions, the commonality of humankind, for which he has only contempt. *Birthdays Are Not for Dying* is a warning for those social justice
movements that ignore their own imbeddedness in the culture, their
own complicity and psychological dependency, for a narrowly focused political ideology. Osofisan is not necessarily arguing against
the Critical Theory School and the New Left, who have rejected the
notion that the seed of social revolution lies with the proletariat.
Rather, his play challenges the notion of the fearless leader, of the
single cultural hero who will lead the masses in revolt. As the voice of
community wisdom, Moni in *Oriki* advocates for the strength of solidarity as the only remedy for social oppression, a position that successfully prevents Imaro's momentary drift into self-pity. In his
rejection of the traditional heroic leader who will redeem his people,
Osofisan deliberately rebuts his mentor Soyinka's position in *The
Strong Breed* (1973). In that play, a character endowed with heroic
dimensions becomes the traditional scapegoat for the society's ills.
Osofisan's one-act *No More the Wasted Breed* (1982) reveals the fu-

tility of such mystical sacrifice. The play "articulates a conception of individual and collective fate founded on the affirmative potential of a forceful human awareness, in which a tragic conception of life, presented as the effect of a disabling fatalism generated by an ignorant mysticism, can have no operative place" (Irele, 1995, pp. xix–xx). Osofisan's rejection of supernatural forces in the political realm is complete when he ascribes no transcendent value to the ritual sacrifice of the designated individual. The playwright's *raisonneur*, Saluga, goes so far as to subvert the very notion of the transcendental worth of myth and ritual. He rejects the gods and goddesses of the metaphysical realm, believing, like Moni, in an imminent community of political consciousness. In both plays, Osofisan regards the role of metaphysical narrative as social control and its propagators as corrupt members of the traditional order.

No More the Wasted Breed, *Birthdays Are Not for Dying* and *The Oriki of a Grasshopper* all approach the individual in isolation from different thematic and dramatic directions. If the first play repudiates transhistorical mystification, the latter two uncover the spiritual impoverishment and psychological dependency of the Westernized cult of individualism within a globalized consumerist ethic. Osofisan seems to reject both traditional Nigerian and Western cultural forms as they have become intertwined in the postcolonial era. His repudiation of traditional Nigerian religious ritual and narrative for the sake of a utopian future parallels Nietzsche's rejection of traditional morality and religion, for, in George Kline's words, a sense of past history that "is too heavy and pervasive is an obstacle to future-oriented cultural creativity in the present" (Kline, 1989, p. 20).

The degree to which Osofisan has rejected Nigeria's cultural past for the sake of a reformulated social future is striking; yet, he also looks upon Western culture and the power of its global capital in similarly negative terms. Although Kunle's Oedipal rejection of his father's friends and style of business reveals an underlying pathology of hatred and megalomania, still, his perception of the ethos of Nigeria's economic and political elite is accurate. His articulate descriptions of hypocrisy and senility among his elders are fully within the satirical tradition of Jonathan Swift. These castigations are dramaturgically powerful and contribute to the rich complexity of *Birthdays*. Kinle's attack on the Councillor is cogent and dramatically appropriate:

Your hands are clean, you don't steal money yourself, but you'll do nothing to stop those who dip their fingers in the wallet behind everybody's back. You're an accomplice, sir, as guilty as the rest. With people like you, nothing will change. You're born to fold your arms behind your back and close your eyes and connive at crime. And that's how you'll die, conniving and pretending to be blind!" (pp. 124–125)

The Councillor's response is to show Kunle the "gift" that the audience never sees, the sight of which terrorizes him. In this state he is poisoned by his resentful wife Bosede. Kunle's high moral standards for his business scarcely hide the competitiveness towards his father who has tolerated such corruptions. Kunle takes pride in examining all the company's books that his "illiterate" father ignored for years. Despite Kunle's outward irreverence towards the status quo and the past represented by his father, Bosede reveals his underlying timidity. Kunle did not expose his father while he was alive out of filial respect but rather because he was afraid of him. "You were terrified of him. Terrified, because you never had the guts he had. You never could face up to men, but you were hungry for the possessions he would leave you" (p. 111). She then predicts his destruction through his own consuming fears and hatreds.

Birthdays uses the popular concept of the Oedipal complex driving rebellious youth, a straightforward admission rare among leftist writers. For Osofisan, social progress cannot be achieved through a facile ideology or a simple faith in political correctness. The transformative consciousness depends upon society's acceptance of values that are constantly adapting to new economic, technological, and cultural circumstances. Enlistment in the cause of social change is difficult, carries few external rewards, and risks social ostracism or even punishment. Osofisan's naturalistic style becomes clinical at times, as he closely traces the hidden motivations behind political consciousness. For such a critique, reliance on the projected values of a nostalgic past and a corrupted present must be superseded by a clear-eyed objectivity tempered by faith in a committed community transcending both class and ethnicity. Osofisan is numbered among the post-civil war Nigerian writers who still take seriously the vital inclusion of the working class and ordinary people into the national ideal (Omotoso, 1996). For Osofisan, this nationalism walks hand in hand with a productive social justice consciousness.

Writing of the worldwide influence of African American rap and "hip-hop" cultural forms, Tricia Rose observes, "The creation, and then tenacious holding on, of cultural forms that go against certain kinds of grains in society is an important process of subversion." Far from being an exclusionary and elitist endeavor, it is "about a carving out of more social space, more identity space. This is critical to political organizing. It's critical to political consciousness" (in Ards, 1999, p. 13). Osofisan has sought to expose the limiting ethos of the pre-civil war political project, not for the sake of a critical rejection of his elders—as his character Kunle would do—but to expand the "social space," the "identity space" of the most disenfranchised. Osofisan's plays deliberately subvert what is taken to be traditional and elitist elements in the drama and fiction of Soyinka and other first-generation Nigerian writers. Compelling through his dramas, Osofisan makes the case that this social and identity space is not easy, but necessary. As his character Moni demonstrates, the only transcendence in such a worldview is to be found in an activist social solidarity sustained over time.

FEMI EUBA'S CRITICAL EXPRESSIONISM

Less psychological and clinical but more intimate and lyrical than Osofisan's treatment are the dramas of Femi Euba. Writing for stage and television, Euba, a contemporary of Soyinka, created a contemporary urban melange with only minimal ritualized elements that in fact function as traditional theatrical devices. Thus in *Abiku* (1972), a symmetrically black and white mask is worn to express the tragedy and promise of life, but also an interracial subject. In this television play, Kole, a young idealistic writer, walks the streets of a (Nigerian?) city in search of subjects for inspiration. His discovery of a broken doll in a park evokes the appearance of the characters Man and Woman, whom Kole questions as to their participation in an infant murder. The nonrepresentational style—for example, the connection between the broken doll and a dead baby is purely evocative—continues throughout the play, as Kole and other characters are momentarily removed from their situations to be placed in symbolist and expressionist scenes. Man and Woman are the generic embodiments of Laura and Willie, who become involved in an interracial love affair. When Laura, an Englishwoman, tells Willie she loves him and that she is pregnant, he rejects her in panic and anger. Hugh, an Englishman and the husband of Laura, confronts Willie in the hospital delivery room and chases him down the street. As Laura gives birth to her child, in a scene of parallel editing, Hugh shoots Willie and then himself in the park. As the shots are heard, the baby dies in childbirth.

Euba's short play is dramatically and thematically complex, easily expandable into a full-length videodrama or feature play. The social justice issues of women's choice, racial divisionism, interracial relationships, mixed motives within social protest movements, and the dependency status of women in general are tightly interwoven. Euba's grasp of the video/cinematic form is demonstrated in several concise scenes that oppose the needs of women with the rigidities of social and institutional denial. During Laura's visit to her doctor to discuss the possibility of aborting the interracial pregnancy, the doctor's indifferent humanistic detachment exposes his insensitivity to her situation. "Well . . . it is a . . . it is a difficult question . . . I am not in any way capable of giving you a moral answer. I mean, as an adult, you are quite entitled to your own opinions and interpretations . . . " (*Abiku*, 1972, p.16). The doctor's feckless approach to Laura's anguish exposes the indifference of the medical profession towards women (a universal problem), and also the unwillingness of modern secular institutions in general to deal with moral issues.

A march of nuclear freeze protesters appears while Laura and Willie discuss the impending abortion. The demonstraters reveal their glee as they make marijuana cigarettes and pelt the police with food. The scene does not critique civil disobedience as such but queries the seriousness of social protest movements. Other social issues are handled with more nuance in the play. Laura's passing of an interracial couple on the street evokes a dialogue between her and Willie where he rejects her love and denies her belief that its fruit, the unborn child, reveals their destiny together. The image of the unborn interracial child becomes a leitmotif throughout the play, powerfully conveying its manifold meanings—life's possibilities for rebirth, the termination of hope, and the birth of new social realizations. The interracial theme elicits a sad remembrance from the writer Kole as he stares at an old photo of himself and a white woman. Consecutive snapshots fill the television screen of Willie and Laura, the white and black couple on the street, Laura and the white man, Kole and the black woman, Willie and the white man, Laura and the white woman, and finally an interracial baby. Immediately afterwards is heard the spiritual "Sometimes I feel like a motherless child," associating the theme of social indifference and denial. The montage of images reifies race as an absolute boundary formation but also emphasizes the reality of interracial relationships that transcend race. The resulting ambiguity creates a tension in the play that is never fully resolved. The deaths of the black and white men, Willie and Hugh, and the concurrent death of the interracial child leave the dichotomy of racial divisionism and racial integration unresolved, an ambivalence that only heightens the tensive political themes of the play. Kole's unspoken reflection on his own past interracial relationship perhaps reflects Euba's unresolved position on racial identity and universalist notions. It is never clear whether the condition of "motherless child" results more from political oppression, traditional views of racial prejudice, or from the indifference of modern, Western values. Most likely, Euba finds false values pervading all these aspects of postcolonial and First World society.

In Part Two of *Abiku*, mythic elements enter more clearly into the performance, as Kole appears as the oracle-priest of Abiku counseling Hugh, accused of killing one of Willie's friends who has stolen Laura's money for the abortion. When the distraught Hugh claims the interracial shooting was an accident, Kole as the priest responds, "there can be no accident other than the deluding mask of fate." Abiku's identity becomes a generalized unborn child who at once functions as the victim of social evils and the fate that determines social history: "He comes with one leg out, the other in . . . One half crying for life, the other steeped in blood, crying death" (p. 22). Hugh is then given the mask of Abiku by Kole. Symmetrically black and white, it leads him to the final scene in the hospital where he confronts Willie and shoots him and then himself. The black and white mask represents Abiku's traditional double nature as both arbiter and victim of faith, and also the ethos of racial separation that drives Laura to consider aborting the interracial child she wants. This lyrical scene contrasts stylistically with the scene following, which becomes an expressionistic nightmare where obstetric patients and their men become automatons in a monolithic institution.

The hospital scene is introduced when a cinema screening of a war picture is interrupted by a loudspeaker announcement asking for Miss X075 to go to the delivery room. A chorus of "puppets" mechanically wail good-byes as a woman puppet, representing Laura, enters the delivery room. A similar announcement for Mr. X056 interrupts the war movie again, and a puppet representing Hugh proceeds mechanically to the hospital. In the delivery waiting room women characters express their vulnerability to the social norms against women and attitudes towards birth control that have compelled them to become pregnant. "I would have said, another year, Billy, maybe another year when I feel capable . . . Would I ever feel capable." Another woman repeats her husband's objections, "Don't use that thing today, love! Gets in the way, love! God, how selfish men are!" (pp. 26–27). The newborn's death is an ironic consequence of Laura's ambivalence towards having the child, but even more so an expression of the futility of the false values and denial perpetuated by social attitudes towards sex and women's freedom. The play's merging of mythic and expressionistic elements is clearly influenced by the European expressionistic tradition and its U.S. derivative through Eugene O'Neill, but Euba's videodrama remains thematically more complex through the juxtaposition of powerful Nigerian metaphysical elements and secular expressionistic scenes and political references. The setting, which could be any postmodern city in the first or third worlds, is pervaded not only by prejudices of the past but also by the commodification and institutionalization of life, both of which limit human freedom.

Abiku projects a dystopia in which Habermas' life-world remains under-appreciated by positivist experts who shun real human needs (the doctor), pseudo-activists unable to overcome the seductions of a gluttonous consumerism (the demonstrators), and institutional structures that cast people into compliant automatons (the hospital). Like Osofisan, Euba postpones a positive political agenda, wishing his audiences to first understand the negativities that perpetuate the postcolonial social order.

Beyond Myth: Transgressive Drama Takes Center Stage

Nigeria's post-civil war writers engaged in a productive dialectic but not over the binary opposition ritual/myth tradition versus political realism. Rather, they placed an uncritical appreciation of traditional African values on one side, and, on the other, a political iconoclasm that targeted both traditional African culture and the Western values of extreme individualism and globalized markets. Soyinka's wariness towards the younger playwrights of the Nigerian university system derived in part from his unwillingness to subscribe fully to their highly critical analyses of postcolonial culture. Soyinka's remarks, "It results, as in [Osofisan's plays] in throwing out the baby with the bathwater, denying even the virtues in his history—a strange position for a writer to find himself as interpreter of his own culture. . . . It is as if such writers are still wrestling with the options of socio-political development, in dynamic interaction with race-culture" (*Art, Dialogue and Outrage*, 1988, pp. 241–242). But Soyinka's objection ignores the discourse of myth and ritual, which derives, as Irele (1995) notes, "not from a concrete grasp of 'essences' but is related to the fabric of existence. For Soyinka . . . myth is often presented as substantial, with ritual as its signifying text. In doing so [he disregards] the mobility of myth as reference, and of ritual as a form of social practice, a condition of the intentionality with which they are invariably charged and which therefore constitutes them into social forces" (p. xxxiv). Far from being autonomous systems, myth and ritual in African culture comprise strategies of negotiation between social actors. Irele's point is that second-generation Nigerian writers can use myth and ritual to present a fully transgressive perspective on postcolonial hegemony.

Going further, it may be said that the involvement of the rhetorics of myth and ritual in the social order renders them subject to legitimate critical attack, insofar as a culture's metaphysics and mythology have been used not only to critique present evils but also to reinforce such evils. That Osofisan, Euba, and other Nigerian playwrights have chosen to utilize the deconstructive capabilities of myth and ritual does not preclude them from becoming objects of critique by future Nigerian playwrights. Indeed, women playwrights, as becomes evident in the following chapter, have been more forthright in their questioning of traditional belief systems as they affect social practice.

Brecht's distancing agenda in the drama has always been a difficult concept to grasp, particularly as the theorist himself writes ambiguously about it and produced few appropriate examples among his dramatic works. Still, distancing in drama remains an important device for transgressive discourse, since it remains the only effective way to overcome the complacency of theatregoing attitudes and the obligatory protocols of commercial theatre. Many theorists mistrust theatre spectacle when used as alienation devices in Epic Theatre. Sandra Richards' comment on Osofisan's works is typical: "The distancing or alienating devices . . . may work effectively, thereby stimulating audiences to reflect upon the explicit social critique. But there exists the alternate possibility that sensual delight in the ingeniousness of the theatrical spectacle overtakes a critical sensibility" (1992, p. 128). However, the social occasion for theatre and the directorial style of particular political productions can make or break effective political messages. Brecht's own theatre experience at the Berliner Ensemble led him to prepare carefully all elements of the Epic Theatre performance, including the sense of occasion for the audience. Control over the social circumstances of production and the directorial style has been carefully planned in Nigeria as well. Far more significant in the discourse of social justice drama is the willingness of its practitioners to focus on uncovering the social causes of their characters' conflicts. This can be done either explicitly or implicitly, the latter being far more common. Perhaps because of its television provenance, Euba's *Abiku* is undeviating in its exposition of the institutional structures and attitudes affecting gender and race issues. The underlying causes of oppression are demonstrated through character (the doctor's interview; the demonstrators), and through stylistic performance devices (the expressionistic hospital scene; the cinema scene). *Abiku*'s theatrical complexity enhances rather than hinders Brecht's distancing goals. With uncompromising critical analysis and artistic richness, Euba and other postcolonial Nigerians have produced a stagecraft that transcends the traditional dramatic forms of West Africa and Europe.

Chapter 3

TESS AKAEKE ONWUEME: REWRITING HISTORY

Commenting on the willingness of the writer to confront the reality of the other in socially conscious literature, Derek Attridge (1999) concludes that "what is foremost in the creative mind is the issue neither of originality nor of communication; it is the demand that justice be done to thoughts that have not yet even been formulated as thoughts" (p. 24). Thus the reader must be engaged in the rethinking of old positions "in order to apprehend the text's inaugural power" (p. 25). Perhaps even more so in the dramatic form, spectator and dramatist together create a kind of willing suspension of dominant social values. The subaltern voices in drama by women demand just such rethinking of social justice issues and possibly the recasting of dramatic structures. This chapter will consider the dramatic form of Tess Akaeke Onwueme, her perspective on Nigerian political theory, and her contribution to current social justice discourse.

Onwueme's generation has looked critically and with some impatience at the way in which noted first-generation Nigerian writers circumvented the political implications of their own works. Second-generation drama by contrast is more straightforwardly realistic, using myth and ritual not to examine and revitalize tradition but as means to ends, as theatrical devices in the service of politically based issues. African Marxist critics in particular have lost patience with playwrights such as Soyinka, who, they contend, abandoned social and economic issues in their pursuit of essentialist notions of a West African—even Yoruban—culture that was fast fading into historical obscurity. Biodun Jeyifo (1985) expressed this viewpoint succinctly by implicating Soyinka's steadfast preoccupation with the particulars of African humanism, with "the imponderable verities of [humankind's] physical and cosmic environment." Grounding this outlook is "the reactionary notion that human nature is indivisible or inseparable from nature in general" (p. 60). Jeyifo and other postcolonial theorists have sought a more critical examination— rather than celebration—of West African traditional cultural formations, understanding that the language and other aesthetic forms of traditional Nigerian society lend support to dominant anti-democratic systems. Non-African postcolonial theorists also have attacked this tendency throughout the Third World to, in Edward Said's words, "abandon history" for the sake of a traditional metaphysics, which seduces by its powers of nostalgia for a past now safely unapproachable (1990).

Whether Soyinka has in fact abandoned the realities of history for the sake of his mythopoeic forms is less significant, perhaps, than the conviction that the exposition of immediate social justice concerns should take (a distant?) second place to the recreation of these traditional aesthetic and religious forms. During the 1980s, second-generation Nigerian thinkers took Soyinka's major dramas as formalist and apolitical if not counterproductive. Though Onwueme followed Soyinka by employing traditional West African settings, she created issue-oriented dramatic conflicts closer to the European "problem play" tradition of realism than to Soyinka's complex and evocative forms.

THE POLITICAL AND THE AESTHETIC

Writing of the relation between aesthetics and ethics in her own political novels, Mary Beth Tierney-Tello (1999) reflects on the issue of accountability and how it shapes her audience's response to the representation of real human suffering. She quotes Diamela Eltit's view of the reception of her *testimonio* work *El Padre Mio*.

Nothing could be more irritating for me than to read a book that treats the social margins from a compassionate perspective. That type of approximation seems classist and reductive for me. . . . It seems to me that what happens there is that they "steal the soul" of those spaces, of those inhabitants. My project was to restore the aesthetic that belongs to and mobilizes those spaces and to give narrative status to those voices traditionally oppressed by official culture and ruined by a redemptive narrative. (p. 82)

Eltit taped the speech of a "delirious street person" and in the main let his words speak without commentary. Her intent was the democratic inclusion of the excluded. To achieve this, the author strayed from the typical practice of the Latin American *testimonio* form by avoiding what Tierney-Tello calls "empathetic or sympathetic solidarity with the testimonial subject." By refusing to allow the reader to identify with the subject, *El Padre Mio* "puts in question an easy political or social solidarity, a solidarity based on identification and identity politics" (p. 84). Eltit means to create an ambiguity between the subaltern subject and the privileged status of the reader, creating, in effect, a circumstance that is close to what David Haney (1999) describes as an "openness" towards the subjects of literature. The means through which the "truth" of a literary text happens—Haney speaks specifically of poems—"is instructively similar to the unconcealing that goes on in the ethical hermeneutics of being open to (instead of imposing, asserting, or conceptualizing) the truth of another person" (p. 38). Both Eltit and Haney prefer a truth of authentic human relationship to the merely epistemic truth in the representations of social consciousness. Accordingly, "*El Padre Mio* refuses to be read, much as it refuses to read itself, as an identitarian construction" (Moreiras, 1996, p. 218). Tierney-Tello concludes that Eltit's work "puts in question an easy political or social solidarity, a solidarity based on identification and identity politics" (p. 84).

In their concern with providing—or transparently reproducing (!)—authentic subaltern voices, these critics may be devaluating the expository side of what Tierney-Tello somewhat condescendingly terms "identity politics." If Eltit's aim in *El Padre Mio* is to avoid "pity" through an acknowledgment that "the subject is a producer of culture, of a haunting, disturbingly powerful language that gestures at the psychopathology wreaked by the political violence of authoritarian culture," she nonetheless trusts in the ethical orientation of her audiences to recognize the "disturbingly powerful language" of the disenfranchised. Eltit and Tierney-Tello wish to overcome the false dichotomy of aesthetics vs. ethics promulgated by current theorists by using aesthetic form to achieve the dignification of their subjects. They also wish to promote the indictment of authoritarian culture (which, in Eltit's case, is the Pinochet government of Chile). Haney's notion of being open to the other, in this case the other of the culturally marginalized, is confirmed by Terry Eagleton's valuation of the aesthetic in socially oriented art, which forces recognition of the uniqueness and integrity of the oppressed subject: "what the aesthetic imitates . . . is nothing less than human existence itself, which needs no rationale beyond its own self-delight, which is an end in itself and which will stoop to no external determination" (1992, p. 30). Tierney-Tello concludes that the mere celebration of difference does not change anything. In fact, readers realize their own participation in the systemic power that created the suffering of the oppressed. "In this sense, one of the possible functions of such texts is to bring this complicity to the fore and not to attempt to assuage it through fantasies about the power and reach of literature and cultural critique" (p. 93).

What then of the efficacy of literature and art in general in the political sphere? Here Tierney-Tello is less assured. Acknowledging the inevitable ambiguities of the aesthetic product and its reception situation does not block her recognition of committed art, but she describes such endeavors as "reimagining our world" through the representation of cultural practices, a process necessary but not sufficient for positive change (p. 93). While it is true that a kind of creative rethinking of the status quo may be necessary to form agendas for political movements as well as individual actions, and that this mental activity can be enhanced by art and literature, it may just as well be said that the presentation of subaltern groups and individuals within their own cultural space can lead to a kind of complacent acceptance of the way things are. It can reinforce the inevitability of fixed social classes that persist because of something like Francis Fukuyama's metanarrative in *The End of History and the Last Man* (1992), which attributes the individual to his or her place in society because of natural endowments or limitations. Is the mentally ill person of *El Padre Mio* on the street because of his own limitations or because of the moral insufficiency of cultural systems? Art that would attempt to explore such significant queries is dismissed early on in Tierney-Tello's essay as self-serving and unwilling to acknowledge the oppressed and silenced as persons of integrity and uniqueness.

Indeed, the bases of solidarity—rationality, identification, and comprehension—are thrown into question [by *El Padre Mio*]. The text forces us to confront a complex other who resists identification, whose identity is diffuse and ungraspable. . . . *El Padre Mio* puts into question an easy political or social solidarity, a solidarity based on identification and identity politics. (p. 84)

The wider question of whether Latin American *testimonio* literature, or any other literature or art form, should avoid politically based agendas for the sake of a vague authenticity created through an artistic form is never raised by Tierney-Tello. The result comes dangerously close to an *a priori* acceptance of a formalist view of art, if not in the same category as nineteenth-century "art for art's sake" theory, certainly within the narrow confines of the New Criticism, wherein the integrity of literary form is prioritized over such momentary preoccupations as social and political justice. Tierney-Tello dismisses partisan literary endeavors as "false identity politics," a label that apparently justifies her turn away from considerations of political efficacy in literature to an unexplained valorization of the author's (Eltit's) artistic preoccupation: "One must be careful not to endow Eltit's project with more political ambitions than it takes on itself" (p. 93).

Still, Tierney-Tello offers a qualification to Eltit's apparently apolitical work. "While we might hope that profoundly disturbing literature like Eltit's could transform hierarchies and the status quo, they remain for the most part unchanged" (p. 93). The question remains whether Eltit's *testimonio* of the oppressed should be viewed as transcending both identitarian politics and the regressive status quo, creating an art work that somehow essentializes the ontology of the oppressed, or whether it should be seen as dodging wider social and political issues of systemic oppression. That Eltit's unique literary approach captures an (the?) essential character of her oppressed subjects may or may not be true, but does this justify a dismissal of the political implications of such exposition? Are we not back to preferring the sacred realm of art over the mundane—and certainly more psychologically difficult—task of exposing the hidden negativities of Third World capitalist formations? In any case, the tension between, on the one hand, literature as a craft demanding training and the special sensitivity obtained from relatively privileged social positions, and, on the other, the underprivileged nature of its subject matter remains an important concern in the First as well as the Third World.

ALTERNATIVE FORMS OF REALISM IN ONWUEME

For women playwrights who present social justice issues in Third World contexts, the binary of art versus politics remains less consequential than the promotion of positive identity formation and consciousness raising for political change. While these writers have been concerned with issues of artistic and ethical authenticity, they have also sought congruencies between what Eagleton (1992) defines as the "glorious futility" (p. 92) of the aesthetic and partisan commitments. To accept, as Tierney-Tello argues, one approach to the exclusion of the other—the individual subject as paramount versus political statement—is to commit needlessly an either-or fallacy harmful both to artistic freedom and to political efficacies. Onwueme makes no such distinctions but instead attempts to enlist aesthetics for political goals. For this purpose, she associates the integrity of her characters as members of oppressed groups, avoiding stereotypical formulations and other overdetermined distortions. In this respect, she differs from male writers, such as Soyinka, who prefers well-articulated characters representing broad social and political forces within Nigerian society. Onwueme's stagecraft accepts more straightforwardly a realist tradition of uniquely defined characters, plots centered around a specificity of social issues, and a general rejection of presentational elements, such as modified ritual, symbolist imagery, stylized dance, and characters with mythopoeic associations. Hence the critical and subversive ends of Onwueme's didactic drama are realized more through the particularity of reality-based settings and circumstances. Whether this is because ritual and myth are too much associated with traditional, and hence patriarchal, projects is another question.

Women's voices in social justice drama have received less consideration by critics and theorists. Crow and Banfield (1996), for instance, do not feature a woman playwright in their otherwise insightful *Introduction to Post-Colonial Theatre*. Beginning in the early 1980s, feminist scholars have moved away from forging a grand social theory of the causes of sexist practice. Since Nancy Chodorow and Carol Gilligan, who proposed the study of women's moral discourse—as distinct from traditional male-oriented projects—female counter-models of moral development have been charged, in turn, with false generalizations, especially by Third World women (Fraser & Nicholson, 1988). First World feminist theory, increasingly stirred to revisionism by the criticism of Third World women's groups and subaltern groups within the First World, has generally shunned universalistic statements about women's identity and the nature of women's oppression. Instead, it has stressed the specificity of historical oppression and the particularities of hegemonic formations. For instance, functionalist categories such as "reproduction," "nurturing," and "homemaking" generally have been discarded as ahistorical in favor of historically generated terms such as "the modern," "restricted," "male-headed," and "nuclear family" (Fraser & Nicholson, 1988, p. 101).

The result of this particularistic approach to women's issues has been a greater worldwide emphasis on documenting the struggles of delimited groups of women. Within world drama, this has led to a proliferation of play productions by and about distinct social formations along lines of ethnicity, race, sexual orientation, and class. The plays of Tess Akaeke Onwueme articulate a uniquely feminine approach to Nigerian dramatic representation. As such, they also qualify in the general trend away from universalistic notions of women's identity by contributing to a distinctly national culture—in the case of Nigeria, as we have seen, an incipient national culture of multiple subcultures. In turn, Onwueme's dramaturgy remains open to the charge of universalizing Nigerian women's experience, since that country remains a postcolonial pastiche of diverse ethnic and religious groupings. Onwueme's approach is distinctly different from the first generation of male Nigerian playwrights, but does show affinity with second-generation male playwrights in the turn towards the dialectic of specific social issues, especially concerns common to the relatively privileged groups within a West African university community.

Eagleton's (1992) concern that the aesthetic need only reflect "human existence itself, which needs no rationale beyond it own self-delight" becomes a less conscious aim when the aesthetic is used in socially conscious fictional creations, such as drama and the novel, than in biographical forms such as Latin American *testimonio* literature of the marginalized and oppressed. Far from viewing the literature and art of social subjects as inherently self-indulgent and exploitative, creating, for Tierney-Tello, "an easy political and social solidarity" dependent upon "pity or a false identity politics" (1999, p. 84), Onwueme is openly factitious in her intent to evoke through artistic artifice the appropriate audience response, highlighting the aesthetic for ethical purposes. In this regard she consciously follows Brecht's Epic Theatre method of artfully breaking the theatre's fourth wall: "When you break that fourth wall, then there is participation. . . . It becomes a communal effort. Everybody becomes a part of it" (Onwueme, 1993, p.12). Onwueme's grasp of the Brechtian paradox, to use art to transcend art for the sake of ethical awareness, leads directly to a progressive agenda whose goal is nothing short of historical transformation. "I feel that history is made, not by accepting history as it is, but by people rewriting it. . . . I consider writing to be a dialogue between the writer and the society. . . . People create social conditions and people can change social conditions for the better" (Onwueme, 1993, p. 11).

Here may be a distinction between First and Third World approaches to the aesthetics of social justice. Whereas theorists such as Tierney-Tello, Alberto Moreiras, and George Yudice seek to defend the compassion of the reader for the disenfranchised and are wary of the tendency of postmodern texts to marginalize their subject matter for the sake of "the thrill of the postmodern sublime" (Yudice, 1988, p. 225), Onwueme by contrast seeks first "a dialogue between the writer and the society" that engages social justice issues. Her approach depends on the willingness of readers/audience members to construct a meaningful dialectic with her characters and settings. This faith in the reception of her texts assumes a relatively self-actualized audience free from both the indoctrinating powers of global capital and the complacencies of traditional feudal culture. Writing and producing within the comparatively rarefied environment of Third World university theatre departments and regional theatres, Onwueme can assume much about her audiences.

The Broken Calabash

The Broken Calabash was premiered in 1984 at the National Theatre in Lagos by the Federal University of Technology's Owerri Theatre Troupe. It was presented forthrightly as an exposition of the "revolt of intellectual modernity against a decadent traditional value of the caste system" (from introductory notes to the first edition, quoted in Redmond, 1993, p. 15). Traditional feudal culture is subverted through an interpersonal conflict involving a love triangle within the nuclear family, a formula well within the traditions of Western tragedy and comedy. Onwueme found her heroine close to home—Ona, a contemporary Nigerian university student, newly converted to Christianity, who, in the tradition of Antigone, Juliet, and Cordelia, suffers in pursuit of "the individual conviction of insurmountability of genuine love for another person in spite of traditional and unholy attitudes of discrimination" (*ibid.*). In contrast to Soyinka's major plays, such as *The River* and *Madmen and Specialists*, the *Broken Calabash* focuses upon the intimate life of a single class within Nigerian society. The depiction of a particular privileged family sets the drama within the dominant inner circle of local social structure—the family is not from among the ruling elite of Nigeria but has profited indirectly from the preservation of the economic and cultural status quo. As a young woman, the protagonist represents a marginalized group within a relatively privileged class. The dramatic conflict defines a tensive ambivalence between, on the one hand, all that fosters privilege and traditional prerogative, and, on the other, a willingness—callow and feckless though it may be—to subvert such hegemonic values.

Like Moni in Osofisan's *The Oriki of a Grasshopper*, Ona is a university student influenced by Western concepts of equality and individual freedom beyond traditional caste and gender. However, both characters occupy opposite ends of a spectrum of personality and moral commitment. Moni embodies what Martha Nussbaum (1986) would suggest is a well-balanced appreciation of the Greek ideals of *techne*—"the aspiration to make the goodness of a good life safe from luck through the controlling power of reason" (p. 89)—and *tuche*—the portion of human living we do not control (p. 3). Nussbaum finds that both Antigone, Sophocles' righteous heroine who will not yield to social pressure or threat of death, and Creon, her king who remains equally unyielding, are "engaged in a ruthless simplification of the world of value which effectively eliminates conflicting obligations" (p. 65). Neither will look beyond their own black-and-white ethical norms nor yield to love and compassion in the usual way. By contrast, the best of Greek ethical culture, according to Nussbaum, balanced the ethical rationality of *teche* and the loving responsiveness to concrete particularity of *tuche*. Thus, "[t]o perceive the particulars fully it may be necessary to love them" (p. 70). Osofisan's Moni possesses this balancing of opposites, an ethical capacity to break through the fortified walls of social complacency and hypocrisy. She also shows a sensitivity towards human contradictions that produces a feeling responsiveness within a torn world. However, Ona possesses neither of these qualities in their appropriate degree. Her carelessness and ambivalence towards the complexities of the postcolonial life world prevent any sort of fulfillment on the personal and social levels within the scope of Onwueme's drama.

By presenting a protagonist whose articulate denunciations of traditional West African hierarchies are undermined by the powerful seductive forms of Western culture, Onwueme's dramaturgy avoids the clichés common to postcolonial liberation discourse, with its two-dimensional characterizations and oversimplified dichotomies. First-generation Nigerian theorists had criticized such distorted representations of Afrocentric virtues and European (neo)colonial villainies in an attempt to bypass false binaries in favor of truly creative identity-forming cultural texts (e.g., Soyinka, *Art, Dialogue and Outrage*, 1988). The generation of Onwueme understood the shortcomings of the Negritude Movement and recognized the need to induce a healthy balance of Western and African cultural elements for the sake of social change. The difficulty of this project precluded facile solutions and syncretistic formulas derived from African as well as Western thought. Hence *The Broken Calabash* avoids easy messages by utilizing the potentiality of drama—and art in general—to challenge both the demagogic discourse of the Negritude Movement and the uncritical accommodation to Western influence, with its globalized capital and culture of commodification. In this attempt, Onwueme understands drama as a politically ambivalent cultural text. Like Eagleton, she recognizes "the very glorious futility" of the aesthetic, using its exposition of the particular and circumstantial in human life to challenge those ideologies and movements that utilize only the *teche* of truth and avoid the elusive in human living. To this extent, the didactic element in *The Broken Calabash* functions as critique rather than transparent political formula.

Ona's university training allows her to express criticism of the hierarchical culture to her fellow students and to her father, Courtuma, a chief and former court messenger in the traditional society. Her dissidence in the first scenes contrasts with the conventionality of her fellow student Ugo, who prefers romantic intrigue to serious political discussion. Ona scolds Ugo for succumbing to the new global culture of commodification.

So you think and are made to feel. But in actual fact, it's all a make-believe—mere phototrick which is a necessary insurance (or antidote?) for self-survival and self-realization in a world with neither worth nor direction. We all wear more than one face at a time in this society. (*The Broken Calabash*, 1993, p. 25)

While Ona's speechifying has merit, it sounds less than genuine, a projection of her classroom notes and discussions with faculty and fellow students. Moreover, her criticism is self-reflexive, since her point that everyone in Nigeria assumes multiple identities applies foremost to herself. This irony becomes more blatant as the drama develops. Although Ona speaks social truths without fully comprehending her own complicity, her reproachful generalizations foreshadow what becomes all too particularized in her own family relationships as the action develops: The "stagnant air of tradition" will absorb "[t]hose *directly* flowing with the new current which the wind of the old insists on drowning" (*The Broken Calakabh*, p. 25).

Ona's hybridity remains shallow and affected. Although she has converted to the religion of the colonialists, her practicing Christianity serves only as a youthful rebellion from her parents, who remain within the indigenous faith. She uses the excuse of going to Sunday church service to make love to her boyfriend, Diaku. This deception provides distance from her parents and the private space that her Westernized individualism requires. Thus church becomes for Ona a source of ideological rebellion and at the same time a self-serving means to a social life. Although she lacks Ona's critical vocabulary for political dissent, Ugo appreciates Ona's wish to make her own decisions about dating and marriage. Both agree that parents "insist on roping their experiences around you" (p. 29). In their conversation, the young women enjoy youthful exuberance and independence, preferring the typical adolescent forms such defiance takes— sex with whomever they, not their parents, choose; experimentation with new and controversial practices like Christianity. Neither takes seriously actions of protest against the political structure. Thus, Ona remains a political ideologue with no motivation to serve the cause of social justice if it does not further her immediate and personal desires. Ugo is more perceptive than she knows when she characterizes Ona's fight with her parents as "a battle of wits" (p. 29). Throughout the play, the dialectic between the characters remains more pathological than sincere, mere buzz words intended for self-serving ends than groundwork pursuant of social change.

Oliaku, Ona's mother, reminds Courtuma that Ona as the only child and daughter must either "marry a wife" for her father "to propagate that line" or become an *Idegbe* to bear children by her father (p. 34). This local custom rests uneasily with the parents, not because they have questioned this traditional practice on ethical grounds, but for immediate issues of propriety. They fear that "[l]ife is no longer as simple as that. Times are changing, and we must not pretend as if the harmattan wind cannot char our skin, too" (p. 34). For Courtuma, Ona's Eurocentric education has become a trade-off between economic realities and traditional ways, both of which he and Oliaku define in self-serving ways. They have sent Ona to the university to learn how to acquire "the white man's wealth" for the family, which they feel is under threat from other Nigerian families who have also exposed their children to Western learning to keep their families financially solvent. This ethic of keeping up with the Joneses also appears among the extended family members, who purposely write letters to Oliaku in English to display their knowledge of the former colonizer's tongue. Oliaku's anxiety about not being able to read her relatives' letters can only be relieved by Ona's capacity to read English. But the shallowness of the parents' views extends even to their own traditional culture, evident when Courtuma reminds his wife that she could not read her relatives' letters from Lago even if they were written in Igbo. Caught between the deterioration of their first culture and the frightful uncertainties of the globalized Western culture governed by transnational capitalism and enforced by a ruling military clique from rival tribal confederation, Courtuma and Oliaku can only regard the future with dread. Their commitment to the past and the future of West African culture, like Ona's speechifying, is shallow at best and at worst disingenuous. Courtuma resolves to remind Ona of her obligation to bear her father's children or marry a substitute for herself, but even this traditional practice is undertaken in a devious and secretive manner.

Courtuma attempts to seduce Ona with words while Oliaku is away. Although Ona pushes him away, her ambivalence appears when she wishes that "God gives me a husband like him, my father" (p. 39). However, she also realizes that the feelings between them threaten her integrity and independence. "Why must you tear me away from myself?" (p. 39). Ona's social statements at the beginning of the play are seen to foreshadow the far more literal way in which Ona must break free from parental authority. Courtuma continues the conversation with his daughter, which becomes a dialectic against Christianity as the most visible form of Western neocolonialism in Nigeria. His arguments are shallow and emotive, indicative of the real reason for his disquisition against the sacraments of Christianity—Ona's time spent at the church is a betrayal of his romantic feelings for her. In this he may sense Ona's use of Christianity to cover her relationship with Diaku. When Diaku visits the house under the eye of Courtuma, he and Ona pretend to read the Bible while Diaku holds her thigh. Like Ona's decision to wear her hair straight to rebel against parental traditions, her Christianity remains, on the surface, a means to achieve immediate ends.

When Oliaku speaks to Ona about having children by Courtuma or finding a wife substitute, she reminds her daughter that she was given to Courtuma and has no choice. At least Ona can choose between two options. Ona's response has for the first time the ring of sincerity. Her anger is directed at the attack on her freedom as a woman. "You people have a very ambitious murder plan. You will not only slaughter me on the altar of your decadent tradition, but would also want another female head. I say to hell with your tradition" (p. 56). Her outburst is the first earnest confrontation in the play, revealing a progression from secretive subversive acts to genuine political discourse. At this point also, Ona's words take on a lyricism that associates with the poetic cry of the choral characters in the play—the Town Crier and the satirical dancers: "Let the wind blow— let the shaky homestead be blown. Anything that cannot stand the force of change must be uprooted into oblivion by the storm heralding the new season!" (p. 56). Her outcry, reminiscent of King Lear's storm speeches, marks a rite of passage from the old to the new values. Nature and time become politicized in her speech, just as the Town Crier sings earlier, "We are in a period of transition. *Kom!* / New yam must be eaten. *Kom!*" (p. 42). Nature as changeable and human values as malleable stand in opposition to the chant of Dibia, the village priest: "Each youth is for Ine. / As we did this year . . . / Every year, every year / The day and then the night / The day and then the night" (p. 53).

With a newfound strength, Ona now seeks to rebut Courtuma's arguments from traditional authority. Pointing out that having her father's children or marrying a wife for him will not bring the "pure blood" that Courtuma feels Diaku's family lacks, she concludes by condemning the traditional system as "indirectly encouraging prostitution" (p. 56). Ona raises the argument to a broader plane by appealing to the vacuity of the old traditions in the current era. "If the homestead is too shaky, it must come down with the storm. If the tree's root is not firm, let it show its face to the sky" (p. 57). Ona has expressed openly, to her parents, the perspective she used hitherto only privately to Ugo, when she was parroting the language of her teachers. Her final rebuttal is underscored by the Town Crier's "*frightening*" cry, "Courtuma, the moon will soon be out. It shall be full, but it shall be red. A new season comes. . . . Let the wind blow" (p. 57). Courtuma is silenced by these authoritative words of condemnation.

In the final scene, events turn unexpectedly. Ona lies sick at home and the Jester implies that she is pregnant and perhaps seeking an abortion. News arrives that Ugo and Diaku have married, confirming Ona's fear expressed in the first scene that other women will steal her man. What follows are a series of disturbing questions offered by the Jester. Is Ona sick? Pregnant? Ill from an abortion? Attempting suicide? But the Jester's queries are grounded in political and social concerns. His ideal view of Ona places her among those who do not wear makeup or "whitewash their skin." As the only child of Courtuma the chief, Ona must abandon Western pursuits and rejoin the propitiatory rituals that mark traditional culture. "Will Ona join us at the festival to satirize those who have defiled the land? Will the land be purged? And the new season see its new yam?" (p. 58).

The traditional village priest, Dibia, arrives to revive Ona, who quickly accuses her father of paternity. When Courtuma protests in horror, reminding her of their homestead and of what will happen to him under the new laws against incest, Ona reveals her plan of vengeance: "that is why you're the father of my child. You asked for it, and you got it" (p. 60). Courtuma runs away in fright throwing off his beads of office. As soon as the pregnancy is revealed, Dibia runs away hastily, underscoring the frailty of traditional religion. As Oliaku and the entire village cry in panic and grief, Ona is seen running back and forth between the crucifix and the traditional shrine in Dantesque despair. Her frenzied act of desperation stems from a confused cultural hybridity. The Town Crier concludes the play with a poetic lament for these catastrophic occurrences during the festival of transition from the old to the new season: "The new yam will be eaten, but it is streaked with blood" (p. 61). As he ponders the disruption of the old culture and the failure of the new, postcolonial culture, Ona continues to run between the African and European religious images.

In many respects, *The Broken Calabash* parallels Sophoclean tragic structure. Choral figures periodically comment on the misfortunes of a leading family and their implications for the larger community. Poetic verse connects nature, cyclical time (the seasons, the harvest, the yearly festivals), and cultural decay, lamenting the degeneration of the old ways and the shallowness of the new commodity culture of global capitalism). Choral dancers satirize new, confusing identities, most theatrically in the performance of cross-dressing men and women who dress defiantly as men. Sophoclean pessimism fills the play: The traditional religion is corrupt and timid; the new religion of Christianity is practiced without the spirit; traditional practices supporting local leadership are taken with ambivalence and even outlawed by the postcolonial government; and the meaning of the religious festival is challenged by Courtuma's suicide and Ona's disgrace.

In fact, the story bears striking similarity to Sophocles' most famous tragedy, *Oedipus Rex*, where a royal family falls into disgrace through incest and suicide. Still, Onwueme has managed to create a distinct tragedy by weaving West African characters, rituals of belief, and metaphysical perspectives into a bitter criticism of value systems that have weakened the social fabric of Nigeria and led to corruption and group divisionism. The play succeeds most remarkably in the difficult task of presenting class, gender, and religious injustices within a traditional African religious milieu. Even more, Onwueme's complex depiction of cultural ambivalence reveals a preference for verisimilitude over ritual celebration and simplistic political agendas. West African religious rituals and customs are scrutinized rather than used as nostalgic markers.

Psychologically, Onwueme's characters are among the most developed in Nigerian literature, yet her dramatic works remain primarily political in orientation. Behind the lust and hypocrisy of a prominent family, larger issues of justice and civic consciousness are presented. Onwueme's unwillingness to present transparent equations of new/good, old/bad, or to take immediate sides in the battle of generations, religions, and genders renders the political issues all the more compelling.

Parables for a Season

In her next play, *Parables for a Season*, Onwueme presents the drama of political succession in true Shakespearean proportions. Women as heroic figures speaking lyrical verse are featured. All the same, the chief characters remain complex and the theme of corruption and lust for power in high places prevents any romanticization of the past. In language of power and beauty, Nigerian social history becomes a straightforward struggle for women's rights and democratic values. Whereas *Calabash* contained complex female characters with ambivalent motivations and ineffectual actions, *Parables* offers strong, authoritative women whose resourcefulness and cunning make them major players in the struggle for royal succession. Their artfulness and considerable strength cross traditional gender lines, in contrast to the women of *Calabash*, whose mostly passive roles afford them only supportive power for their male leaders. (Ona manages only belatedly to stand against paternal authority, but her strength is motivated more by personal revenge than political cause, a circumstance that confirms her dependence upon momentary passions.) *Parables* also offers a range of ethical perspectives among its women characters, who are governed more by individual willpower than by the strictures of conventional social authority. For example, like the daughters of King Lear, the queens of Ogiso present a wide spectrum of views on the right to succession. They are as much independent players as the men in the drama. The heroine, Zo, disguises herself as a young girl, Wazobia, a name that combines the names of the three youngest, and therefore most vulnerable, queens, Wa, Zo, and Bia. This symbolic solidarity in the main character lends an allegorical element that associates with organized resistance in the cause of democratic development, extending the promise of positive social change.

Even more than those of *Calabash*, the characters of *Parables* are preoccupied with time's natural manifestations—the change of seasons, the evidence of decay and growth. The Town Crier and Chorus of commoners sing not of measured time (the classical Greek *chronos*), but of special time, the noncalendar time of fulfillment (*kairos*). Ogiso, the wise foreign chieftain, observes the contradiction of the seasons—that the fullness of life, time's promise of fulfillment, also leads to its downfall and death. "A time comes when the pear fruit / Ripens and must fall. / A time comes when the coconut laden / With milk goes on its downward journey / In ascent of powers above" (p. 69). The upward and downward movements of organic nature express the fortunes of both individuals and societies. But the cyclical movement of nature is not always progressive. The characters are aware of the general corruption of the time, a falling off from the halcyon days of King Ogiso, now faded to a distant past. The threatening dualism of fruitfulness and corruption permeates the play's psychology. The foreigner Ozoma, outside the play for power, speaks candidly of political realities: "King, Your parables Are for a generation With imagination on wings. Ours is a generation With thick scum on our ears" (p. 75). Emblematic of the falling away from social fulfillment is the looming "uncompleted monument," product of the labor of the commoners, but, unlike the pyramids of Old Kingdom Egypt, a "mound" that serves only to remind everyone of the moral inadequacies of the times.

Whoever succeeds King Ogiso will right all wrongs, completing the monument before it crumbles from neglect. A royal woman must succeed to the throne, but the queens jealously fight among themselves for power, some conspiring with male chiefs to aid their cause. The most senior queen, Anehe, reveals her jealousy of the younger queens, Zo and Bia. "You think we are now Equal because the king raised You to his shoulder against The will of everyone else?" In a long tirade to Zo, Anehe tells of the perils facing royal women at court. Their beauty initially attracts, but soon fades in favor of younger beauties. It takes courage, cunning, and sacrifice to endure. The election of the female king-surrogate is complicated by the appearance of the commoners, who, like the queens, express the injustices of the system. The commoners are more articulate than the queens about the need for democratic values. Sotimo: "That's the tragedy of our times, That issues are not considered on Merit but on solidarity, numerical Strength and atavistic concepts Of race and superiority." Adamawa: "It makes nonsense of democracy" (p. 85). The elections are rigged in favor of the landowners, but the voices of the commoners are not enough to bring in the time of fulfillment. The younger queens, feeling most strongly the injustices of the system at court, finally realize that the social structure has caused the evil of the times. Wa: "Even the best of us at the best Of times is a toy in the hands Of power and men" (p. 98).

At the critical moment, Zo disguises herself as Wazobia, proclaiming, "Why must we strive to accept the imbalance?" Her solution follows traditional West African polity—social transformation is initiated by a powerful leader with a religious mandate. Though her language uses traditional organic imagery, her program of reform is democratic in spirit: "And I am the wood That will give fire to the kingdom's herbs To enkindle light in this dark abyss." Moreover, Wazobia perceives her reform reign in feminist terms. Woman's traditional childbearing role is widened to include political creativity: "The task of woman is to build—to create" (pp. 103, 104). An aristocratic coup is quickly thwarted, which prompts the outrage of the commoners, who challenge the exclusivity of the election and the inequalities of the feudal system: "While some ride free on the Backs of others, Others trudge on through and Through to the end" (pp. 112–114). Their call for power sharing is abruptly halted by Wazobia, however, who uses gender issues to momentarily appease the commoners' demands for social equality: "No! I am woman! I carve my Own path. . . . A female leads you in The new dance step. Up!" (p. 121). Her call for universal support of her reign leaves open the question of the extent to which she will seek to finish the social monument along democratic lines.

The Reign of Wazobia

Zo as Wazobia the new regent king rules the Aniocha Igbo community now bifurcated by issues of gender, class, and culture. More than the other Onwueme plays of the trilogy, *The Reign of Wazobia* uses dialectic to present these issues. The characters—divided between aristocratic men and women, commoners, who tend to be more egalitarian in gender and class concerns, and younger aristocratic women—debate using a "purpose, passion, discussion" method familiar to Shavian drama. Wazobia tells Iyase, the conspiratorial male chief, that the feudal, exclusionary ways must be replaced by a broad program of social reform and inclusiveness. Her language demonstrates to a suspicious feudal society conviction and dramatic effect. "I do not see any reason why women and youths must be kept away from matters of state concern. Matters of state affect them much as they affect chiefs and princes" (p. 149).

Onwueme achieves in *Wazobia* what Brecht rarely demonstrated in his dramas, a presentation of characters and situations that offer clear programs of action. The reactionary chiefs bring a wide range of issues into the argument against a woman's reign, from break-dancing to women's liberation. By contrast, Wazobia's program of reform is presented systematically in Movement Three, as a direct response to Iyase's reproachful attacks on her power. When Wazobia organizes the loyal women to oppose the recidivist faction, her speech stresses women's self-sufficiency. Like Aristophanes' Lysistrata, she affirms the power of women to form their own lives. "And so on and so on. With or without man, make a meaning of your life" (p. 154).

Wazobia's program is grounded on the optimistic premise that social structures can be fundamentally improved through solidarity movements. But her viewpoint does not go unchallenged, even by her own lieutenants. Bia's cynicism follows from her awareness of the duplicity of the male and female conspirators: "In the final analysis, every man fights his own battle, only teaming up when there is a common enemy. This is the secret of their mission. Men tread and tend crooked paths" (p. 162). However, Wazobia's social vision places faith in a communitarian equality wherein all, men and women, poor and wealthy, share domestic as well as civic duties. The conspirators are defeated when the women achieve a solidarity foreshadowed in Zo's chosen name, Wazobia. Omu, the respected woman priest, takes up Wazobia's cause, uniting the Chorus of Women, who are now able to defeat the feudal forces by breaking taboos of gender: "Together we stand. What they plan is abominable, and we shall match force with force" (p. 166). The women appear in their "natural state" and surprise the men who have come to assassinate Wazobia. In these and other stage actions, Onwueme is overtly influenced by Euripides' *Lysistrata*, but her united women's movement calls explicitly for democratic reform.

Chapter 4

CINEMA IN CUBA AND BRAZIL: THE INTELLECTUALS AND THE POPULACE

Brazilian filmmaking during the 1950s and Cuban filmmaking during and after the 1959 revolution greatly enhanced the turn to social justice in Latin American cinema. Even as the revolution triumphed, Cuban directors theorized a focused, committed cinema that would further the cause of social transformation at home and abroad. Accordingly, the Cuban Institute of Film Art and Industry (ICAIC) was from its inception tightly focused, its limited budget and personnel enabling its commitment to produce political films that departed stylistically from what was taken to be the too narrow conventions of Soviet Social Realism. In seeking this break with Russian orthodoxy, Alfredo Guevara called for artistic pluralism and freedom for the individual artist, but at the same time for a uniquely Latin American approach to social justice themes. While at first ICAIC filmmaking stressed documentary, directors like Santiago Alvarez, leading the newsreel unit, produced highly confrontational and creative pieces with global themes. *Now* (1965), *Hanoi, Tuesday the 13th* (*Hanoi martes 13*, 1967), and *LBJ* (1968) became unique Third World voices in the international public sphere of human rights.

When domestic and international success threatened to transform Cuban cinema into a Hollywood studio formula-producing system, technically superior but thematically impoverished, Julio Garcia Espinosa demanded a polemical art that prioritized social justice and challenged the complacency of its audiences. What he called the "Imperfect Cinema" admonished Cubans that the virtue of necessity—small, committed production crews with limited budgets and simple equipment and production values—was the appropriate method for a cinema that sought to reveal the nature and causes of Third World social conditions. He observed that,

> in the underdeveloped world technical and artistic perfection are false objectives. . . . [T]here is more to be gained by engaging the audience directly and with a sense of urgency, roughness included. The aim . . . refuses to fix meanings and thus invites the active participation of the audience. (in Chanan, 1996, p. 745)

Espinosa's imperfect cinema shows similarities to the artistic method of the Polish stage director Jerzy Grotowski's "Poor Theatre," which emphasized minimalist *mise-en-scène*, politically committed performers, and the idea of the theatre as an encounter (Grotowski, 1968, pp. 55–59). Grotowski's Laboratory Theatre, also a state-sponsored organization, regarded stylistic innovation as an important method of disrupting audience expectations for conventional performances and plot structures. Both movements were informed by Bertolt Brecht's Epic Theatre philosophy, which above all sought to surprise and "alienate" viewers by departing from fixed meanings and instead leaving open-ended denouements, final scenes that raise questions rather than provide facile solutions. Revolutionary Cuban films and Brazilian *cinema novo* have sought several ways to startle the sensibilities of their audiences, not the least of which has been the close juxtaposition of accepted dichotomies, thus achieving a thematic irony that invites the viewer to question social contradictions. For example, in Tomas Gutierrez Alea's *Strawberry and Chocolate* (1995), a young communist vigilant attempts to expose an openly gay citizen with religious leanings while he and his fellow vigilants watch a state-approved documentary about the human rights violations of the U.S.-sponsored dictator Anastasio Samoza. Such disruptions are often self-reflexive, implicating doctrinaire attitudes of the official committed left, including socialist filmmakers, while also taking on the global perpetrators of transnational capitalism.

Alea, Cuba's most acclaimed director, began producing straightforward films documenting the revolutionary struggle but soon began experimenting beyond the confines of neorealist drama as defined by postwar Italian cinema and the older Soviet cinema tradition. Alea characteristically mixes comedy and drama, using light and heavy satirical elements to uncover ambivalence within the revolutionary movement. Following the tradition for films about Latin American slavery begun by Brazilian Carlos Diegues, Alea produced historical films that pointedly reflect upon present social practices, allowing an anachronistic approach to theme in the Brechtian manner.

Death of a Bureaucrat: Bureaucracy Lite

Alea's *Death of a Bureaucrat* (1966) satirizes life under social planning in a nation recently released from neocolonial and transnational corporate control. That Cuba was and remains unique in the Americas for sustaining a social structural alternative to the dominant, military-supported capitalism of North America has not prevented its state-financed film industry from producing self-critical satires. Alea's satire was made during the years when the First World undertook a general movement towards the left—the 1968 protests in Europe and the civil rights and Viet Nam war movements in the United States were its salient features. The film retains a confidence in the socialist system in that sympathetic humor for the "common man" theme prevents a more acerbic criticism of the state as inhuman monolith. Unlike the devastating futuristic novels of George Orwell (*1984*) and Aldous Huxley (*Brave New World*), Alea does not indict the regulated society as soul-destroying and deprived. Rather, his perplexed protagonist, the Nephew, confronts the contradictions of the Cuban revolution's bureaucracy without surrendering his social or personal identity, or forfeiting his body and mind. *Bureaucrat* functions more as constructive criticism from the loyal opposition than as an external indictment of the 1959 revolution.

Whereas Charlie Chaplin's common man character in *Modern Times* becomes a literal cog in the wheel to industrial exploitation under capitalism, Alea's Nephew uncovers the lusts, petty professionalism, indifference, self-absorption and neuroses of state bureaucracy without himself experiencing an inhuman transformation. The Nephew's series of predicaments—some inspired by the physicality of screen comedians such as Harold Lloyd and Buster Keaton—result from the vagaries of bureaucratic structures, but they only momentarily frustrate his purposes, rather than threaten self-identity. Death assumes multivalent meanings in the film. The funereal elements are reproduced with ironic intent within a distinctly Caribbean colonial *mise-en-scène*—rococo angels, plumed horses, and brass bands. These associations of the old order contrast with the posters created in the Revolutionary Office of Graphic Arts, which proclaim "Death to the Enemies of Socialism" and, most ironic of all, "Stamp out Bureaucracy." In fact, the film's title, *Death of a Bureaucrat*, is easily transposed into Death of Bureaucracy. What must die in Alea's film is the hypocrisy and insularity of institutional structures, which substitute professionalism and careerism for the ideals of the revolution.

A model worker is buried with his work card as a spontaneous gesture of tribute by the mourners for his invention of a machine that reproduces mass assembly statues of socialist heroes. When the deceased's nephew and widow go to the pension board, they are informed that no allocation can begin without the deceased's work card. When the Nephew visits the cemetery office to access his uncle's coffin for the work card, he is informed that a Certificate of Exhumation is necessary, even if the body is not actually moved from the cemetery. After the nephew moves the coffin himself by night and retrieves the work card for his aunt, he learns that he cannot bury his uncle again without a Certificate of Exhumation. At the Office of Exhumation he learns that his case is special, since he does not actually want to transport the body from the cemetery, which in any case would not be allowed for two years. He is sent instead to the Office of Expediting, where there is a long line of applicants. The office closes just as he reaches the clerk. Hiding in the deserted office, he finds the stamp of approval for his certificate, but cannot get out of the office building. His desperate attempt to crawl along the building ledge at the top floor draws a crowd, who assumes he is attempting suicide. Meanwhile his uncle's body is taken from the aunt's house by public health officials guiding the cemetery workers. As the narrative ends, bureaucratic planning has been superseded by seemingly random acts by isolated but powerful institutions.

In fact, the bureaucratic fastidiousness of state planning is interrupted throughout the film by outbursts of interdepartmental squabbling, street fighting, and lustful trysts among the public servants. These low-comic elements move the film towards a more sympathetic treatment of institutional functionaries, who are represented as all too human under a thin facade of formality. Unlike Kafka's bureaucratic figures, whose amiable tone hides a nightmarish malice, Alea's managers, clerks, and bosses seem less threatening when they reveal moments of humanness. In the Office of Pensions, for example, the chief clerk and the manager reassure the Nephew that they will "personally handle the pension" when the work card is produced, and express great sympathy for the "desire to take articles of value for the afterlife, like the Egyptians of old." Though their congeniality never questions the institutional forms they follow, and their interest in the Nephew's case derives more from the boredom of office routine than from simple kindness, their behavior reveals a stubborn humanity rather than evil intent. For example, the manager's eyes stray to the figure of a woman filer while he is reassuring the Nephew of his full cooperation and sympathy.

Even the Nephew's nightmare about his predicament becomes a parodic tribute to Luis Bunuel's well-known surrealist scenes in *The Andalusian Dog* (1929). In the dream the Nephew pulls a coffin with a rope along a dusty road. The coffin becomes two nuns whom he pulls with great effort. In Bunuel's famous scene, two priests are pulled by a dreaming character with great struggle in an apparent reference to the burden of conventional morality. Alea's use of surrealism loses its critical edge because the filmic allusion to Bunuel turns the sequence into comedy. Another scene that offers the potential of Kafkaesque and surrealist nightmare includes the moment when the Nephew discovers that all doors to the bureaucratic office lock from the outside, preventing his escape. This would work as Brechtian social gest, as a critical metaphor showing the inability of escape from institutional structures. However, the general comic pace of the scene, carrying over to the walk on the top floor ledge of the building—a filmic reference to Harold Lloyd's famous scene on the skyscraper, including a large outside building clock—neutralizes any deeper interrogation of institutional planning. Other comic devices that mitigate social critique of the injustices of state planning under socialism and advanced capitalism under Third World statism include the characters' superstitious fear of the graveyard at night and the vampire fangs of the waiter in the restaurant by the cemetery. Even the miniature rocket ship used for passing interoffice paper forms is amusing rather than threatening as an allusion to Cold War nuclear power.

Alea's references to technology critique the techno-optimist ideologies employed by institutional power, but the low-comic treatment of these scenes prevents a more significant statement about the relations of technology and power. The Nephew's psychiatric examination parodies Freudian, Skinnerian, and Pavlovian praxis, but Alea never connects in a serious way these deterministic ideologies to social systems of control. The deceased uncle's machine for producing busts of revolutionary heroes suggests the ubiquity of triumphalist ideology under the revolution rather than the tyranny of the machine under structures of power. Although the Nephew is caught in one bureaucratic entanglement after another, is diagnosed for mental illness twice, and is accused of all manner of crimes against the bureaucracy of death—even necrophilia—he remains only partially affected by the fiasco of red tape and duplicity that characterizes the film's bureaucratic milieu. Near the end of the day he still can absentmindedly take the ice shavings for his rum drink from the block of ice that preserves his uncle's body, much to his aunt's consternation. Alea presents a revolutionary society capable of being satirized but not critiqued for fundamental injustices.

Memories of Underdevelopment: Postrevolutionary Detachment

Perhaps Alea's most important film for narrative inventiveness and thematic richness is *Memories of Underdevelopment* (*Memorias del subdesarollo*, 1968). Made during the year of euphoric activism in Europe and North America, it presents an individual caught between his sensitivity toward the ideals of the Cuban revolution and his intellectual solitude. As the bourgeois intellectual of Marxism, Sergio represents a modern Latin American whose ambivalence keeps him from fully identifying with any social movement, yet whose personal preoccupations do not prevent him from recognizing the fundamental injustices of the old (Batista) regime. Caught between moral choices, Sergio can comment on social needs, including issues related to revolutionary government policy, but lacks the ability to move decisively in any direction. An inside observer at his typewriter, deserted by wife and family, he remains a socially isolated outsider.

The film begins in 1961, two years after the revolution, when members of the property classes are leaving Cuba for the U.S. at the Havana Airport. These scenes of bridled anger and relinquished class dignity contrast with the opening sequence of scenes showing vibrant salsa dancers, who are among the people remaining in Cuba to continue the social transformation. Sergio bids his mother and father farewell for their flight to Miami, but he and his wife Laura do not kiss, instead they exchange looks of hostility and contempt. Sergio's narrative voice-over, the words from his apartment typewriter, predicts that Laura will work for a while until she gets tired, then marry someone who will take care of her. His bitterness and loss are explained in an innovative narrative sequence where he and Laura fight violently over his decision to remain in Cuba. Sergio has audiotaped their conversation and replays the bitter words throughout the film as a voiceover. At one point, the fight scene is visually reproduced. This narrative repetition evokes the self-centered materialism of the lifestyle Sergio abandoned to remain part of the Revolution. Although he has distanced himself from his family and former life, he remains unattached to the new society.

Back at his apartment, Sergio looks through a telescope at Havana and pronounces it unchanged. Soon after, however, he remarks how everything has changed. His personal transformation seems to happen unconsciously, as Sergio plays with his wife's abandoned clothing and jewelry, at one point trying on a luxurious robe. The cross-dressing reflects the general role-playing that characterized his former life recently rejected. He supports the revolution intellectually but denies its reality through self-imposed isolation. As Sergio's voiceover narrates the general social injustices plaguing Latin America, using poverty statistics for argument—"twenty million children die of malnutrition every decade"—he also fantasizes a lovemaking scene with his new domestic, an attractive young woman who is a newly baptized Protestant. Sergio embraces her in a river, replacing the minister as baptizer. The harsh realities of Cold War politics intrude into this fantasy when actual newsreel shots of the atrocities of the Bay of Pigs are shown. In a particularly devastating newsreel scene, the captured invasion leaders face their accusers. A woman describes the torture and death of her family as the perpetrators stare at her defiantly. The radical evil depicted in the newsreel footage contrasts with Sergio's sexual daydreams, represented in soft-focus fantasy scenes. Sergio's prurient preoccupations derive from his seductive lifestyle of abundance before the revolution, but these class associations do not prevent his intellectual and professional commitment to the new egalitarian ideals. Still, he remains emotionally and psychologically distant from these ideals and cannot commit interpersonally.

Two people who represent the lack of commitment and social isolation rife in the early years of the revolution are Pablo and Elena, who have their own stories in the film narrative. Elena has a relationship with Sergio soon after his wife and parents leave. She shows little interest in political issues and cultural matters. Sergio's approach to her callowness is to see her in some way as a "typical Cuban," who because of underdevelopment has "an inability to relate to things." Their difference in age further serves to distance Sergio from her, making Sergio aware of his inability to relate to people and the social transformation taking place. Elena's teenage interests make her oblivious to the social transformation that affects her, just as Sergio remains unmoved by the immediacy of the structural changes within Cuban society. When he is visited by government assessors who inventory his apartment building, an action that he knows will lead to the confiscation of his property, he remains passive and uninvolved. Similarly, Sergio's friend Pablo insists nervously that he has never given the revolutionary government cause to be against him, yet he remains uninterested in the social improvement programs, seeking only to leave the country. The lack of connection to a broader social life also affects the interpersonal relationships of all three characters. As he sees Pedro off at the airport Sergio dismisses the "stupidity" of the Cuban bourgeoisie, their lack of honesty and social consciousness. Also, his breakup with Elena forces a firey court battle with her parents and brother over her seduction and abandonment. During the courtroom drama Sergio remains impassive, even while Elena's mother physically attacks him.

Antonio Gramsci's concept of the "organic intellectual" is ironically represented by Alea's protagonist. Unlike the Marxist organic intellectual, who, in Iris Zavala's (1992) Latin American context, works from the bottom of the social structure to bring about a new culture of political awareness and criticality, Sergio can only observe in isolation at his typewriter in his politically unacceptable apartment. The personal contradictions that overwhelm Sergio reflect the wider social and political contradictions that precede revolutionary change. Georg Lukacs (1983) has observed about the increase of social collision before a revolution,

A real popular revolution never breaks out as a result of a single, isolated social contradiction. The objective-historical period preparatory to revolution is filled with a whole number of tragic contradictions in life itself. The maturing of the revolution then shows with increasing clarity the objective connection between these isolatedly occurring contradictions and gathers them into several central and decisive issues affecting the activity of the masses. (p. 98)

Lukacs finds that some social contradictions can continue even after the revolution; in fact, some are strengthened. Alea's postrevolutionary Cuba remains distant from the middle-class intellectual, whose personal contradictions are not healed by the revolution, even when his individual rights remain relatively intact. Sergio's political awareness and high standards of human rights are profound, yet he cannot join the spirit of his own country's revolution. While the Cuban revolution has not prevented tragic contradictions on the personal level, it has offered hope through its utopianism and popular enthusiasm. But these social forces are not embraced by all, especially the propertied classes and intellectuals with private lifestyles like Sergio.

Sergio is included among "the concrete children of their age," to use Lukacs' view of historical fiction, in that he clearly represents as a fictional character "the inter-relationship between the psychology of people and the economic and moral circumstances of their lives" (1983, p. 40). As a middle-class intellectual, Sergio cannot fully identify with the revolution that has divided his family and taken away his ownership status. But neither can he identify with the transnational forces of imperialism that have robbed his homeland and perpetuated inequality in Cuba for a century. His education and political awareness allow him to silently critique even the academic theorists of the Cuban revolution, as he does at the seminar on revolutionary progress, but his lifestyle remains detached and his positive actions remain nugatory and ineffectual. To an extent autobiographical, *Memories of Underdevelopment* presents the intellectual as feckless and the working class as oblivious to the work of social justice; only the bureaucrats—such as the humorless inspectors who seize Sergio's apartment building—are effective actors in the revolution.

The Last Supper: Enlightenment Ideas and Cheap Grace

The narrative and photographic experimentalism in *Memories of Underdevelopment* influenced other Latin American directors to depart from the tenets of Italian neorealism, not least Alea himself (Chanan,1985). Turning to history for themes, Alea began two films about the hypocrisy of religious piety, *A Cuban Struggle Against the Demons* (*Unda pelea cubana contra los demonios*, 1971) and *The Last Supper* (*la ultima cena*, 1976). Based on a true incident in late eighteenth-century Latin America, the latter film presents a wealthy plantation owner whose Enlightenment education and traditional religious piety bring him a sense of guilt over slave ownership. The master's conscience is, however, compartmentalized and fickle. His decision to host a reenactment of Christ's last supper for a selected group of field slaves, in the church tradition of footwashing and other forms of ritualized humility, is a kind of tokenism familiar to multiracial societies in the post-civil rights era. While the master's plan to place himself in the role of Christ shows a decided lack of humility, his scheme to invite only the lowest status of slave, the field-hand, to his meal annoys the house servants, local notables, and his friends. The film's bitter satire attacks a type of intellectual distinct from those in *Memories*—the hypocritical brother of the masses.

While the master's preparations for the ceremony are elaborately undertaken, rumors of slave revolts are rife throughout the territory. The slaves have reacted to the ruthless efforts of the owners to step up sugarcane production to meet worldwide demand. To such threats, the master responds no differently than the other slave-holders of the Creole class. He will not hesitate to use brutal and immediate force to end outbreaks of freedom. During the last supper he is drunk from wine but still manages a speech filled with references to brotherhood and the commonality of all souls under God. His disquisition seems a hybrid of universal verities from the Ages of Science and Belief. He delights in the perplexity of his slave guests, one of whom is a leader of the underground rebellion. The diners respond to his speech with a dialectic on the vagaries of freedom and enslavement, but the master's intoxication prevents him from grasping the meaning of his slaves' observations. Presented with the opportunity to hear the anguish of slavery firsthand, his self-absorbed drunkenness prevents his true enlightenment. Concerned only with the outward form of both Enlightenment brotherhood and Christ's preference for the poor, the master, like Organ in Moliere's *Tartuffe*, uses such pieties only to feed his narcissism. The master's hypocritical complacency is reminiscent of Dietrich Bonhoeffer's (1967) notion of "cheap grace," the tendency to accept the Church's promise of forgiveness without heeding its more difficult—and socially unacceptable—call to moral transformation.

Alea's pious plantation master and postrevolutionary intellectual have in common their "inability to relate to things," as Sergio sadly observes about himself and others. The slavemaster lacks the intelligence and political awareness of Sergio, preferring instead, like Sergio's friend Pablo, to profess a facile association with the righteous cause while perpetuating structures of oppression. Sergio's keen awareness of hypocrisy prevents his ready seduction by both revolutionary institutional structures and the lucrative enticements of First World intellectual culture. Still, his personal relationships are few and his brief romance with a visiting European activist after his breakup with Elena reveals a superficial affinity with socialist agendas but an estrangement from political life, even while he is quite articulate about the revolution's shortcomings. Alea himself has certain affinities with Sergio the middle-class intellectual, since the slavemaster's facile religious righteousness—like bourgeois hypocrisy—demonstrates for him the incapacity of privileged classes to be fully aware of the class struggle. Sergio's predicament is not an obvious shortcoming, because his form of alienation may just as easily presage an authentic response to social transformation. Sergio's sensitivity results, after all, from a discernment of the possibilities of social justice not yet realized by North American capitalism or Cuban state planning. The ambivalence of *Memories* contrasts with the dogmatic blundering of *The Last Supper*, where the slavemaster's myopic view of righteousness precludes any need for social transformation. The politically aware slave at the supper table functions in this respect as an ironic Judas figure, one who will betray the master-as-Christ not for 30 pieces of silver but in the cause of the social transformation Christ himself urged.

Gomez, Alea, and the Revolution: Involvement and Isolation

Other Cuban filmmakers have taken a more involved orientation towards the 1959 revolution, presenting characters immersed in the daily work of social transformation while documenting the problems inherent in such programmatic political causes. Manuel Octavio Gomez's *Now It's up to You* (*Ustedes tienen la palabra*, 1974) analyzes the dynamics of popular justice, in contrast to the abstract justice of political theory and bureaucratic enactment. A counterrevolutionary is brought to trial for burning a warehouse on a Cuban forestry collective. As the court investigation unfolds, the motives of the entire community are brought into question. The film becomes, in Michael Chanan's words, "not so much a matter of facts

and sworn evidence as the investigation of the state of consciousness in the community" (quoted in *Stagebill*, 1999a, p. 4). The contradictory political consciousness of the collective leaders who allowed the destruction to happen reveals the broader implications of
the crime. Gomez demonstrates that the question of guilt becomes
quite different from a popular justice perspective, removed from traditional jurisprudence and standards of social planning.

On one level, *Now It's up to You* is a didactic work that explores
revolutionary praxis and challenges traditions of justice that pre-
sume individualistic, property-oriented societies. The broad spectrum of community members represented in the film invites an
allegorical interpretation of the various pitfalls of universal standards of justice. Divided by personal and familial desires, the collective members reveal different levels of altruism and political commitment. The two central characters, a husband and wife team responsible for the management of the collective, function as norm figures.
The wife becomes a *raisonneuse*, who strives for the integrity of the
collective under the tensive circumstances of mutual accusation
and hypocritical sloganeering. While Gomez represents a socialist
society still relatively healthy and intact, capable of intense internal
scrutiny, his didactic orientation, evident from the film's title, is an
admonishment for vigilance in the pursuit of new social structures.
He reminds his audience that there is no clear demarcation between
counterrevolutionary thinking, political apathy, and social hypocrisy. Preferring to document the revolution from inside, within a forestry collective—rather than from Alea's position as isolated
outsider—Gomez revives the naturalism of Gerhart Hauptmann and
other German playwrights of the early twentieth century, who used
group protagonists to document the nature of popular justice from
the context of industrial capitalism. But while Hauptmann's factory
of weavers responds affirmatively and with solidarity to the demands
of social justice under industrial oppression, Gomez's fragmented
forestry community reveals different levels of commitment.

Alea soon departed from the unequivocal political commitment of
his first film produced immediately after the 1959 triumph, *Historia
de la revolucion* (1960). In *The Twelve Chairs* (*Las doce sillas*, 1962),
Alea satirized aspects of the young Revolution. In his *Strawberry
and Chocolate* (*Fresa y chocolate*, 1995) he continued to include satirical elements critical of the revolution. David, a young doctrinaire
communist, visits the apartment of Diego, an openly gay intellectual
with religious leanings, to report on his political heterodoxy. However, he comes to admire Diego's tolerant outlook on life. Caught between the strictures of political belief and the humanism of his new
relationship, David begins to question his deepest political supposi-

tions. Nominated for the best foreign film Oscar in Hollywood, the film received unprecedented critical and popular acclaim internationally. In fact, its clear argument for the acceptance of homosexuality as natural to all cultures has few rivals in First World cinema. At the same time, Alea's portrait of the common human frailties of the neighborhood vigilance member and David's own ability to change his outlook while retaining his political orientation reveals a fundamental faith in the relative tolerance of Cuban socialism.

The critical perspective all but disappears, however, in Alea's *Guantanamera* (1995). Tremendously popular as an export product, the film attempts romantic comedy and offers only passing reference to social and political concerns. Like *Letters from the Park* (*Cartas del parque*, 1988), its social discourse lacks even political overtones. *Up to a Point* (*Hasta cierto punto*, 1983), like *Memories of Underdevelopment*, a self-critical exploration of the ambivalence of the socialist intellectual, best shows Alea as an *auteur*. Gomez and Alea represent opposite ends of the Cuban cinematic spectrum: Gomez, the didactic recorder of the contradictions within the struggle for social change, Alea, the explorer of the ambiguities of social change. Their probing of the contradictions and ambivalences of the Latin American social struggle contributes to Cuba's reputation as a compelling and informative locus for social justice discourse.

Alea's critical complexity challenges simpler notions of identity as residing entirely within the individual subject and suggests a social construction of identity. Louis Althusser's investigation of the relation of individuals to their conditions of existence led to his argument that ideology invests individuals as subjects through the mechanism of recognition. Ideology summons individuals into place and bestows on them their "identity" (1971, p. 163). The view that consciousness is constructed challenges the traditional humanist positioning of the subject at the center. Sergio's isolation is debilitating in its artificiality and self-centeredness. The exploration of identities in *Strawberry and Chocolate* argues for the decentering of heterosexuality as a dominant social determiner. This approach to identity and human rights gains support from recent research on homosexuality, which, according to David William Foster (1994), has departed from "the concept of homosexuality as a group of deplorable acts to be dealt with in judicial, religious, or social-custom terms and toward research formulations that seek to understand how homosexuality may be part of an economy of psychosexuality whereby it performs an integral function within the social dynamic" (p. 26). The implications for human identity in general lead to a view of social construction where social fixity is replaced by the dynamic of human relationality. Looking at Latin America, the sense of difference applies at various levels—national, linguistic, racial, gender, sexual orientation, as well as class. In their different approaches, the films of Alea and Gomez explore human identity as integral to the functioning of social life. Within such a world, individual isolation and its consequence, divisionist thinking—but not "difference"— becomes problematic and inhibitive of human rights.

Brazil's *Cinema Novo*: Witnessing Human Rights

When the left-leaning elected government of Joao Goulart heightened the class struggle and alienated the United States in the early 1960s, the subsequent military overthrow cast Brazil into a turbulent period that influenced the incipient *cinema novo* movement. Unlike Cuba, which began its film movement from almost nothing in 1959, *cinema novo* grew from the Higher Institute of Brazilian Studies (ISEB), founded in 1955 expressly to construct a national ideology of development. Members of ISEB perceived the social contradictions they would uncover in films through the dichotomy of "nation" versus "antination"—not foreign versus national—because they perceived imperialism as an "internalized" force of the Brazilian class structure (Johnson, 1987, pp. 88–89). The "populist pact" that emerged called for a gradualism that sought *conscientizacao*, a critical consciousness that sought to uncover the injustices of underdevelopment in the cause of social liberation. This directly didactic approach, together with an emphasis on an independent and inexpensive production method, shows its close affinity to the "Imperfect Cinema" of Cuba's ICAIC during the same years. The simplified understanding of film production in the 1960s remained unique in Brazilian film history (Johnson & Stam, 1982). For Glauber Rocha (1982), perhaps Brazil's most acclaimed filmmaker, the movement "ultimately [made] the public aware of its own misery" (p. 69).

Hector Babenco's *Pixote* (1981) is a bleak depiction of the effects of poverty on children. The film's prologue, introduced by Babenco, offers startling statistics on the social conditions in Brazil's urban slums. This neorealist approach is enhanced by the unusual device of introducing Fernando Ramos da Silva, the actor playing the principal character, Pixote, in front of his home with his family members. The long pan shot of Sao Paolo's shanty neighborhoods used as background for Babenco's recitation on the demographics of poverty thus gains concrete, human quality when Fernando, his mother, and siblings appear within the panorama in a fixed long-shot. The actor's life setting, presented in the midst of the broad landscape of urban poverty, creates a unique filmic identity beyond the actor/non-actor binary. Through the documentary prologue, Babenco establishes the social reality behind his film, leading the audience from bleak but abstracted statistics—half of Brazil's 120 million people are children, more than 28 million live in poverty—into the intimate world of his characters.

Pixote and other children and young teenagers are sent to a brutal and corrupt reformatory where the director offers socially responsible platitudes to the visiting professionals and journalists. The director's tour speech becomes a discourse of self-interest that reassures his visitors that the harsh treatment the boys undergo is a thing of the past, "No, we don't lock dormitory doors anymore, all that's gone." "You will see the miracles we do on limited budgets for the boys here." The brutal warden for the boys sleeps with one of their mothers for special treatment and conspires with corrupt police detectives to cover up the killing of two boys. When the scandal is disclosed in the media, the manager and warden arbitrarily implicate one of the boys, who is savagely beated to death when he vows to expose them. Pixote and three other boys escape the reformatory and begin a life of crime that involves adults who take their drug sales without payment and a prostitute, Sueli, who lures customers to her apartment where the boys steal their money. When a gringo customer resists, Pixote accidentally shoots one of the boys and in a panic kills the customer. Alone with Sueli in the film's final scene, the prepubescent Pixote seeks comfort at her breasts, but she rejects him and tells him to leave, claiming she is "nobody's mother." Alea's characteristic juxtaposition of contradictions is poignant, as Pixote, rejected for his attempt to be nursed by Sueli, rises from the bed and checks the magazine on his gun before leaving. This powerful denouement confirms the statistics presented at the film's opening, that many of Brazil's young population are without family and guidance and have become, against all nature, destroyers of humanity.

The straightforwardly realist aspects of the film are expanded by innovative narrative techniques, the creative mixing of tones—humor, irony, sympathy, and bitter commentary—and cinematography that typify the Brazilian *cinema novo* tradition. The mixed-tone approach is seen clearly in the use of orchestrated music in the beginning scenes that contrasts with the utter ruthlessness and inhumanity of the boys' lives. Such mixing heightens the film's pathos without sentimentalizing or sanitizing the story. Other themes, such as the positive treatment of homosexuality and the hypocrisy of illegal prostitution, broaden the focus of social justice. Lilica, a gay teenager, falls quickly in love with two boys who are killed in the film and becomes the conscience in matters of love throughout the film. His capacity to understand genuine love in relationships presents a positive gay character within a traditionally homophobic culture and a verbal commentary on the vagaries of conventional love relationships.

Tent of Miracles: Forgotten Views of Miscegenation

Nelson Pereira Dos Santos' *Tent of Miracles* (1977), based on the novel by Jorge Amado, begins with the arrival of professor James Livingston, a North American Nobel laureate who is revisiting Brazil to remind the nation of its intellectual debt to the long forgotten early twentieth-century figure of Pedro Archanjo. A mulatto of humble origins and beadle for the local legislature, Archanjo introduced an early theory of micegenation and social justice. Livingston's announcement of Archanjo's political significance baffles the Brazilian journalists and publicists, who have never heard of him. The distinguished academics are equally unaware of their important predecessor. When a film team receives funds from Livingston to begin a documentary on Archanjo, the director struggles to understand his subject's life and theory of race mixing for social progress. Mercedes, the director's fiancee, sleeps with Livingston hoping to be cast as the female lead. The narrative moves to flashbacks of Archanjo's life, when his relationships with white, light-skinned, and black women put into practice his theory. When a wealthy white liberal takes offense at his request to marry his daughter, Archanjo's life is threatened.

Amado's humor reveals the shallowness of Livingston's interest in "underdevelopment," the topic that brought him the Nobel Prize. More interested in the mulatto Mercedes than in explaining Archanjo's genetic assimilationist theory, Livingston remains the uninvolved North American celebrity, distant from contemporary Brazilian life and hedonistic in his orientation. The popular culture of advanced capitalism immediately exploits the notoriety of Archanjo's assimilationist theories. Publicity agents want to sell a brandy label using his name and mystique. Only the film director and a few of his colleagues concern themselves with uncovering the true significance of Archanjo's life. His friends argue over the significance of racial gradations and social status in Latin America, while Mercedes thinks only of the glamour associated with the Livingston visit.

The satire of Amado and Dos Santos attacks the middle class' indifference to political history and its obliviousness to the wider Brazil, as represented in the novel and film by the African-Brazilian culture. Throughout the film the spirit-binding strength of this culture, centered on the poor and disenfranchised, disrupts the world of the power elite. Amado's novel featured the Yoruban West African spiritual tradition, called *candomble* in Brazil. This intense ritual had many forms, some controlled by women and some by men. The worship of such "saints" as Ojouba and Shango was often violently suppressed by local police throughout Brazilian history (Thompson, 1999). Dos Santos actually underrepresents the violence involved in suppressing non-European cultural expression among the poor. The police actions are instead transformed into comic versions of the tables turned. The local thug hired by the police is put in a trance by the *candomble* priest and turns on the local official who hired him to break up the ritual dance. A learned humanist is distressed into drunkenness when his mulatto colleague tells him he still believes the ritual practices throughout Bahia have unique power to comfort the meek. Although the shrines of these African gods, the so-called tents of miracles, survive efforts to suppress them, and Archanjo's interracial community achieve a unique commonality, in the later flashback scenes, signs of racial divisiveness appear. Archanjo in his old age learns about the Nazis and refuses to believe they pose a danger to racial integration, but a young black peasant woman corrects his optimism by exclaiming that they are indeed capable of such retrogression.

The scenes in the present offer less hope for the simple equation of interracial union and social justice. The complexities of Brazilian popular culture of the 1970s reflect a highly self-conscious preoccupation with the sensationalism of interracial trespassing, best represented in the relationship between Nordic-looking Livingston and the sensuous mulatto Mercedes. Instead of explaining Archanjo's utopian goals to a society just as unequal as in his day, Livingston gallantly praises Mercedes as "a superb representation of what interracial union is all about." The postmodern narcissism in the film is self-reflexive in its commentary on social commonality. Livingston, Mercedes, the director, and the other journalists and academics relate only to their fellow darker-skinned Brazilians at African-inspired dance receptions for the Nobel laureate's tour. Unlike Archanjo's interracial group earlier in the century, the postmodern Brazilians and their North American visitor are mere spectators to African culture, and not its social peers. Mercedes becomes the true postmodern intellectual/artist as her interest in the apostle of miscegenation derives solely from a narcissistic interest as performer and role-player. In Amado's words, "she proved to be a marvel at making contracts" (1971, p. 390). Thus the tent-of-miracle celebrations that once gave meaning to a harsh reality of oppression and social disdain becomes a postmodern ploy for cultural publicity and corporate advertising.

Archanjo's vision of ethnic unity as presented in the film can be critiqued for its universalist and assimilationist assumptions. Moreover, the view that the races would come together out of a sense of commonality and mutual attraction is represented in the early

flashback scenes through a heavy reliance on stereotypical notions—the presumed African penchant for exuberant celebration,
nonconceptual communication, and emotional warmth. Lost in the
Dos Santos' social satire are the grave political circumstances of the
historical Pedro Archanjo's world and his courageous pursuit of
what has since become termed multicultural thinking. *Tent of Miracles* represents a filmmaker caught between his desire to uncover
the real Archanjo and the contradictions of his own complex
postmodern life. Archanjo is left in prison in the last flashback scene,
the film's message tentative. Alea as the real director leaves his audiences with the political ambiguity common in his films and which
the historical Archanjo rarely settled for. The early films of *cinema
novo* expressed, in Beat Borter's words, the "philosophy of cinema
as intervention, of creating new ways of seeing, expressing a new revolutionary self" (1997, p. 156). This focused political orientation gave
way to cinema perhaps richer in ambivalence and nuance, but without the sustaining eye on social injustice evident in such films as
Pixote. The international popularity of such films as Walter Salles'
Central Station (1999) confirm the general trend in Brazil away from
films that analyze the structures of power in favor of films with
charismatic main characters. Even with its shortcomings, *Tent of
Miracles* offers a particularly clear argument that a people's struggle for identity and representation also involves a struggle among
power groups.

_____ Chapter 5 _____

SOCIAL JUSTICE CINEMA IN IRAN:
DISTANCE AND INTIMACY

IRAN'S "GLOCALIZATION": HYBRIDITY AND INTEGRITY

During the 1970s, cinema in Iran became a chief target of revolutionaries against the Pahlavi government of the Shah regime. By the advent of the Islamic government in 1979, 180 cinemas had been destroyed (Naficy, 1996, p. 675). While clerical leaders were not opposed to film in itself, they associated most commercial films with unwanted secular and Western cultural influences. In 1982, the Ministry of Culture and Islamic Guidance was founded to enforce guidelines for subject matter and treatment. Instead of discouraging artistic development, however, the effect of change had the unanticipated result of commercial success. As a consequence, Iranian banks offered long-term loans for film production. During the late 1980s into the 1990s, filmmakers received praise at international film festivals, a source of national pride for the Islamic government. Following the success was a gradual loosening of strictures on film content. Women characters, for example, moved center stage from the background. Moreover, the relationality of gender changed significantly. "The averted gaze became more focused and direct, sometimes charged with sexual desires" (Naficy, 1996, p. 677). Women directors also appeared for the first time.

Since then, Iranian cinema's reputation has grown even more internationally, becoming a major source of cultural hybridity at home. Today Iran faces an embarrassment of aesthetic choices.

Which direction to pursue with a new and dynamic cultural institution has been a cause for concern. As the Islamic government showed clear signs of liberalization in the second half of the 1990s, the question of cultural identity remains paramount. Throughout history, those in power have decided what becomes the remembered sources of identity and unity for a society. Whatever is consistent with the aims of a particular social group is remembered, embroidered, and reconstructed. What is inconsistent and threatening is erased or denied (Zelizer, 1995). To what extent the new liberal government of Iran will make itself "the masters of memory" (Le Goff, 1992, p. 54) remains an open question. For good reason suspicious of the economic and military hegemony of Eurocentric cultural forms, Iran has remained, like its Arab Muslim neighbors and China for hundreds of years, opposed to such cultural trespassing by official policy. When Western cultural forms, especially those involving the mass media, have controlled the image of non-Western identities, reality is experienced through "white" eyes. The experiences of "black" people are thus devalued, simplified, marginalized, decentered, and subordinated relative to the experiences of "white" people (Madison, 1999, p. 409; see also Orwell, 1953).

Still, the prospect of a mass global culture dominated by First World power sources has been questioned in recent years. Although Stuart Hall (1991) acknowledges the homogenizing consequences of such cultural forces, he perceives the significant role of local reception in shaping the communication of outside forms. Hence, global cultural capital can only "rule through other local capitals" (p. 28). Following Hall, Marwan Kraidy (1999) has proposed a definition of hybridity that more accurately describes the reality of globalization. Given the fact that "both global and local cultural formations are inherently hybridized," Kraidy proposes that "Hybridity is thus construed not as an in-between zone where global/local power relations are neutralized in the fuzziness of the melange but as a zone of symbolic ferment where power relations are surreptitiously re-inscribed" (p. 460). The implications for Iranian cultural forms are significant. Iran's struggle for cultural integrity against opposing forces is real. However, those opposing forces are not monolithic, but hybrid themselves, even as Iran's own culture remains hybrid. Within the resulting melange, in Hall's positive view, room exists for the forging of progressive cultural integrity through both outward and inward hybrid influences.

MAKHMALBAF: REVOLUTION AND CHANGE

Central to the development of the Iranian cinema has been Mohsen Makhmalbaf's unique style of what has been termed "poetic realism" (*Stagebill*, 1999b, p. 8). Unlike most filmmakers of social jus-tice, he creates a rich fabric of ambiguity and tone, treating his sub-jects at times with gentle humor, at other times with poignant silence. Continually experimenting with narrative form and characteriza-tion, Makhmalbaf rebuts the long-term misconception that Third World cinema follows the lead of First World creators. *A Moment of Innocence* (1996) challenges the dichotomy of the play-within-a-play format. At times, the viewer is not sure what comprises the "re-ality" of the storyline—the actors in their real-life decision-mak-ing—or the fictional recreations of the rehearsed film under production. Complicating this reality even more is the fact that the important characters in the rehearsed film are playing themselves in part of the film, while young actors are being recruited to play these actors 20 years before. Moreover, the story—an incident from the 1970s Iranian liberation movement against the Shah's dictatorial regime—is nonfiction, while the film script is novelistic in point of view and treatment. Finally, the film's layers of identity are self-re-flexive, since the film under production is based on a significant in-cident in Makhmalbaf's personal life during the revolutionary struggle. Today's commonplace binaries—the generation gap be-tween idealistic youth and cynical age, "truth and reality," "the per-sonal and the political," fiction and nonfiction, the story itself and its retelling, rehearsal and final product—are all transcended in the search for the truth of a society's struggle.

Moving beyond Luigi Pirandello's largely apolitical situations, Makhmalbaf breaks another binary opposition accepted *a priori* in the post-Cold War era, that political and partisan drama cannot bridge the gap between personal worlds and the broad world of polit-ical struggle. In fact, the filmmaker answers Judith Mayne's lament about this separation:

[T]heoretical writing about the "politics" of "critical" spectatorship [in cin-ema] usually remains locked into an either/or situation—a micropolitics where everything is a contestatory act, or a macropolitics where nothing is contestatory unless part of a globally defined political agenda. (1993, p. 172)

A Moment of Innocence (and *The Silence*, 1988, discussed below) goes beyond thinking only in terms of master narratives of social revolution and structural change. Like the contemporary films of Latin America's new cinema movements, Makhmalbaf's works break the boundaries between the personal and the political, the macro- and micropolitical worlds of literature and ideology to create a new space where the life-spans of individuals converge and unite with the expanses of large social movements. In this cinematic world, identities reveal that the personal not only *is* the political, but

that the duality itself becomes inadequate to describe the transactional nature of human experience.

The real incident that undergirds the complexities of *A Moment of
Innocence* involves a plan devised by Makhmalbaf himself as a
young anti-Shah militant. Using his new girlfriend as a decoy, the
young Makhmalbaf surprised and stabbed—not fatally—a young
police officer. The scheme cost him five years in prison, where he
feared for his life under torture. The director wishes to compare his
world (Iran's world then) with his world (Iran's world today), in an attempt to explore the inner lives of himself and the other principlal
agents of the revolutionary incident. By juxtaposing the older and
younger versions of himself and the same versions of the still-living
police officer he stabbed, he aims to fathom those deeper motivations left unconscious over a two-decade period of profound social
change. Vestiges of prerevolutionary days continually break through
present realities (of the film actors and of Iranian society). For example, in an important narrative element that instances the director's
adroit use of humor for thematic purposes, the actor-playing-him-
self-as-police-officer threatens to leave the set over the casting of an
actor playing his younger prerevolutionary self, then over his discovery that the woman he loved 20 years before is the woman involved in the scheme to disarm him. Such incidents in the film
ignore traditional conceptions of character development. Makhmalbaf
does not so much "refictionalize" his narrative as examine bio-
graphically macropolitical concerns through the intimacy of
micropolitical realities. In the process, the play-within-a-play format is quickly transformed into a narrative where perception and
reality play off one another to probe Iran's tumultuous history.

In the opening scenes, Makhmalbaf plays himself-as-director of
the film-in-rehearsal, creating a Federico Fellini-style thought game
on filmmaking itself. But if the film's early scenes pay tribute to such
cinematic classics as Fellini's *8 1/2* (1963), they move beyond artistic self-preoccupation to reveal the jaundiced inner lives of the filmmaker's aging revolutionary generation. The young woman whom
the director loved is now a married homemaker in exurbia who does
not want to get involved with either Makhmalbaf's film or his personal life. In contrast, her daughter, the same age as the woman
when she became involved as a militant with the director, is eager to
play her mother in the film, but is prevented by the mother, who desires a more traditional role for her. The director plays himself in the
film as the character Mohsen, a jaded director who distances himself from the principal actors in his film, using his director of photography to play both therapist and acting coach for them. Mohsen's
low profile allows the director to keep some perspective on his pro-

duction, preventing an otherwise narcissistic presence from intrud-
ing upon the film's wider explorations.

In the opening scenes, the policeman-turned-actor watches the
casting process for young actors to play his younger self. He chooses
a handsome young man to play himself, an attempt at self-flattery
that fails when Mohsen instead casts a less attractive young man to
play the young policeman. The young actor looks more like the policeman 20 years younger, but the actor-policeman takes a while to
warm up to him. His subsequent coaching of his younger self reveals the general militaristic attitudes of prerevolutionary Iran. The
younger actor does not possess the martial bearing of the older actor, a study in contrast between Iranian culture under the Shah and
present-day Iran. In much the same way, the young actor cast as the
revolutionary Makhmalbaf is idealistic to such a degree that he
wants "to save the world" and "plant flowers in Africa." Through the
young actor's callowness, the director satirizes the youthful exuberance of his own (former?) revolutionary ideals, and by implication
the general naiveté of his country during the 1970s, when an altruistic internationalism combined uneasily with a turning inward towards religious traditionalism. At one point the actor playing the
young Makhmalbaf refuses to rehearse the stabbing incident with
the young policeman and woman. His sensitive weeping reveals a
conception of masculinity quite different from the martial callous-
ness reflected in the actor-policeman's coaching of his younger self.
Moreover, the young woman cast as the director's prerevolutionary
beloved is more ambitious than sensitive in her new role as actor, as
she stares perplexed at the young man's weeping. This breaking of
gender coding through traditional role reversal comments on the ex-
tremes of gender role conformity still present in Iran during the
1990s. The young woman—played by the daughter of the real woman
involved with Makhmalbaf in the stabbing incident—trades traditional female sensitivity for her new opportunity to transgress gender boundaries as a film actress.

If Makhmalbaf's social commentary is subtly imbedded in the responses of his characters/actors, the important moments of the
narrative are given critical perspective through the device of the rehearsal process. Enlisting a variation of the *cinema verité* production approach, the film's rehearsal process often crosses between
reality and fiction. In addition to the device of actors reacting to their
own involvement in the nonfictional incident, attempting, as in the
case of the policeman-turned-actor, to justify and change the social
injustices of the prerevolutionary society, the narrative interlards
scenes of present-day reality with scenes from the stabbing incident
of the 1970s. Moreover, the actors do not rehearse scenes in the

standard industry manner—particular scenes rehearsed on particular days of a production schedule—but as private actor coaching sessions leading to a one-time take for the camera. This method creates the unrehearsed effect of the French *cinema verité*, but, more significantly in the film's narrative, eliminates the separation between the pretense of drama and the reality of actors' lives. Suggested in the title, the film's moment of innocence critically compares present-day Iran with revolutionary Iran, revealing not only generational gaps in ideology and sentiment, but also the disparities in a single individual's acceptance of social ideals. The obligatory question of the film, at which moment in history is innocence embodied—the present-day consumerist culture of the globalized village, or the youthful exuberance of 1970s revolutionary Iran?—is left open at the end as a comment on the complexities of historical movements and individual lives.

The Silence: Justice from a Child's World

In a very different film, Makhmalbaf explores the harsh realities of poverty and child labor through the unexpectedly lyrical and visually radiant *The Silence* (1988), a film that, like Akira Kurosawa's *Dreams* (1990), explores the human spirit nonconceptually, beyond words. Makhmalbaf's dialogue is sparse but important, conveying a minimum of exposition and intentionality. Characters first observe, becoming a part of a situation before they speak, allowing the ineffable elements of human relationality to form and speak before words are exchanged. But if what the film attempts is the unutterable in human living, it more than makes up for its nonconceptual focus with a clear, uncomplicated plot structure and a realism firmly rooted in the particularities of locale and culture. The simplicity of the story creates a universality within the particular that defies the common binaries of universal versus particular, relativism versus essentialism, in human culture.

Khorshid is a 10-year-old blind boy who works for an old stringed instrument maker, tuning his products. He became the primary support for his mother when his father emigrated to Russia for work. Apprehending the world through sound and touch alone, Khorshid explores a society beyond the social coding of class, gender, and age. Hearing the patterns of life itself, the music of social striving, he intrudes upon the everyday tasks of people around him, demanding that their lives change to produce more harmony. His alternative approach to daily living succeeds through a childish innocence that demands from others their participation in his vision of a life more human. Khorshid's unceasing appreciation of the common details of living presents a heightened self-awareness and inspires a deeper searching among the sighted characters around him.

The rich visual and aural elements of the film have drawn reviewers to its subliminal appeal. "*The Silence* works a kind of aesthetic synethesis: a blind child who hears mise-en-scène as music is imagined by a director whose eyes see images as part of the delicate yet indestructible weave of poetry" (*Stagebill*, 1999b, p. 7). But the director is after more than aestheticism, more than a cinematographic and musical study. His characters suffer the harsh realities of unemployment, child labor, and a threatening government oppression that has just begun its rigorist policies of forced religious conformity. Filmed on location in an impoverished Tadjikistan, the characters' lives offer little time for aesthetic appreciation. Khorshid is able to evoke such awareness because of his youthful exuberance and his nonthreatening status as a blind person. However, he dreads the daily knock on the door from his mother's landlord, who demands the back rent payments. Threatened with dispossession and eviction, he attempts to turn such severe economic realities into an everyday beauty that he can comprehend. While passing a brass tub factory, he hears the cacophonous sounds made by boys employed to hammer the metal into rounded forms. When one of the boys offers him money, he rejects it, stating that he is not a beggar, but asks them to beat their hammers with the same melody as the landlord's knock on his mother's door—da-da-da-daah. As the boy sings the melody for the boys, the landlord's imperious knock is heard in the background. The boys soon begin hammering according to this rhythm, creating a harmonious working space. Khorshid's other attempts to transform his world into a more harmonious place include his singing on a bus to work, where he inspires girls his age to offer fresh bread and red apples; and his influence on his childhood friend, a young girl who dances and adorns herself with Dahlia petals for her fingernails and cherry stems for earrings.

Often distracted from his work routine by the sounds of people and nature, Khorshid is reprimanded by his boss. When a school music director accuses the instrument maker of selling inharmonious products, the boy is fired. Despondent, Khorshid asks his favorite musician, a poor itinerant composer, for help. The musician offers to play for the landlord, hoping that his heart will soften when he hears the beautiful music. Khorshid, however, is not entirely convinced. The film's ending is left open, leaving the contingent nature of life as a permanent counterargument to life's fulfillment. The film's mellifluous realism presents social justice issues without offering answers. The unresolved ending leaves an ambivalent denouement that supports the theme of life's contradictions—beauty amid injustice, generosity of the dispossessed, and harmony within bleak poverty. References to particular political movements occasionally appear but are kept at a distance. For example, while Khorshid and his companion enjoy the sounds and smells of nature, the girl notices a man angrily commanding a group of young women to wear their head scarves. The couple avoid the unpleasant confrontation by taking another path through the woods.

In its visual and aural lyricism, repetition, and unhurried pace, *The Silence* can be compared to Makhmalbaf's *Gabbeh* (1996), a film set in a remote part of Iran where the stark beauty of the landscape serves as a metaphor for the marginal lives of a group of nomadic herders. Intensely visual and symbolic, the film uses folktale narrative to tell of an old couple who value a rug (*gabbeh*) that depicts a dark horseman riding with a young woman in a barren landscape. As they wash the rug in a stream, the young woman appears to them and tells her sad tale. Her poor family would not allow her to marry the young man of her dreams—the dark horseman. Flashback scenes reveal her anguish and the loneliness of the poor wanderer, who only appears on horseback at extreme distances, singing stridently to her of their mutual longing. Their unhappiness embodies the fleeting nature of hope in a land of migrant poverty and deferred rights. If the young woman can find no love in this world, she finds affinity with the old couple, who still fight between themselves over old regrets. Threatened by rural poverty and official restrictions, the characters reveal the harsh life of a repressed minority—the so-called Iranian "nomadic culture"—neglected for centuries by governmental policy (Tapper, 1997).

The young woman's family will not let her marry anyone until others in her family are married. She grieves the unfairness and uncertainty of the situation, wondering if her beloved will wait so long without satisfaction. As in *The Silence*, the problem is left unresolved, a comment on life's contingency and unfairness. Presenting the injustices of women's place in rural Middle Eastern society, the theme is evocatively developed with such feminine imagery as the magical rug and its haunting design, made by women's labor; the long suffering of the young woman and isolated rider; and the hope for a better future, often conveyed through the nuances of soundtrack music and photogenic nature imagery. Avoiding political statement and prescriptive solutions, the film nevertheless leaves audiences questioning traditional notions of the role of women and poverty's neglect of human values. In *A Moment of Innocence* and *The Silence*, Makhmalbaf depends upon a slow unfolding of his theme through nonconceptual forms, such as haunting music and nature imagery. Departing radically from most didactic narrative methods in the twentieth century, his films present the discourse of social justice through nonrealistic techniques and figurative language. This approach directly disputes contemporary understanding of the binary opposition, political narrative/private-based aestheticism, challenging Eurocentric notions of the separation of social subject matter and the depiction of individual sensibility.

Avoiding overt confrontation in these films, Makhmalbaf instead moves to a place of quiet illumination, affirming a progressive toler-ance of human difference. His cinematic tone creates the kind of ex-pressive authenticity that Vivian Gornick recommends in her commentary on politically motivated art: "Accusation engulfs in-sight, prevents a point of view from developing. Without a point of view . . . there is only a recital of disturbing feeling" (in Linfield, 1999, p. 32). Rather than denying social repression by avoiding its reali-ties in his culture, Makhmalbaf distances himself from its emotion-ality, the better to interpret the lives of ordinary people, whose life-affirming worlds remain overshadowed by the wider controver-sies of repressive governments and institutions. If his characters seem to avoid direct political confrontation (*The Silence*) or have abandoned their once youthful civil disobedience for a tolerant skepticism (*A Moment of Innocence*), they nonetheless demonstrate through their wise humanity alternatives to official ideology, in this way exposing its ethical and aesthetic limitations.

Leila: Convenient Piety and the Family

While Makhmalbaf offers characters who have strayed from their social personae as defined by official propriety, breaking through delimited categories to forge new identities not always known even to themselves, director Dariush Mehrjui creates a world where cus-tom and traditional relationships dominate the characters to the point of despair. His Iran is one where misfits and skeptics have no place and where social coding is questioned only at the breaking point. Set in the affluent but restricted Iran of the 1990s, *Leila* (1997) is claustrophobic where *The Silence* is broad and open in its imagi-nation and *A Moment of Innocence* ranges diachronically between generations of people with thoughts and feelings of their own. In Mehrjui's story, independent behavior and contentious opinion are sublimated for the sake of a consensual ethic of family respectabil-ity. *Leila* is above all a feminist tract that contains no argumentative discourse in its dialogue. Rather, its dialectic is imbedded in the irony of unspoken thoughts and contradictory actions, undertaken for the sake of family, marriage, and religious custom. Recalling Ingmar Bergman's studies of psychological repression under religious strictures—*Fanny and Alexander* (1984), and the nuanced trilogy of faith, *Through A Glass Darkly* (1962), *Winter Light* (1962), and *The Silence* (1963)—*Leila* informs through moments of painful silence in a world of deferred gratification.

Leila and Reza are soon married and seem the perfect couple for understanding and mutual respect. Their liberalism and conventionality are apparent within the melange of prosperity and enforced conformity of 1990s Teheran. When Leila is told that she cannot have children, Reza affirms that his love for her will overcome the prospect of no children. To lift Leila's despondency, Reza insists that they will be happy with just the two of them. His mother, however, begins a campaign to divide the couple, harassing her new daughter-in-law until Leila agrees to allow her husband to take a second wife who will provide the family with an heir. Leila is overwhelmed by guilt and a sense of responsibility, unable to stand up to her mother-in-law or retain the full affection of her husband. When the new wife is found and the wedding celebration under way, Leila isolates herself in her room and experiences the heartbreak of love lost. Reza breaks away from the wedding party to comfort Leila, but he confronts a changed situation. Both are unable to continue their former relationship under the new circumstances. In the chilling denouement, a flash-forward scene reveals Leila resigned to her loneliness and disillusionment as she gazes from a distance and unobserved on the young son who was the fruit of the second marriage. Although Reza left his second wife, Leila has refused to see him until now. The film ends at the moment when Leila observes the boy from afar. Her face registers compassion for a child caught between separated parents. This moment of selfless tenderness is the first such feeling in the film, signifying perhaps the hopeful prospect of the couple's reunion with the child. Mehrjui does not allow his audience to see the resolution. Instead, the film ends on a silent moment with Leila, the observing observed.

Leila discloses an hypocrisy of selfishness behind the altruistic ideals of the revolution in Iran. Where the characters in *A Moment of Innocence* are critical or overtly perturbed by the events of recent history, responding to a time when they were innocent and wanted to change the world, Mehrjui's people keep a low profile, are seduced by materialistic values into conformity, and consider only the good of the family. Within the upper-middle-class world of urban Iran, traditional hierarchies mirror the theocracy of the state, and daughters-in-law become easy prey when the interests of the family predominate.

The film concerns the deterioration of love under the constant and overwhelming force of traditional values. At first, Reza and Leila seem the perfect yuppie couple. They possess what most people envy—looks, money, health, a certain tolerant liberality, education and urbanity—and seem to have achieved a degree of independence from traditional obligations. Mehrjui's story, however, reveals in gradual stages the deterioration of this apparent happiness. Under family pressure, the couple begin to argue, reassuring each other that love is stronger than the desire for children and the demands of parents. Soon these reassurances become demands, and Leila begins to yield, at first to her husband's anger that she should doubt their love, and then to her mother-in-law that she should do the right thing for Reza and step aside for the sake of the future. Confused by the conflicting values underpinning the demands of family and love, Leila at last resigns herself to being a co-wife. For his part, Reza reacts angrily when he discovers his mother's calculating attempts to undermine his marriage to Leila. Motivated by youthful ideals of love over duty, he is indignant towards an older generation that would willingly sacrifice his love for the sake of family respectability. Throughout the film Mehrjui explores a theme common to modern literature: the distinction between respectability and integrity. Reza's personal pride and integrity do not allow him to betray the ideals supporting his love relationship, but the pressures of family respectability in the end win out. However, Mehrjui will not let the dialectic end at this point. The second marriage fails almost before the wedding is over, and eventually the mother-in-law is forced to raise the baby on her own, much to her chagrin. Her dread at the prospect reveals the shallowness of her traditional values and is a rare moment of critical humor in the film.

The heart of *Leila* remains the devolution of the marriage, a narrative of extreme verisimilitude and subtlety. One motif that frames the deterioration of communication between Leila and Reza is the automobile, a Freudian symbol of control but at the same time of freedom. When the couple reluctantly agree to the taking of a second wife, it is with the understanding that it remains only an obligatory action, necessary to produce an heir and not affecting their own marriage significantly. Thus, the conversation of the two at first is lighthearted and sarcastic, as Leila accompanies Reza in the car for his first interview with a prospect. After the meeting Reza ridicules the whole procedure for Leila's benefit, making fun of the attitudes of the respective families and commenting on the features of the woman candidate. However, as the interviews continue and the family pressure mounts, Reza becomes progressively less talkative and Leila gives way to sullen passivity. On the way towards the final interview, a subdued Reza simply drops Leila off on the street while he continues on his own, their mutual silence deadening. The automobile has become a place of departure, an exit from the intimacy of a love now overruled by mistrust and contained bitterness.

Encircling the couple are two families whose varying attitudes towards their situation only serve to aggravate the emotions and introduce a pervasive feeling of claustrophobia. While Leila's family is predictably more empathetic to her misfortune, they prove incapable of preventing the deteriorating relationship. Reza's family is presented with more fully developed characters, some of whom are sympathetic toward Leila and are against the second marriage. Especially the men in Reza's family show either open indifference to the need for an heir or challenge the mother-in-law at certain moments. In the end, however, the traditional demand for an heir overcomes such arguments, and the faction for the co-wife succeeds in turning Reza against his original vow to preserve his love for Leila above all other considerations. Mehrjui creates a tension between the genders in the internecine struggle of extended families; however, the generally sympathetic or passive attitudes of the men—Reza's father, for example, is completely dominated by his wife in the whole matter—and negative attitudes of the women in Reza's family may be an attempt to balance the political vehemence of Leila's sisters, who advocate her liberation from all enslavements. By so doing, Mehrjui avoids direct engagement with the particularities of gender politics, allowing the gradual isolation within Leila and Reza's relationship to remain the chief focus.

The film presents a strongly deterministic narrative structure in that a sense of inevitability haunts the marriage relationship from the beginning. However, Mehrjui offers certain *raisonneur* characters in both families who argue forcefully, though not successfully, for alternatives to the traditional marriage culture. Reza's family includes an unconventional uncle who has remained single and takes a sardonic attitude towards marriages intended to satisfy the need for male heirs. Two of Leila's sisters are especially outspoken on the oppression of women in traditional Muslim society. These alternative norm characters are favorably treated and personable, in contrast to the characters propounding the traditional responsibilities of child raising, who appear selfish, disingenuous, and hypocritical.

The varied reactions within the film to Reza and Leila's dilemma create a deeper, more nuanced narrative, situated not within a static world of fundamentalist dictates—the conception often assumed by the Western corporate media—but within a world beset by the contradictions of a society in rapid transformation, influenced by competing ideologies. In this sense, Godfrey Cheshire's observation in a positive, but unintentionally ethnocentric review may have missed the point: "At a time when 'Iranian Cinema' internationally connotes a certain distanced exoticism, views of rug-weaving nomads or impoverished children against crumbling buildings, Mr. Mehrjui's sleek, educated, post-modern Teheran is clearly anomalous" (1998, p. 28). Given the rapid economic development of Iran in the 1990s, the family lifestyles represented in the film—driving BMWs and wearing designer *chadors*—far from being anomalous, typify a materialism uneasily wedded to a traditionalism fast becoming anachronistic. The self-centered uses to which traditional "family values" are placed in the film show an affinity with contemporary U.S. culture, where wealthy politicians cynically spout pious formulas and pray for votes, but religious forgiveness is overlooked in prison systems that have long ago abandoned rehabilitation. Mehrjui's Iran, like much of U.S. culture, prefers convenient piety to substantive duty, selfish aggrandizement to love of neighbor.

THE SUITORS: CONFINEMENT AND OBLIVION

If Mehrjui discovers hypocrisy amid an economy of rising expectations, in Ghasem Ebrahimian's *The Suitors* (1988), self-serving pieties are replaced by straightforward attitudes of domestic repression and misplaced affinities. While a social claustrophobia motivates Leila's desire to leave her husband for the reassurance and relative freedom of her family's household, Mariyam in *The Suitors* is completely overwhelmed by traditional social control. Her situation is in certain ways more anomalous than Leila's, a fact that brings with it more devastating consequences, since the traditional structures in Muslim culture that would protect her rights to privacy and mobility are absent. Although the setting is the New York metropolitan area, not Iran, part of the power of Ebrahimian's film is the reach of gender repression, a cultural feature that seems unaffected by international boundaries, indeed, that may increase some forms of gender repression.

Arriving in JFK Airport in New York, Haji and his wife Mariyam experience a culture clash when the federal customs agent insists on seeing Mariyam's full face behind the veil. The scene, exhibiting in its awkwardness the ambivalence and uncertainty of the couple, foreshadows the tragic separation of a woman from her society, who flees in desperation to an unknown future. Much older than the beautiful Mariyam, Haji had sent his mother and sister to ask her mother's permission to marry Mariyam. With little money in Iran, Mariyam's mother agrees to the marriage, feeling that in the United States her daughter will have a chance for a better education. The new relationship is without passion, and Haji's sudden death at the hands of a city police department SWAT team leaves Mariyam numb and confused. Unable to speak English well and unfamiliar with First World culture, she makes unsuccessful efforts to buy her own food and medicine. She removes her veil, but feels awkward on the street without it. When she asks directions to the post office, young men harass her, and she returns frightened and defeated to her confined apartment.

Mariyam's life soon becomes controlled by Haji's friends, who visit her with mixed feelings of concern and desire for her beauty. Ali, the most enterprising "suitor," questions her for not wearing a veil in public and insists on buing anything she needs. It is hastily arranged that she will marry him. She is invited to his family's house, a large and isolated estate in upstate New York. There her depression worsens and the attempts of Ali's sisters to inspire her enthusiasm for the marriage are met with disdain. Mariyam attempts to leave the estate in desperation, but is soon found by the men and taken back to her guest room. With no freedom, virtually kidnapped, and surrounded by strangers in alliance with each other, Mariyam stabs Ali in the back of the neck as he speaks enthusiastically about the wedding. She hides his still-living body in her bathroom and calls Reza, the only friend of Haji's group who shows genuine personal concern for her. He picks her up secretly from the house and Mariyam offers him Haji's inheritance money for support if they leave the country together. He agrees, but at the airport they cannot fly together because she is without a passport. Reza suggests he return to the estate to get her passport, but Mariyam insists she will not see Ali's family again, not explaining to him her stabbing of Ali. She devises a plan whereby she will stow away in a suitcase on the flight while Reza rides with the other passengers. They buy a large suitcase, and the plan seems to be working, but Mariyam opens the suitcase on the baggage cart and escapes from the airport on her own as the film ends.

The film's unanticipated ending confounds audience expectations, a central feature of Brechtian analysis. Ebrahimian confounds audiences, who now wonder what will happen to Mariyam, where she will go, and what new relations she will establish. Perhaps even more interesting is why she deliberately plans to desert Reza, the only person in her life who shows any feeling for her on the personal level. Perhaps she wishes to break from all past relationships, seeing them as entanglements preventing her complete break to freedom in a new world. This is aptly foreshadowed early in the film when she momentarily loses Haji at the airport, and her veil flies away when she awkwardly struggles to recover it. Later, after his death, she attempts to leave her apartment alone without her veil and the experiment fails when she is overwhelmed by the strange relationality on the New York streets. Throughout the film Mariyam tries and fails to break from the claustrophobia of her exploitative world, governed by the men whom Ebrahimian ironically terms "suitors" in the title. The word "suitor" would imply a subservient position in that it requests rather than extends favors. However, the men in the film dominate Mariyam, even the minor characters who are identified as friends of Haji's group of recent Iranian immigrants to New York. They are like the famous suitors of Penelope in Homer's *The Odyssey*, who soon forget their suppliant status to dominate and threaten her household in the absence of her husband Odysseus. Mariyam's claustrophobia stems chiefly from cultural assumptions, now misplaced in a new world none of the characters understands. This obliviousness to the new culture around them is revealed in the opening scenes of the film, where Ali's circle of friends are attacked in their apartment by a New York City Police SWAT team when a suspicious non-Muslim neighbor reports them for murder. In fact they were sacrificing a sheep for religious observance in the apartment bathroom. With blood covering their shirts, they seem unaware of their suspect status as outsiders in Western culture. The characters' general disregard for the new culture surrounding them extends to the wives and sisters of Ali and his wealthy friend Amin, who prepare Mariyam's wedding dress without comment on her lack of choice.

Only Mariyam—and perhaps Reza—seems to sense the new culture. Alone in her apartment, she wistfully examines high fashion magazines, envying the mobile, detached images of women on deserted beaches, free from the impediments of traditional culture. Mariyam's brief confinement in the suitcase becomes an emblem of her lifelong confinement, a situation that she alone breaks through to make her escape. But the resolution remains equivocal—how will she survive independently when she was unaware that she needed her own passport to leave the country? One possible answer given her physical attractiveness would be the bleak scenario of call girl solicitation or even street prostitution, where she would perhaps fall under the control of a male pander. These unsettling eventualities refuse a comforting closure to this story of women's struggle for personal/political rights. It is this Epic Theatre element that forms the political consciousness of Ebrahimian's film. The commercial happy ending is replaced by an awareness that even women possessed of beauty and substantial inheritance can remain the treasured property of economic and cultural elites.

WHERE IS THE FRIEND'S HOUSE?: ETHICAL CHOICE IN TRADITIONAL CULTURE

The rights of children have been recognized over several decades through the United Nations' various first- and second-generation human rights agreements (Over, 1999). In Iran, traditional culture has placed children in protective relation to established institutions. However, problems remain when the sort of rapid economic development of recent years leads to unanticipated social change. Iranian cinema has featured the world of children in several important films, revealing the value placed on education and nurturance sought in Muslim culture. Abbas Kiarostami's *Where Is the Friend's House?* (1992) represents a child who defies parental authority for the sake of his concern for another child. The oppositionality of the film is in part softened by the youth of its protagonist—a boy of late grammar school age—and by the filmmaker's adroit handling of the narrative, which situates the characters' actions within the calm routine of everyday village life, presenting a lyrical film of spacious agrarian landscapes and village street scenes. Within a setting created by adults, a boy goes on an unauthorized journey of self-discovery. His independent decision unfolds a new world transformed and appreciated only through the eyes of a child.

When a schoolmate is reprimanded in class for not having his homework assignment, the boy feels badly that he accidentally placed his friend's notebook in his own satchel. After school he implores his mother to let him return the notebook, but she refuses to listen to his explanation, telling him repeatedly to do his homework as she finishes the laundry. Unable to forget his friend's humiliation that day, he secretly leaves the house and runs to the other village. He does not know where his friend's street is, and the busy adults do not bother to answers his questions. Only a boy his own age helps him to the street where a village friend of his friend lives. After repeated attempts to find the house through winding streets, he discovers a pair of trousers hanging on a line that he thinks may belong to his friend. When this proves false, he becomes discouraged and runs home quickly as it gets dark. Later he tries again, and now he is helped by an elderly man who knows where the friend's house is. As the man walks with the boy, he tells him about his own life as a maker of window latticework, pointing out as they go the beautiful windows and describing the people he made them for. The lighting from the windows radiates through the dark streets, creating a wondrous world of strangers and their relationships. Although the boy fails to find his schoolmate, the next day in class he secretly returns the notebook to him under the desk, having filled in his homework assignment for him.

The story recounts a typical experience of a school-age child caught between the demands of parents and his own conscience. As the boy discovers perhaps for the first time his own moral boundaries, the film profiles a transition in life, one that almost always occurs unnoticed. Produced by Iran's Institute for the Intellectual Development of Children and Young Adults, the film is at once didactic and aesthetically developed, another example that challenges the limited binary of political drama/aesthetic drama. The coming-of-age theme involves an act of defiance in a world where adults hardly listen to children and often never notice their presence. Hence the narrative contrasts the moral development of a child with the moral laxity of the adult world. The adults, busy with their daily routines and profit-making enterprises, have no time for the humanity around them. Only the retired window maker—another person ignored by the society of working adults—takes an interest in the boy, telling him his life's story and about the people he knew in his vocation. Windows are a central image in the film, functioning something like William Blake's "windows to the soul," the eyes of perception that reach out to others. They open what has been shut by the daily routine and prejudice of adults. Only the young and old remember to see the humanity around them and help those in need. The boy, unable to get his mother to listen to his moral concern for his friend, defies her wishes and begins his own journey of life. *Where Is the Friend's House?* describes life's quest, which can only be achieved positively by establishing boundaries between authority and the individual. Kiarostami's film shows affinity with Jafar Panahi's more famous *White Balloon* (1996) and Majid Majidi's *Children of Paradise* (1998), about the unnoticed world of children who learn that the world of reality does not match the demands of parental authority. In their oppositional celebrations of childhood, these films argue for the rights of children in a flawed world governed by adults.

Part II

THE DRAMA OF MOVEMENT

_____ Chapter 6 _____

DRAMA OF IMMIGRATION:
THE CINEMA OF INVISIBILITY

Political scientists have seldom attended to displaced people, refugees, and immigrant populations, largely considering such movements tangential to the central concerns of international politics. Yet, as Elizabeth Ferris (1993) predicts,

Virtually all of the international political and economic trends seem to point to an increase in the forced migration of people in the years ahead, not a lessening of it. The pressures of population, economic scarcity and environmental degradation will all become even more compelling reasons for people to leave their communities. (p. xii)

The relation of immigrant and refugee status to U.S. foreign policy has been well documented statistically. Immigrants from countries with governments accommodating to transnational corporations (so-called "pro-business" governments) are less likely to receive refugee status and have a more difficult time entering the U.S. as ordinary immigrants (Ferris, 1993, pp. xx, xxv). At the same time, international organizations have created human rights laws that remain inadequate in form and interpretation. While the Universal Declaration of Human Rights grants individuals the right to live free of governmental persecution and to leave countries where such conditions exist, it is not recognized as a basic human right that such individuals be *accepted* by other nation states.

While there is some cause for hope that particular governments will extend individual rights to its noncitizens, many countries, including those, such as the U.S., with the largest number of refugees and immigrants, have not moved progressively in this way (Hammar, 1990, p. 137). Confronting recent immigrants and refugees in the United States is the new character of jobs for immigrants. The restructuring of the U.S. economy has meant fewer jobs in manufacturing, which requires stable, semi-skilled labor, and more jobs in the growing service areas, which require a much higher percentage of temporary, unskilled employment. This means short-term benefits for relatively elite groups—businesses, middle-class consumers—but long-term disadvantages for the society as a whole, as large numbers of undereducated and illegal immigrants begin to affect negatively the society as a whole (Cornelius, Martin, & Hollifield, 1994, pp., 12–13). For immigrants, however, the negative effects are immediate and unforgiving. Police in New York City have recently ignored blatant acts of brutality against Manhattan's 60,000 sweatshop workers perpetrated by management (Riker, personal interview, 1999). Needed is a link between trade negotiations of transnational corporations and their governments with workers' rights legislation. This connection has commonly been ignored by such institutions as the newly established World Trade Organization (WTO) (Levinson, 1999, p. 43). Until international organizations are able to raise awareness among the populace of their member states to press for universal labor laws, the abuse of immigrants will continue. Meanwhile, the discourse of social justice for immigrants remains nugatory, confined typically to listener/viewer- sponsored media and politically aware news journals in the First World, locally organized events and protests, and the occasional depoliticized "human interest" story in mainstream media. Similarly, cinema in the First World has remained distant from such subject matter, with a few notable exceptions. These attempts are significant for their failures—often noble, often less so—as much as for their sterling successes, the latter of which we can learn from as examples of drama that entertains and reveals at the same time.

The everyday experiences of immigrants recently arrived in their destination countries have received at best comic interpretations from Hollywood studios. Most popular in this regard has been *West Side Story* (1961), based on the Broadway musical and Shakespeare's *Romeo and Juliet*, and films such as *Born in East L.A.* (1987), the latter's cogency at times turning the straightforward comedy into serious political satire. *El Norte* (1983) gained a degree of popularity, and its story of the perils of a young brother and sister escaping the terrorism of Guatemala's military government was timely, but its light-hearted commentary, in typical Hollywood formula fashion, avoided relevant foreign policy issues and the implications of refugees fleeing from a U.S.-sponsored terrorist state. Far surpassing all of these in verisimilitude, relevance, poignancy, and political consciousness is David Riker's *The City* (*La Ciudad*, 1999), an independent film that captures the despair and injustice experienced by Latin American immigrants to New York City in the 1990s. Its four distinct stories tell of anger coupled with powerlessness, love hindered by ignorance, parental attachment amid homelessness, and the isolation of inhuman labor conditions.

THE CITY: INTIMACY AND THE INVISIBLE

In "Home" a young man from rural Mexico walks the streets of New York's outer boroughs unable to find the address a relative has given him. Tired and perplexed, he walks into a banquet hall of a "sweet 15" celebration and finds Maria, the young woman of his dreams. They discover they are from the same district of Mexico. Maria, serious and shy, presents a laconic front, but soon warms to the young man's sincerity and loneliness. Since he has nowhere to stay, she invites him home to her uncle's apartment. There a hesitant flirtation begins and Maria receives a tender kiss from the young man before she goes to her room to sleep the night, promising that she will make him breakfast in the morning. The young man enters Maria's bedroom in the early morning to gaze upon her sleeping and look at a family photo. On his way back for groceries to fix a surprise breakfast for Maria, he is unable to find her apartment amid the towering project buildings. He stares at the monolithic urban environment. Myriad identical windows stare back at him, as he clutches the grocery bag in despair.

"Home" conveys pathos and relevance through its simplicity and the generic force of its identities—the young man and woman remain typical and yet individual, the details of their lives rendered less significant and kept to a minimum for the sake of the compelling story. In this way characters and setting remain universal and yet particular to a First World city of the 1990s. The vignette is an instance of the effective use of universally human subject matter—first love and innocence within a threatening melange of struggle and alienation—to uncover the particularities of social injustice. The ordinariness of the characters, their mutual affection, vulnerability, and innocence, raises the hope of overcoming an inhuman world. In the end, however, the utter anonymity of the city defeats budding love, which represents an essential humanity in the vignette. The unique authority of the story derives almost entirely from the sadness and suddenness of its ending. The young man's abrupt disorientation is brought about by his own ignorance of inner-city life. His desolation also falls suddenly upon Maria, who at that moment is wondering why the young man deserted her unexpectedly while she slept.

If "Home" represents innocent love defeated by the social forces of alienation and inhumanity, Riker, who also wrote and edited the four tales, includes moments of humor that enhance the story's cultural setting. The young couple laugh along with the film audience when the young man compares his small foot with the large shoes found in the apartment of Maria's absent uncle. This reference to the love triangle of traditional comedy—two young lovers prevented from merging by a parental male blocking character—registers the familiarity of their situation and the innocence of their motives. Other parallels to the classic comedy of young lovers include the fact that the young man could easily have found his relative's address by asking Maria or one of her friends at the celebration, thus discounting his claim to be without a place to stay. Both innocents are in this way subtly manipulative of their first love encounter, an observation as old as Greek New Comedy. Maria adroitly ends the awkwardness of their first kiss alone on her uncle's apartment couch by promising the young man breakfast in the morning. Such moments lead the audience into a comedy of romance, making the forlornness of the ending all the more powerful. This intentional disruption of conventional plotting is pure Brechtian Epic Theatre, a deliberate challenge to the audience's complacent expectations for the happy ending of comedy. Riker's surprise ending trespasses on the conventional resolution of commercial theatre and cinema, confronting audiences with the reality of the immigrant's precarious circumstances.

However, the intimacy and optimism of the characters also allow audiences to rediscover an invisible and often despised minority— Latin American immigrants. In this way Riker transcends the either/ or fallacy often perpetuated by naive interpretations of Brechtian didacticism. In all four stories of *The City*, empathy for the characters is combined with such distancing devices as unresolved and unhappy endings. In fact, to allow audience identification with characters whose existence is unobserved or denied by society's majority is in itself a break from conventionality. Permitting an audience to identify with a previously invisible or disdained group creates a critical distance from the power structures of society. This narrative capability Brecht himself largely overlooked in his theory. Thus Riker's film succeeds didactically at two seemingly opposite agendas—evoking empathy for his characters and establishing distancing devices that invite thoughtful reflection.

In "Bricks," perhaps Riker's most inconsolable story, a group of male day-workers line up for work in the back streets of an anonymous outer-borough neighborhood. There are too many workers and not enough jobs. The men jostle for position when the Italian-American boss arrives. He can only take so many workers in his truck and a boy is at first prevented from accompanying his father, who has nowhere else to send his son for the day. But he is eventually allowed to come. The ride to the work site is long and the men cannot see where they are going because the truck is locked and without windows. The worksite is a vast warehouse lot devastated by demolition. The boss offers the men 15 cents for every brick cleaned of mortar with hammers and scrapers. When the men protest that this offer is not what they were promised, the boss' brusque manner and their need resign them to their labor. He abandons them for the day, falsely promising to return soon with water and supervision. After first turning their anger upon one another, the men reluctantly begin stacking individual piles of cleaned bricks, carefully separating them from the others. Some men continue to argue the injustice of their circumstances in a wealthy country; others impatiently reject such talk as pointless and defeatist. Their frantic discourse reflects similar lines of argument and denial within the mainstream society, where unfair social conditions are dismissed as inevitable and even necessary to separate the strong from the weak. Despite their outbursts of anger and ideology, the men soon find common ground for human decency when one of them is seriously injured under a collapsing wall of bricks. Their boss has deserted them, and their scouts cannot identify the neighborhood or even the borough. Unable to find help for the injured man, they lament their abandonment and powerlessness. Despair brings them together once again as they watch the injured worker die. Their vigil for the one sacrificed to poverty and anonymity allows them to forget for the moment their individual piles of bricks. The fatalism of the denouement is increased by the boy's profound reaction to the horror of pointless death. His perplexity robs his innocence, and he joins the adult world in despair and grief.

"Bricks" shows clear influence from the Theatre of the Absurd. It features a bleak, generic setting of decay; human abandonment; faith in a savior figure who does not return; the love-hate character of comradeship; and above all, a fatalistic plot structure. Nevertheless, Riker's tale elicits pointedly political issues. Whereas Samuel Beckett and Eugene Ionesco generally dissociate their dramaturgy from political commentary, only occasionally offering characters who satirize the manners of known social types, Riker's social agenda is didactic in its exposé of immigrant life and attention to verisimilitude. The only hope posited in "Bricks" is the political one of worker solidarity. Among the men, the words of the labor organizer gain more credibility when the tragic consequences of their working conditions unfold.

"The Puppeteer" elicits the most acted performance from Riker's non-actors. Jose Rabelo's role as the homeless street performer elicits a more complex range of emotions. Ill with tuberculosis, he refuses to stay in a city shelter for fear of exposing his young daughter to contagious diseases. They live in an illegally parked station wagon crammed with possessions. The vacant lot where they are permanently parked functions as performance space for puppet shows, and the daughter assists with collecting money and dressing puppets. But when the father sees his daughter making up stories to go along with the pictures in her children's books, he is determined to put her in school. He learns that every child in New York City is entitled to free education and takes his daughter to the local school. When he is unable to prove residency in the city, he returns with his daughter to the vacant lot in anger and despair.

Unlike the other tales in the film, "The Puppeteer" relies upon a slower-paced acting style, much in the tradition of Italian neorealism. While the father is a neighborhood success with the mothers and children, he feels the failure in the traditional masculine role of provider. Worse, his love for his daughter cannot grant what he most wants for her, the education he was denied. Riker uses the play-within-a-play motif as ironic comparison. The wondrous and adventurous world of the puppet show contrasts with the determinism of urban desolation. Riker's black and white photography is most operative here, as the disparity between the colorful world of the imagination and the bleakness of illiteracy and poverty is emblematized through black, gray, and white. Despite their daily performances before spectators, the father and daughter are the most isolated of the film's characters. The young girl has no other children to play with and instead contents herself with blowing a horn and making up stories. Their social isolation has also created a barrier between them, as they commonly turn away from each other into their own worlds and lack the spontaneity of playful interaction. As in Riker's other vignettes, "The Puppeteer" ends with little hope for the characters. Bureaucracy and indifference defeat the invisible cry for help.

"Seamstress": Silence Turned Around

If immigrants are silenced, fragmented, and denied culture in the first three tales, in the concluding piece, "Seamstress," the invisible gain an unanticipated visibility through their collective silence. This most politically proactive of the four vignettes concerns a young woman who works in a crowded sweatshop where no one has been paid for weeks. When she learns in a letter from home that her sick daughter needs $400 for an operation, she begs her boss for the back pay. She is told harshly that the checks have not yet arrived. Her desperation leads her to ask relatives in the city for money, but they are unable or unwilling to help. The other seamstresses and male pressers try to raise money for her, but it is not enough. In a state of despair, she cannot work effectively at the fast pace demanded by the factory and is bullied by the manager. At last she clings to her sewing machine while her boss pulls at her. This violent moment is the most compelling in the film, but Riker produces an unexpected reversal. As the woman convulses with anguish under the boss' abuse, the other workers begin an unplanned work stoppage. Their silence within the factory is deadening. The Asian couple who manage the shop are paralyzed, as are the workers and the film audience. Riker prolongs the moment with a succession of closeup shots that reveal the contained anger on the faces of various seamstresses and pressers, the beads of sweat signifying their working conditions. A sustained long-shot of the entire factory loft ends the crescendo of rapid closeups, revealing the solidarity of a spontaneous work stoppage.

All the more cogent because unplanned, the stoppage effectively galvanizes the workers, who until then have passively accepted delayed paychecks, an overheated and unventilated building, piece-work wage schemes, and long hours. Riker stops short of the prolonged organized strike most memorable theatrically in Gerhart Hauptmann's *The Weavers* (1965), where peasant workers take to the streets in protest. Instead, this vignette leaves the future open. The ambiguity of the denouement effectively attracts a certain pathos for the workers and even the managers, who themselves are browbeaten by nervous corporate executives. However, by leaving audiences with a high level of emotionality, the ending misses the Brechtian aim of alienation. Epic Theatre above all wishes to replace the elicitation of pathos and empathy at the drama's conclusion with a perspectival analysis. By distancing audiences from the climactic feelings of the drama, robbing them of the pleasure of vicarious tragedy, a socially responsible objectivity could uncover the structures of power underlying the characters' plight. Nowhere is this possibility more evident than in "Seamstress," which contains all the ingredients of pathos and discloses systematic class and racial exploitation. Riker's decision to present a more postmodern ending—actually closer to the ambivalence of Theatre of the Absurd—wherein clear answers are suspended in favor of the anguish of uncertainty, prevents his final film statement from becoming partisan drama.

While Riker avoids clear answers in his urban immigrant stories, he effectively presents a didactic aim—making visible the invisible. *The City* answers to this extent questions of fact rather than policy. While Brecht sought pragmatic solutions to concrete but structural problems in society, Riker's discourse instead depends upon allowing immigrant subjects to reveal their lives in a straightforward manner, using verisimilitude to evoke empathy rather than the more mainstream glamorization and lighthearted treatment typical of the Hollywood studio formula. His use of non-actors, naturalistic dialogue in Spanish with English subtitles, an urban *mise-en-scène*, and most of all the harshness of his subject matter preclude facile Hollywood treatment. Stereotypes and other over-determined identities common to First World treatment of Third World subjects are rejected in favor of three-dimensional characters who invite audience empathy.

Brecht never gave enough attention to the matter of postcolonial identity as a dynamic in didactic drama. Since Frantz Fanon (1986), the identity of the colonized has been recognized as problematic, a reconstructed image perpetuated by colonizing institutions. In the words of Homi Bhabha (1994), "[t]he image is only ever an appurtenance to authority and identity; it must never be read mimetically as the appearance of a reality" (p. 51). In the world of transnational corporate labor practice, where labor rights are as invisible to the global village as the laborers themselves, stereotypes help refill the vacuum left by the indifference of world media and the obliviousness of intergovernmental bureaucracies with investment priorities (Kernaghan, 1996; Ledbetter, 1997). Riker's portraits of New York immigrants do not succeed by "understatement," as a sympathetic reviewer, Stephen Holden (1999), observes, but rather by a recognizable—i.e., neorealist—uncovering of everyday pain hidden by hegemonic constructions of reality (p. E12). By representing the real problems and living conditions of Latin American immigrants to New York, *The City* dispels over-determined images of identity, an achievement that in itself must qualify as an alienation effect (*Verfremdungseffekt*) in the Epic Theatre tradition, since audience expectations are challenged and the sources of social denial are exposed by implication, if not explicitly. In this way Riker expands the Brechtian aim of creating a drama that teaches rather than fetishizes.

MAINSTREAM CINEMA TRIES HARDER

First World film production has all too rarely acknowledged the immigrant presence, generally with fragmented images and tenta-

tive development. Richard Attenborough's internationally popular
Ghandi (1982) traced the life of its subject with attention to objectivity and balance. Scenes of mass emigration employed casts of thousands on location and revealed tableaux of religious conflict
between the Hindu and Muslim populace as they passed one another towards their new borders. One startling scene shows a young
father in anguish over his child, who died perhaps from violence or
disease, pick up a stone in anger and run wildly towards the long
line of emigrants moving in the opposite direction. The subsequent
mass violence is meant to encapsulate the widespread violence that
accompanied the division of India and Pakistan. Attenborough's
scene succeeds as film spectacle, helped in part by the use of thousands of South Asian extras. However, as a dramatic documentation
of social justice and human rights, it remains insufficient and oversimplified. Unable to present the father and infant in their individuality, or the circumstances of their recent flight, the film instead
relies upon overdetermined conceptions of Hindu and Muslim tensions—precipitous violence, mutual intolerance—that justified the
colonialist presence in the subcontinent. Unable to separate itself in
such scenes from the ideology of colonialism, *Ghandi* emphasizes
the biography of a world-famous national leader while keeping the
reality of forced mass mobility as a peripheral spectacle.

Perhaps garnering the most attention as a film specifically focused on the reality of immigration from the Third to the First World
has been Gregory Nava's *El Norte* (1983), a film that in many ways
succeeds where other didactic films have failed. A teenage brother
and sister are forced to flee their isolated mountain village in Guatemala when government death squads threaten their lives. The couple lack the sophistication to journey through Mexico to the United
States without help from various people. A "cayote," that is, a hired
clandestine guide to help them across the border into California,
tells them to crawl through an abandoned water pipe under a mountain for several miles. The terrifying experience leaves them bleeding
and sick, but they soon arrive in San Diego to begin a new life. The
brother, more resourceful than his sister, becomes a waiter and
works his way into the confidence of his employers despite problems
learning English. The sister finds domestic employment with a
wealthy suburban family, but she becomes ill and dies of rat bites
resulting from the journey through the pipe. In a poignant moment,
the brother attempts to hide his grief while planning to fly to Chicago
to better his career.

The film's documentation of the Latin American immigrant experience reveals individuals who undergo hardships to escape tyranny.
However, the film obscures more than it reveals. There is no attempt

in the beginning Guatemalan scenes to document the long-term political oppression of the U.S.-backed military government. Rapid editing, a shrill musical score, and closeup shots of night-and-fog violence inadequately substitute for the details of a social setting that would establish the context of systemic violence. In the flight through Mexico and later in San Diego, when the siblings are looking for work, humor is used as a momentary diversion to lighten the bleak implications of the refugee experience. Rather than providing insight, humor in *El Norte* often becomes associated with stereotypical ethnicities. For example, the boisterous Mexican truck driver who gives the brother and sister a ride north uses profanities unknown to the rural couple, a low-comic moment reproduced when the white U.S. border patrolmen remark to one another that the two young refugees "don't sound Mexican." Comedy layered between serious scenes marginalizes the film's political commentary, an unintended ambivalence that diverts the theme of refugee flight from Latin America and the exploitation of illegal immigration. Instead, humor serves to slight the harsh realities of movements between the Third and First worlds, transforming the film into something closer to the common Hollywood formula theme of the newcomer's successful struggle in the land of opportunity.

While the sister dies tragically from complications related to the illegal border crossing, the brother experiences a rather easy rise to middle-class status through his skills as a waiter, a service occupation that the film reveals as depending for success upon flattery and self-deprecation. In the restaurant kitchen the brother practices various forms of flattery for his customers, a use of comedy that appeals to the complacency of mainstream audiences, who may find the Latino male less threatening when he willingly assumes a subservient status. Even the surprise raid on the restaurant by the INS (U.S. Immigration and Naturalization Service) is treated lightly. The pursuit of illegal refugees in the scene sacrifices potential tragic poignancy and becomes instead an opportunity for a farcical, Keystone Kops-style chase. Similarly, the sister's first experiences working as a domestic in an upper-middle-class suburban household ignore the implications of cultural isolation and class division inherent in the situation. Instead, the sister's work as a domestic becomes a Lucille Ball-style replay of the daffy housewife. Focusing on the farcical situation of her inability to comprehend computerized washing machines, the sister's domestic work experience becomes an amusing struggle against the machine rather than a purposeful exploration of the loneliness of the foreign house worker so brilliantly achieved in Ousemane Sembene's *Black Girl* (*La Noire de . . .*, 1966). Very much a collaborative effort, *El Norte* dilutes its political message beyond recognition. While the film was under production, Guatemalan refugees were touring the U.S. speaking out against the military oppression of their country, urging citizens to speak out against Washington's long-term support of the regime. *El Norte* succeeds in expunging all traces of the Washington connection to its story.

By turning into comedy serious geopolitical realities made timely by the direct international involvement of governments, mainstream cinema at once presents social conflicts and ignores their provenance. Heavy use of ethnic stereotyping serves to implicate the victims themselves in their own plight and redirects the potential indictment of geopolitical forces towards common preconceptions, thus rendering innocuous commentary. Much more popular than *El Norte*, Robert Wise's *West Side Story* (1961) reproduced on the screen the Broadway musical hit about recent immigrant life in New York City. Conceived as a twentieth-century version of the Romeo and Juliet story, the play and its film version enlist satire rather than comedy to advance the theme of the consequences of group prejudice. Particularly evident in the musical number, "I Like to Be in America," social satire directs audiences to a debate between the Latina women, who approve of the opportunities of America, and the Latino men, who point out to the women the consequences of segregated neighborhoods and employment discrimination. Brechtian in its biting use of song lyrics for political commentary, the play and film also include "Officer Krupke," a satire on First World bureaucratized social service systems that fail to help families of recent immigrants. While the film's deeper social analysis must contend with a romantic plot structure that prioritizes desire between members of competing ethnic groups, the wide distribution of the film and its sustained popularity over several decades has made *West Side Story* in many ways the most influential film about immigrants. Still, the film's major lacunae are apparent when significant aspects of immigrant life are considered. The play and film do not focus on the immigration process itself, an element of agency that would reveal primary motivational elements of immigrant life. Nor do they attempt to uncover the specific forms of social injustice through the drama's most significant form, its plot structure. Housing discrimination, police brutality, employment "glass ceilings," and other oppressive forms are relegated to allusions in the song lyrics. Finally, the commercialization of the story precludes any serious analysis of immigrant life in a large First World metropolis. The tragic ending plays to the sort of emotionality Brecht so lamented in the boulevard theatre of the 1930s, leaving audiences in tears but also fatalistic about "life's tragedies."

The ambiguities of so much didactic drama produced in both the First and Third worlds are perhaps inevitable, given the nature of theatre and cinema as public, mass art forms. About cinematic "negotiation" in the marketplace, Judith Mayne (1993) has observed, "no 'negotiation' is inherently or purely oppositional, but . . . the desire for anything 'inherent' and 'pure' is itself a fiction that must be contested" (p. 100). However, didactic films about the immigrant experience that are straightforwardly oppositional and confrontational, such as Riker's *The City* and, in moments, Cheech Marin's *Born in East L.A.* (1987), are decidedly different from compromised fare that have "gone mainstream" in avoiding—the sometimes obvious—implications of their subject matter. More important than determining the degree of authentic oppositionality in a work of social relevance is the open nature of its aim. Here the mere reproduction of unjust social practice is not as significant as the clarity of the drama's "message." On this point Jean Starobinsky writes, "the law of authenticity does not demand that an utterance *reproduces* a given reality, but that it *produces its truth* in a free and uninterrupted development" (in Perego, 1998, p. 337). Marin's *Born in East L.A.* creates such a context through its dedication to uncovering mainstream attitudes towards subaltern groups in late-twentieth-century California.

Born in East L.A.: Satire and Border Crossings

Cheech Marin's film remains one of the few singularly oppositional independent films about immigrants produced in the U.S. for primarily U.S. consumption. Its comic/satirical base melds contemporary Chicano humor of self-deprecation and understatement with a realistic social milieu to produce an effective discourse of confrontation. Marin's satire is keen and cogent, but softened somewhat by the lead actor/director/writer's insouciant performance style and humorous base. Marin's observant nonchalance, though well within the classic film tradition of Charlie Chaplin, W.C. Fields, Bob Hope, and other grand performers, creates a running commentary that serves to make more vivid the disparities between the experiences of mainstream culture and Chicano life. Marin's targets include the power structure of suspicion; ethnic stereotypes; the treatment of migrant workers; INS violations of civil liberties; and the economic gulf between white and Chicano Californians, epitomized in the *barrio* of East Los Angeles. Born, raised, and currently living in that large urban area, Marin's character Rudy is unable to convince his fellow white citizens of his residency status, a fact that becomes the premise of Marin's astute political satire.

Marin's film begins in the low-comic style typical of his film series about Chicano life in the *barrio*—a world that combines flamboyant cruising cars, women-gazing, succinct social commentary, and family life—but soon becomes satirical when Rudy is caught in an INS raid of a local sweatshop where he has gone to meet his cousin. Without his wallet, he is unable to prove his U.S. citizenship and is abruptly transported to a Mexican border town. The local INS office does not believe his story despite his flawless English and East L.A. slang. Looking Mexican is enough to keep him from entering his own country. Despondent, he takes a job with a white U.S. national running a strip joint for tourists. One of his jobs is to teach a group of would-be illegal Asian immigrants how to dress, walk, and talk like a California Chicano. The social stereotyping he teaches becomes an ironic comment on the same fixity that led to his own mistreatment by mainstream authorities. Adding to the satire is Rudy's inability to speak Spanish or even know the significance of the *Cinco de Mayo* celebration. Rudy is believed by no one except a young woman from El Salvador, who sees him give his fruit produce to a poor woman with children. This act of kindness finally reveals his true identity— that is, his inner character—to someone.

Rudy's attempts to cross the border to the U.S. become a comic treatment of the reality behind gatekeeping policies, boundaries that are permeant for the lowest class of worker, a group essential to the U.S. economy, but to no one else. Open only to the exploited, Rudy's U.S. citizen status casts him among those inessential to the U.S. economy. In another act of kindness, Rudy substitutes his own seat on a illegal border-crossing truck to a woman who is separated from her husband. This moment of pathos changes the tone of the film, which ends when Rudy leads thousands of Mexicans over a hill towards the border, an onslaught that the surprised border patrol is unable to stop. Marin's comment seems to be that the disparities between the First and Third Worlds can never be perpetuated by maintaining institutional boundaries and self-righteous reactions masquerading as patriotism. As Rudy comments early in the film, his predicament was caused by the color of his skin—"brown"—not by his character, a challenge to institutional and attitudinal ethnocentrism.

Central Station (1998) won critical acclaim for its strong acting and human sentiment. Director Walter Salles cast the famous Brazilian actress Fernanda Montenegro in the role of Dora, a misanthropic woman who has lost connection with life. Reluctantly befriending a small boy whose mother is killed in front of Rio de Janeiro's Central Station, Dora at first "sells" him in a shady deal, but thinks better of it and agrees to take him to his home village in Brazil's impoverished Northeast. Their bus trip together becomes a journey of self-discovery, as the characters draw closer together and deeper into themselves. While the boy searches for his family, Dora seeks her heart. In an interview, Salles (1998) comments that the film "is about the ability to start all over again at [age 67]" (*Angelika Filmbill*, p. 23). The panoramic landscape of the journey and the pathos of the characters made the film internationally popular, but focus on the destitute emigrating from rural Brazil to the urban areas—the social milieu of the film—is sacrificed for a commercialized "human interest" story and a facile sentimentality centering on a middle-class woman's reinvestment in life.

Dora's bitter disillusionment is revealed early in the film in her attitude towards the illiterate immigrants who hire her to write letters home. Uninvolved in their personal anguish over separation, poverty, and cultural isolation, she often does not bother to mail the letters once she is paid. Disdainful of their commonality, gullibility, and ignorance, she has long ago fortified herself against compassion by hardening her heart. Still, Salles' story never succeeds in connecting Dora's personal anguish with the larger pain of Brazil's disenfranchised, through which she—and others in the middle class—derives income. Although the young boy's simple faith in humankind inspires her to help him find his family, the story retains its focus on Dora's regeneration. Her ability to begin a relationship with a truck driver on the journey demonstrates a rediscovery of life, but the poverty of Northeast Brazil remains only a backdrop for what amounts to a romanticized account of the young and innocent helping those who have become old before becoming wise. The sentimentality of the relationship between the boy and Dora prevents any further reflection on the structures of oppression within their society, leaving audiences with the sort of complacent reassurance Epic Theatre sought to move beyond. More disturbing details of the plot are conveniently avoided, such as the activities of the couple to whom Dora wished to sell the boy, and the ease with which she is able to retrieve the boy from their apartment. Departing from the didactic tradition of Brazilian *cinema novo, Central Station* keeps the disenfranchised at a distance appropriate for commercialized pathos but not for the probing confrontation with hegemony and powerlessness.

Journey of Hope: The Invisibility of Refugees

The condition of refugees seeking sanctuary from the actions of oppressive home governments has received little attention in First World cinema. Such films as Peter Weir's *The Mosquito Coast* (1986), about the "rescue" of indigenous groups along the Eastern coast of Nicaragua, and Weir's *The Year of Living Dangerously* (1983), about a flight of refugees from a vaguely conceived Southeast Asian dictatorship, typically focus on First World characters—played by notable box-office draws—at the expense of the committed uncovering of particular Third World political histories. *Mosquito Coast* was also intended to embarrass the Sandinista government of Nicaragua, a then new socialist government out of favor with Washington (Herman, 1988). One notable exception is Xavier Koller's *Journey of Hope* (1991), which won international laurels, including an Oscar for Best Foreign Language Film. It concerns a Kurdish village family who decide to emigrate for Switzerland for an illegal entry when their farmland becomes infertile. Haydar and his wife Meryem anguish over separating their family, but reluctantly decide to take only one of their seven children with them. The boy is the youngest and also the most rebellious child. Along the way they confront middlemen who continually raise the smuggling price. After a dangerous trip in a locked container within a cargo ship, they face blizzards on the slopes of the Alps and treachery from greedy smugglers. Before sending the family over the stormy mountains, a smuggler persuades Haydar to sign an agreement to give half their future earnings in Switzerland to his organization. Abandoned by their guide, the immigrants struggle to climb over an Alpine range. When they are separated and lost, their journey to a better life becomes a struggle for survival. After the boy dies from exposure in the mountains, the parents, now captured and awaiting return to Turkey, feel tragic loss and disillusionment.

Despite its popularity with First World distributors and critics, who promoted the film's realism and sentiment, *Journey of Hope* avoids the political implications of the Kurdish dilemma in Turkey, a NATO member in favor with the West. Harsh treatment of Kurdish villagers at the hands of Turkish authorities is never documented. In fact, the film manages to show no Turkish authorities at all. Moreover, references to the refugee status of Haydar, Meryem, and the other Kurdish immigrants are infrequent and parenthetical. For example, as an elderly religious man is captured by the Swiss border patrol, he cries for "refugee status," but there is no further dialogue about his claim. All reference to the systematic persecution of the Kurdish population by the Turkish government is denied in the film, perhaps as a deliberate stratagem to avoid controversy for access to wide distribution. Instead of persecution, references to the depletion of the farming soil are established in the film's early exposition, a fact that does not explain the long-term use of the same lands by Kurdish farmers. Transferring focus to the perilous journey of the immigrant party and the greed of the smugglers moves the film towards the action-film formula dear to commercial film production.

Opportunities for presenting such details of character and culture that would enrich the context of Kurdish life are often sacrificed for a sketchy exposition of the home village routine. Still, the concise foreshadowing of the youngest child's death is well handled dramatically. In the village, the boy dangerously allows a fast-moving train to pass over him in a game of "chicken" with other boys and is punished by his father. Later, the boy's death in his father's arms from exposure results from the risk-taking of his parents.

Despite an extreme economy of cultural detail, the film's ending brilliantly uncovers the callous indifference of First World attitudes towards refugees. An argument between a health care worker and a police captain raises the issue of who is responsible for the plight of refugees and the limitations of nationalistic and ethnocentric thinking. The most cogent exchange happens in the very last lines of dialogue. When a Swiss citizen offers to help pay for the son's funeral and transport back home, Haydar breaks his dazed dejection and remarks, "I wish I could have been your friend." Surprised by the intimacy of the statement, the Swiss man responds with an unconscious double take, creating a powerful moment of connectivity between cultures. Koller's bleak story leads to a cogent denouement that questions nationalistic divisionism and ethnic suspicion. His unwillingness to offer audiences gratuitous comfort by saving the life of the boy and allowing his parents to remain in their land of promise moves the film away from action/adventure melodrama and towards serious political analysis, but the lack of political specificity hinders his discourse, serving to reinforce Western indifference towards the plight of persecuted groups within Turkey.

DAVID RIKER: PREPARING FOR *THE CITY*

If *Journey of Hope* decontextualizes its message at the expense of political relevance, *The City* begins with the specificity of actual immigrant sweatshop workers in New York City before the formative elements of the film are undertaken. Breaking radically with commercial film production schedules, Riker took six years to complete his four vignettes. He assumed the task of investigative journalist before writing his final screenplays. This production method could more accurately be described as transactional rather than linear filmmaking, since he did not create his film's narratives before gaining the trust and cooperation of his non-actors. To find them he went to "shape-ups" in neighborhoods that hire men on the street for non-union construction work throughout New York's five boroughs. After Riker told these workers about his project and gained their confidence, they agreed to help him on the film. The four stories—with one exception—were the products of this collaboration. At one point, the women he assembled to help create the "Seamstress" vignette asked him to leave the room for an hour while they divided themselves into small groups to discuss what eventually became the film's final story (Riker, 1999, personal interview). This radical departure from an hierarchical to a cooperative method of filmmaking created a product radically different from all other screen dramas. Intimate and engaging, it establishes new areas of discourse beyond those delimited by the established dichotomy of social drama/docudrama. *The City* is neither a political tract nor a melodramatic reshaping of social justice issues. Using non-actors (or, to put it positively, the actual people involved) as performers and collaborators, it combines social documentation with intimacy, exposing the social structures of exploitation by uncovering the private lives of new arrivals to a culture that does not see them. Riker's choice of subject matter in itself creates the Brechtian alienation effect by virtue of its departure from the common representations of the poor, ethnic groups, women, and immigrants. The disruption of categories constructed by the dominant ideology directly throws into question mainstream preconceptions, rendering strange what has been negotiated within the culture and revealing realities that have been hidden. This kind of alienation effect is achieved for partisan drama without choral commentary, multimedia, actors stepping out of their roles in a presentational style, and other performance methods traditional to Epic Theatre in its staged forms. Riker's neorealism rediscovers the capacity of cinema for social critique.

_____ Chapter 7 _____

POINTS OF CONVERGENCE:
SOJOURNS WITHIN THE HOMELAND

Ousmane Sembene, the noted Senegalese filmmaker, began as a novelist but moved to film when he realized how much more appropriate cinema was for reaching the broad majority of his homeland people. One of his early films, *La Noire de . . .* (*Black Girl*, 1966), became the first feature-length film by an African. Its translation to the cinema faithfully kept the theme of Sembene's novel while creating a style unique to the cinema. *La Noire de . . .* represents the pioneering work of a postcolonial creator who has through compelling symbolism confronted the problem of cultural and economic hybridity in an increasingly globalized world. In fact, the film was a quite early articulation of the ambiguities of postcolonial hybridity, a subject that has received appropriate attention from theorists only beginning in the 1980s.

While *La Noire de . . .* depicts the psychological deterioration and social isolation of a postcolonial subject as she moves from a Third World to a First World location, it is also, in part, an instance of the representation of sojourns, returns, and movements within Third World homelands. D. moves from her Senegalese home to live as an *au pair* with a white family in France, where she is so isolated from community and so estranged from her employers that she eventually commits suicide. However, the film returns to Africa where the mask that D. originally gave to the French couple is returned by the husband, only to be worn by D.'s brother as he chases the former employer out of the hometown at the end of the film. Thus the

brother's reappropriation of the religious artifact is a gesture of pro-
testation against the former colonial and present neocolonial power,
embodied in the former white employer of his sister. The mask's recovery and use also becomes a trope for the rescue of African identity within the postcolonial setting. Sembene's storyline moves from
Africa to Europe back to Africa, creating a circular journey wherein
the legacy of colonial/neocolonial subjection—represented by the
lowly *au pair* status of the "black girl" in a First World modern household—is overcome in a powerful denouement. When the mask as
persona of African identity is brought home, its appropriation as
cultural object of subaltern status is erased. While D.'s lonely suicide expresses a spiritual defeat, the African mask, originally representing an act of love and gratitude between her and her French
employers, becomes the emblem of the endurance of African cultural identity under threat from European hegemony.

Sembene's return to Africa in *La Noire de . . .* expresses the power
of location as a metaphor within hybridity and immigration studies.
While the film might have ended typically with the suicide of a
postcolonial servant within First World materialist culture, thereby
rendering a victim status to the protagonist and offering a melodramatic response, instead, Sembene unexpectedly thickens the plot
by returning to the Third World setting. This reversal disrupts the
hierarchical certainty of the film, leaving First World audiences with
an uneasy ambivalence towards the immigrant experience. D. is not
so easily categorized as a victim, nor is the French husband and wife
easily slotted as the callous and indifferent neocolonialists. Instead,
the fleeing husband experiences some of the spiritual abandonment
and loss that his black employee felt on a daily basis under his roof.
Sembene's message defies facile categorizations. The viewer is left
with an uneasy sense of waste, misunderstanding, and remorse.
What would otherwise be easily classified as white supremacy over
black victimhood becomes instead much more reciprocal. A certain
commonality remains of the neocolonial experience, which Sembene
evokes primarily through the change of locus. The film leaves some
room for hope, as the white employer's decision to journey to Africa
demonstrates. His travel to the Third World setting indicates a degree of remorse and responsibility, a sensitivity that must be placed
alongside the brother's sense of outrage and defiance.

In the remaining selection of films, characters experience boundary crossings solely within homelands, that is, Third World settings.
Movements occur between classes, ethnicities, races, genders, and
generations (*Men with Guns, Yellow Earth, The Women's Story*); between urban and rural cultures, often crossing back and forth (*Guelwaar, Yellow Earth*), and between the world of political elites and

subjugated majorities (*Men with Guns, Guelwaar*). By focusing on movements within Third World boundaries, the hope is to discover a more intimate subjectivity, relatively free from the subordinationist frameworks of even the best intentioned films of immigration to the First World. Without the legal, linguistic, and nationalistic problems common to immigrant movement across nation states, these sojourners nonetheless undertake travels of consciousness, memory, disclosure, and liberation (both individual and social). Dilemmas remain for travelers within the Third World—problems of hybridity, cultural commensurability, cultural displacement, skin color prejudice—but enabling experiences also arise—political reawakening, overcoming of denial, the reassessment of tradition, and cultural engagement and coherence.

While postcolonial countries remain profoundly affected by First World foreign policy, cultural globalization, and transnational business interests, they nevertheless need to be understood within their own cultural contexts. The wide popular reception of immigrant films such as those by Hanif Kureishi tend to overshadow the unique value of films where journeys are undertaken within originative cultures. Third World subjectivities are often more fully explored within that locus than within the First World as final destination. We will first examine Sembene's acclaimed film, *Guelwaar* (1966), in many ways the most artistically complex and thematically developed of the films selected in this chapter.

GUELWAAR: HYBRIDITY IN THE THIRD WORLD

Although featuring African characters and set entirely in postcolonial Senegal, *Guelwaar* offers a more socially and politically comprehensive exposition of Third World oppression than *La Noire de.* . . . Whereas John Sayles alters certain details to suit his North American audiences in *Men with Guns* (such as changing barefoot physicians into middle-class medical students, perhaps to make it easier for First World audiences to identify with their deaths), Sembene's Africa is presented with no significant compromise. The tribal groups, religious factions, disaffected urbanites, rural village types, and shunned women accurately represent postcolonial West African culture. Whites appear only as supernumeraries, and then fleetingly, in the official grandstand at an agronomy exhibition. Sembene presents a fractious nation divided by the vagaries of foreign aid programs and Cold War era politics. Still, his broad vision unfolds a drama of intergroup struggle and reconciliation.

The conflict of the main plot centers around the mistaken burial of a Christian political victim in a Muslim cemetery. The two communities at first resist each other's cultural differences but eventually recognize the universal need for a dignified burial. The mutual understanding between the religious groups becomes a hopeful paradigm for the broader political and economic struggles in the film. Tragically, their movement toward reconciliation is not followed by the national and international leaders. When a widely respected political protester is killed by a corrupt government faction that cannot risk losing its lucrative foreign aid package, the young rebel against their elders, threatening civil disruption for the sake of social transformation. *Guelwaar* ends with the various factions—representing gender identities, age differences, and religious sects—united to reaffirm the traditional values of dignity and integrity.

Although trained in France and Russia as a filmmaker, Sembene has consciously sought to produce his films for West African audiences. Thus his filmmaking has been less restrained by the requirements of Western cinematic practice and audience sensibilities. *Guelwaar* conveys meaning largely through a strong storyline, fully developed characters, a rich and complex social setting, and, perhaps most of all, timely political subject matter. When the film was shown on U.S. television as part of Black Heritage Month in 1997, audiences responded positively. The cultural hybridity of most of the characters makes it accessible to many First World viewers. One such character, a young woman who has been disowned by her family after leaving for the city for employment years before, faces dilemmas easily recognized in a globalized world. Her journey from and return to her village is revealed as a cultural separation, a gulf between a previous life within a traditional consensual culture and her acquired life as a westernized urban woman. In fact, her cultural hybridity is not unique, since the other villagers are in various ways also influenced by their colonial and neocolonial history. The chasm that separates the young woman from the village elders, the priest, and the local women is one only of degree. Although westernized in dress and manner, she still anguishes over the loss of her original identity, a circumstance that elicits a degree of sympathy from the chief elder and other villagers.

The young woman's position as the outsider in her hometown reflects a general perplexity in *Guelwaar*. Other characters, including the Christian clergyman, the political advocate, and the group of soldiers—the latter recent emigrants of traditional rural villages— sense the dissociation of postcolonial society. In fact, the film's *mise-en-scène* suggests that all of Senegal is consumed by cultural and geographical dislocation. The characters, often presented in large congregations on dusty roads, seem to be on the move within their country. Protesters boycott First World aid shipments, spill

grain bags on highways, pursue other religious groups that have vi-
olated their traditional space, and travel great distances to hear
oppositional leaders. Like Sembene himself, the political reformer in
Guelwaar has returned from the First World to engage in the overthrow of a corrupt regime run by local political elites. After he under-
takes a radical relocation from a First World university research
environment to his traditional society, his social consciousness
forces him to reject the very culture that has trained him in such ideals as democracy, social justice, and self-determination. Tragically,
the foreign aid programs of First World powers, tied to economic alli-
ances and transnational business interests, have led to his country's dependency rather than independence. For the reformer, the
ambiguities of Western culture become real only when he returns
home and experiences firsthand the negative consequences of the
First World presence, which throughout the film has remained in
the background.

Whites hardly appear in *Guelwaar*, but their presence haunts the
African characters, all the more profoundly for remaining unseen.
Indeed, their invisibility becomes the counterpart of Ralph Ellison's
novelistic conception. Whereas in Ellison's fiction, the African American's invisibility signifies a disenfranchisement within U.S. culture,
the invisibility of the Europeans in *Guelwaar* signifies an ominous
power controlling African society, all the more formidable for being
unknown and remote. Whites are not shown making decisions re-
garding their best interests, but the effects of their damaging policies are vividly represented. The Europeans are not shown
journeying to Africa, but, like demi-gods, they pull the strings that
disrupt African society, setting one Senegalese against another, re-
locating masses of people. By keeping Europeans (and white Americans) out of the picture, Sembene at once focuses on representing
African characters for African audiences and explicating the long-
range effects of First World foreign policy. It is the very inaccessibil-
ity of the white neocolonial world, Sembene tells us, that is the key to
its power within African postcolonial societies. Kept at a distance,
the neocolonialists elude culpability, as one African group in the
film blames another for its social and economic crises. At a political
rally, voiceless white faces appear on the officials' stand, figures of
obvious power and status but only distantly and indirectly revealed.
Within the social space of the film, white remoteness further signifies the difficulty of grasping the prodigious power and control of
First World culture, which remains at the same time both distant
and near through its telecommunications, the marketing of its
products, and the threat of its considerable military force.

Sembene has seen himself as a national filmmaker, interested in affirming the cultural identity of Senegalese society but also chronicling the misguidedness of intra-African conflict. Both goals are complementary in his films, even dependent upon one another. *Guelwaar* demonstrates that cultural identity can be secured only through an enlightened engagement with the political and social struggle unique to the postcolonial world. Sembene was probably familiar with Lorraine Hansberry's play, *Les Blanc* (1966), completed after her untimely death by her husband, Robert Nemiroff (Nemiroff, 1995). In that play, Tshembe Matoseh, a European-educated African, returns to his West African country and becomes convinced that he must resume the political struggle for independence against the white colonialist government. Recognizing that he cannot live fully without facing the political oppression of his people, he joins the anticolonial movement, knowing that his wife and family in Europe will always remain a part of his identity. The dilemma of Tshembe's cultural hybridity is directly confronted and discussed extensively by the characters in scenes of Shavian dialogue, but Hansberry's audience is left with no easy solutions to the contradiction between Western enlightenment teaching and colonial practice.

Like Tshembe, *Guelwaar*'s reform leader is admired by his fellow Africans despite his decision to live between his homeland and Europe, but his success in the independence struggle remains problematic. Similarly, the young girl returned to her village becomes at once an object of curiosity, hostility, and some sympathy; her stay among her people will not be easy. For these characters, cultural restitution remains problematic, a matter not so much of repossession but of the degree to which they both are willing and able to modify altered subjectivities to fit the demands of changing circumstances. Similar dilemmas face the other featured characters, the Muslim imam, the sympathetic police lieutenant, the Christian clergyman. Sembene suggests that the future hope of his country lies in the ability of its various groups to cross boundaries of traditional divisionism to build an authentic culture of commonality while remaining skeptical of First World policies of dependency.

MEN WITH GUNS: JOURNEY OF ACCEPTANCE

John Sayles' *Men with Guns* (1998) is set in Central America, but the particularities of country and government are deliberately unspecified. This generic quality allows audiences to comprehend the human face of suffering under social and economic tyranny without the encumbrances of foreign policy controversy. Instead of creating a Brechtian alienation effect, this strategy, for Sayles, brings the viewer closer to the indigenous characters; their inhuman choices and futile anguish are presumed to become more manifest when the particularities of foreign policy, regime, and nationality remain unknown. Thus First World audiences are able to interpret characters and situations freely, without preconceptions. Surprisingly, Sayles' lack of specificity does not hinder the credibility of the film, since the oppressive conditions represented are apparent in many Central American countries. The particularities of death squads; forced clearances from the land; systematic matching of particular tribal peoples with certain export-oriented crops for harvesting (throughout the film, village peoples refer to themselves as "sugar people," "salt people," and so on); and a class structure that prevents news of human rights abuse from leaking out, are all evident throughout much of Latin America. In fact, the film was made in Mexico with a Mexican cast, except for two U.S. actors playing North American tourists. Sayles' extensive use of non-actors enhances the reality and immediacy of the film, qualities that contribute to its compelling strength.

The main character, Dr. Humberto Fuentes, is Creole (of Spanish ancestry) and knows nothing about the students he has trained as doctors in the poorest mountain villages of his country. Although one of his close patients in the capital city is a high-ranking army general, Fuentes wishes to know nothing about the brutal policies of the government. When he decides to visit his students in their remote villages out of curiosity, he begins a journey of discovery that reawakens his personal and professional commitments. He soon learns that all his students have been murdered by the military. While he is dying of a heart attack in a secret mountain refugee camp, Fuentes realizes that his legacy as a physician will be embodied in a young army deserter, trained as a medic, who earlier had stolen his medical bag but is now, like Fuentes, undergoing a change of heart.

Fuentes' journey into his own country's "heart of darkness" becomes a pilgrim's progress. He meets a young woman, raped by soldiers, who refuses to speak; an army deserter ashamed of his crimes under orders; and a runaway priest who has abandoned his village parish rather than submit to execution in an army reprisal. When he discovers that his former students have been executed by the army, he wants to return to the comfort of his practice in the capital, but his companions convince him to look for the mysterious refugee "city" high in the mountains. The mute woman's faith in the "paradise" of such a place inspires both Fuentes and the guilt-ridden army deserter. Before their arrival at the refugee camp, the priest surrenders to the soldiers who will execute him by identifying himself as "a ghost." His sacrifice confirms the truth to Fuentes and his companions that running away from injustice solves nothing. When at last they enter the refugee "paradise," Fuentes realizes he will die, but the mute woman takes his medical bag and forces the deserter, who was trained as a medic, to become the new doctor for the refugees. The deserter accepts the bag, his remorse overcome by the faith of the woman and Fuentes' consideration. Fuentes dies realizing at last that his vocation has been given new meaning through the legacy of the woman and the conversion of the deserter.

The idea for *Men with Guns* (the title is purposely nonspecific) came from conversations with many friends over several years. One friend, according to Sayles,

the novelist Francisco Goldman had an uncle who was a doctor in Guatemala and got involved in an international health program. A few years later he found that most of his students, whom he had sent off in good faith to serve as barefoot doctors in the poorer communities, had been murdered by the very government that claimed to support the program. Another friend's father was an agronomist for the Rockefeller Foundation—several of the people he trained to increase their corn yield were killed within three years of their return to the countryside. (John Sayles, p. 18)

Sayles developed the screenplay from his comprehension of the oppressive economic and political conditions that foster widespread social denial in Central America. Within the U.S., he was impressed by a Gulf War statistic that showed 65 percent of citizens did not want that war covered with the kind of media explicitness shown in Vietnam. "They didn't want that kind of detail, they didn't want the negative side of the story. They wanted a nice comfortable win to feel good about" (John Sayles, 1998, p. 12). Much of *Men With Guns* was filmed in Chiapas, Mexico, where a recent army massacre took 45 villagers, an event that added a tragic relevance to the film's initial screening. In Chiapas, several thousand people were removed from their homes and displaced as forced workers, much like the poor Fuentes encounters on his progress to "paradise." Actual destruction and random shooting also parallel the events in the film. For Sayles, the hollowness of the media coverage of Chiapas only confirmed the film's theme of denial.

Like Dr. Fuentes, most privileged people are invested in the power structures that create human rights abuse. Sayles' sense of irony is telling, as when two U.S. tourists are willing to stereotype Fuentes as a native Latino, even as his fellow citizens along the journey refer to him as "white." In fact, the verbal means whereby socially perceived groups maintain distancing devices that ensure social divisionism appear throughout the film, threatening to derail the movement of discovery. The film's pilgrimage from denial to curiosity to realization, then to a final reaffirmation of the human potential for goodness, achieves at once an individual and an interpersonal epiphany. "Paradise," the young woman's name for the refugee camp that becomes the locus for the reformed medic's social mission, and journey's end for Fuentes, evokes a utopian promise that transforms Sayles' otherwise brutal realism. *Men with Guns* becomes a passionate, even at times lyrical, cry for sojourns that overcome the indifference to local and international suffering in a globalized world.

Fuentes represents Thoreau's privileged people of "quiet desperation," who begin movements from cynical apathy to social awareness. Although Fuentes, like King Lear, became "old before he was wise," his sojourn, also like Lear's, exposes him to the cruel indifference of nature but at the same time propels him towards a newfound connectedness with his former social inferiors. Thus the transformation of his personal and social identity is achieved in the film through a compelling sense of place. The space of his journey's end becomes a point of convergence, where a tormented, cynical ego finds reconciliation in a social identity that is affirming of a future social program and accepting of its present inclusiveness.

YELLOW EARTH AND *THE WOMEN*: TO AND FROM THE CITY

Chen Kaige's *Yellow Earth* (1984) and Peng Xiaolian's *The Women's Story* (1989) present women for whom change of place becomes at once a joyous promise and a dangerous reality, but also a means of access to their liberation. Both filmmakers are "fifth-generation" graduates of the Beijing Film Academy, the first group of directors to experience a significant loosening of official government restrictions in the early 1980s (Hitchcock, 1999). In *Yellow Earth*, a soldier of the Eighth Route Army travels from the southern Yunnan province to a rural northern Chinese village in Shaanxi province to collect folk songs from local farmers. His mission is to preserve songs that document the oppression of the traditional Chinese class system and to use his collections as marching songs for the army to win over the farmers. He stays at the home of a poor widower with a young son and teenage daughter, Cuiqiag. Betrothed to an older man Cuiqiag has never met, her future life as a daughter-in-law will be bleak because her father has spent her dowry on her mother's funeral and his son's betrothal. Their village is by the Yellow River in a harsh natural region nicknamed yellow earth, where subsistence agriculture is so common that carved wood is substituted for fish at wedding banquets to affect abundance. The soldier, Gu Qing, asked the father about the famous folksongs of the region, but he replies laconically that they are bitter songs, not worth preserving. However, Cui-qiag is curious about the outside world represented by Gu Qing, who tells her about the equal status of women—their short hair, army enlistment, and ability to marry whom they please. Cuiqiag only sings her songs to herself, but soon allows Gu Qing to record them. When he announces that he must return to the south to re-join his army that is fighting the Japanese and Nationalists, she begs him to take her along. He promises to return the following April. Cuiqiag cannot wait, however, because she is "suffering too much," so she attempts to cross the flooded Yellow River in a boat and is drowned while singing a new song about a better life under communism taught to her by Gu Qing.

In the film, Kaige presents a land of promise, Yunnan, where young men and women dance joyously to songs of the revolution, and a land of traditional subjugation, where all generations sing songs of pain and loss. An important aesthetic element of the film, the rural folksongs concern the plight of seasonal workers, young women forced to labor for their parents and indifferent in-laws, and the consequences of lost hopes. The contrast between the tradi-tional rural songs and the new, urban songs forms a binary of op-pression versus liberation, apolitical acceptance of one's place versus a kind of Sartrean authenticity where individual choice both defines one's life and allows for a more honest community of equals. How-ever, Kaige's film transcends any simple binary opposition imposed by the requirements of socialist realism. Ambiguities remain. Cuiqiag dies in her attempt to cross the river into the land of promise (a striking Judeo-Christian image) just as she is about to sing the word "communism" in a song about political liberation. When the brother watches his sister die, it is uncertain whether he will fall back into the muteness he maintained before Gu Qing's arrival.

Yellow Earth presents a highly lyrical, evocative account of place that uses nature imagery and folk music to convey a nonconceptual understanding of everyday deprivation and cruelty. Unlike many films of immigration, such as *My Favorite Launderette* and *El Norte*, cultural displacement stands as a future possibility only. Gu Qing, the traveler, raises the awareness of his host family members gently and indirectly, aware of their potential hostile responses to outsid-ers. Whereas in most Western films, the outsider is subject to local prejudice and the pain of ostracism, Gu Qing remains the privileged misfit by virtue of his enlightened education and status as an army researcher. The poor village people, including foremost Cuiqiag, are enthralled by his vision of an outside world, the urban south, where gender, class, and other distinctions seem transcended by a new, more promising social arrangement where lives find fulfillment. The film's cinematography of the land—as immense and beautiful as it is bleak and empty, unforgiving of the farmers who must work its soil from year to year—places people as small figures within the vastness of nature, evocative of traditional Chinese landscape painting. Sustained panoramic shots of barren steps and eroded fields cover nearly the entire screen, in violation of traditional Western rules of landscape photography. The delicacy of Cuiqiag's soprano voice of lamentation contrasts with the earthiness of the visual imagery. A broad, dangerous river, symbol of life's objectification by commerce, and a subsistence landscape, where social obligation and poverty smother happiness, overpower the tiny human presence.

In this part a pessimistic film, Kaige suggests that the road to the socialist land of promise may be dangerous and wasteful, a political stance that would have earned official censure in China only a few years before. The film's striking dissociation of environment from selfhood suggests an ambivalent interpretation of the promise of human struggle in history. Yet despite the harsh determinism of Cuiqiag's cultural and environmental world, her inner life retains the capacity for hopeful change, conveyed principally through the poignancy of her songs of pain and aspiration.

The Women's Story: Crossing the Great Wall

In *The Women's Story*, the plight of women in a rapidly industrializing China has a more positive directive than *Yellow Earth*. Women debate with men on the hardships of gender roles and unite to confront local patriarchal structures. Peng Xiaolian, the director, is a woman member of the "fifth-generation" film movement. She uses place both as a position/condition to overcome and as a means of comparison where new and old lifestyles are displayed in stark contrasts. Three village women set out for "the city" to sell their yarn. One is escaping her arranged marriage to a mute whom she dislikes; the second, from a family demeaned by neighbors for having all daughters and no sons, is curious about the role of women in the westernized urban centers; and the third, a widow, is in danger of losing her life with her son because of her poverty. The women's divergent responses to the city brings forth newfound identities. The runaway bride is most fascinated by the lifestyles of the city women, their clothes, makeup, and short hair. She also is willing to manipulate customers in the new commercial spirit, but she is checked by the youngest woman, who is the most aware of how the new economic conditions have affected inner lives. She is also the most curious about the different gendered experiences in the new setting. Her brief affair with a factory worker, also a recent rural emigrant, reveals the tensions between men, who see the city as a way to make money, and women, who in addition see it as a place of liberation and empowerment. The mother, the oldest and most traditional of the three, is the most resistant to the new possibilities of the city. She longs for her only child as she watches urban children play, is cheated by a customer, and finds urban people rude and impersonal. However, during their time in the city, all three find that the spirit of freedom binds them together, and when they return to the village, they unite to face two male in-laws who have come to take the betrothed woman away.

Location often achieves the symbolic in *The Women's Story*. The three use the Great Wall at the beginning of their sojourn as a route to the city. Emblematic of China's cultural past and also the divisionism that has enforced traditional social relationships, the Wall becomes a bridge that carries the film's travelers from the old world to the new. On their return to the village, their solidarity and fortitude promise to abolish the Wall of division between old and new, gender, class, and age. In a break with tradition, Xiaolian uses long-distance shots for cityscapes rather than for the rural landscapes. In the film, the city, covered with the newness of emerging high-rises and construction cranes, and separated by the commercial waterway, remains a place of ambivalence as the women move through autonomy. In a visually stunning scene, the three newcomers are confronted by a frantic woman escaping the police because she is pregnant with an additional child. Her two children are both girls and she hopes for a boy. The violation of the official government policy of one-child families has made her desperate. Later in the film, she appears to the women on a wide expanse of urban steps with a newborn boy. Her mixture of joy and anxiety affects the women, one of whom is scorned for her all-daughter family. When the desperate woman is left alone to climb the formidable steps, her future life of hardship is presented in a silent long-shot. Combining such harsh figurative elements with a light-hearted treatment of camaraderie that carries over from the new city to the old village contributes to the power of *The Women's Story* as social statement. The women's movement is circular. They return to the traditional ways, but it is clear that the village will never be the same as a result of their sojourn. The three women, representing two generations, have succeeded in the new land of promise. Their struggle in the village will not be easy, however, although their mobility, their determination to continue their business activities, and their new consciousness in the city is established.

MOBILITY, PLACE, AND POSTCOLONIAL IDENTITY

Writing of the emerging film movements of the Caribbean and other "third cinemas," Stuart Hall asked in 1990, "Who is this emergent, new subject of the cinema? From where does he/she speak?" Hall's answer is what he calls the underlying "oneness" beyond superficial differences that makes "Caribbeanness" (pp. 222–223). Hall would seek the essence—or an essence—of this in African culture, which he describes as "the great aporia" (p. 224). Rey Chow (1996) finds the recovery of the culture of the subaltern more problematic. Chow questions Homi Bhabha's (1994) argument that, "since a discursive system is inevitably split in enunciation, the colonial's text itself already contains a native voice—ambivalently" (p. 91). Chow observes,

But what kind of an argument is it to say that the subaltern's voice can be found in the *ambivalence* of the imperialist's speech? It is an argument that ultimately makes it unnecessary to come to terms with the subaltern, since she has already "spoken," as it were, in the system's gaps. [Moreover] . . . we try to make the native more like us by giving her a voice. (pp. 127–128)

While Chow finds it difficult to approach subaltern authenticity, his examples are taken largely from the observations and remarks of First World academics. The emergence of Third World cinema movements during the 1980s and 1990s has made first-hand exposition of the postcolonial voice more evident. Thus Chow's question in his article title, "Where Have All the Natives Gone?" can perhaps be better answered by looking at Chow's "native" in the homeland rather than in First World locations.

Of course, hybridity remains for the Third World traveler, as *Guelwaar*, *Men with Guns*, and indeed all the films studied here make clear. The fact of heterogeneity, however, only points out what Stuart Hall (1990) describes as the constructive nature of cultural identities, which are "the unstable points of identification or suture, which are made, within the discourses of history and culture. Not an essence but a *positioning*. Hence, there is always a politics of identity, a politics of position, which has no absolute guarantee in an unproblematic, transcendental 'law of origin'" (p. 225). The "positioning" of cultural identities can be discerned in these films of sojourning within the homeland. In Sayles' *Men with Guns*, the characters, who cross gender, class, and racial lines, journey together in a way that combines interior and exterior realities. Fuentes explores his own subjectivity when he confronts the objectification of his fellow humans. Yet his hybridity is not fixed in a simplistic way; rather, his identity as "white" among the rural poor does not determine his future actions or change of heart any more than the deserter's hybridity as a Native American who is also one of the "men with guns" prevents him from rejecting that negative hybridity for another, more positive one as a medic for the refugees. This "politics of position" (Hall 1990) connects with Derrida's "postponement of meaning" that characterizes all discourse (p. 228). Meaning in life is never finalized, nor is human identity.

Part III

THE DRAMA OF IDENTITY WITHIN THE FIRST WORLD

_____ Chapter 8 _____

NATIVE AMERICAN CINEMA AND DRAMA: VALUING IDENTITY

A heightened concern for social justice among Native Americans began with the mobilization around key events in the 1960s and 1970s. The most important of these were the second Wounded Knee protest occupation in 1974 and the Trail of Broken Treaties March on Washington, D.C., in 1975. This activism within the United States inspired in turn the growth of indigenous movements worldwide. These seminal actions, coupled with the general reawakening of identitarian concerns throughout the world during the same decades, created a diffusionary effect. Dissenting indigenous groups discerned a common predicament created by the processes of modernization throughout the world (Wilmer, 1993). Their recognized commonality in turn led to fruitful organizational structures, such as the founding of many nongovernmental organizations (NGOs) recognized by the United Nations. Some of these proved particularly effective for enlistment in the cause of human rights and self-determination issues, and, perhaps most controversial of all, in the formation of self-development agendas. Most important among such organizations were the International Indian Treaty Council, formed through the American Indian Movement (AIM) in 1974, and the World Council of Indigenous Peoples, formed the following year.

THE CURRENT POLITICAL CONTEXT

The new mandate for indigenous self-determination and other autonomous concerns did not lead immediately to sustained dramatic production, either through new theatrical forms or in the cinema, as it did within other liberation movements at the same time. However, the appearance of a more critical awareness of cultural forms among Native American theorists beginning in the 1970s did influence, if not stimulate, the development of these forms. Almost immediately, critical theory became quite cogent and confrontational, most notably through indigenous writer/activists such as Ward Churchill, Vine Deloria, and Annette Jaimes. Churchill and Jaimes work within U.S. academe, teaching at the University of Colorado's Center for Studies of Ethnicity and Race in America (CSERA) at Boulder. Such new institutions have provided critical voices heretofore unavailable to indigenous theorists. Their academic status has made educated mainstream culture decidedly more sensitive to the issues and dilemmas of Native American life, particularly as it has been affected by modern and postmodern cultural formations.

Nonindigenous writers who were perceived by the wider culture as projecting "authentic" voices of indigenous groups, what Churchill ironically terms "friends of the Indians" (Churchill, 1992), have been critically reappraised, with the result that a less naive, stereotypical approach to Native American life has been appreciated by First World academics and activists. Still, hundreds of years of self-serving stereotypical thinking about Native American groups have not succeeded in breaking overdetermined conceptions of their identity among the broad populace. Certainly the socially conscious have gained a much clearer picture of the Native American's cultural expropriation by well-meaning—or not-so-well-meaning—popular writers, filmmakers, and journalists. Still, negative images of indigenous culture persist, no doubt in part because of the still powerful influence of the frontier "cowboys and Indians" mystique within U.S culture known throughout the world. Consequently, Native Americans, representing by far the oldest culture within the United States, remain the least understood and recognized group. Paralleling this lack of discernment within mainstream culture is a degree of invisibility and ambiguity experienced by many Native Americans themselves, who can be equally influenced by the powerful cultural and economic institutions of the world's only remaining superpower.

In the international sphere, self-determination, self-development, and other issues of autonomy for indigenous groups have generated intense debate within legal and diplomatic institutions (Corntassel & Primeau, 1995). Despite such activism, indigenous literary forms that contain social justice themes remain somewhat distant from these arguments, which respond much more to the vagaries of international bureaucracy than is immediately apparent. Recent Native American literary interest is centered on the novel, which is the preferred form of such respected writers as Leslie Silko, N. Scott Momaday, Louise Erdrich, Louis Owens, and Gordon Henry, Jr. Even so, there exists an incipient playwrighting movement. Native American dramatists have arisen at both the grassroots level and through universities in the western U.S. Although writing for relatively limited audiences, they often project a compelling discourse of indigenous concerns.

Typically, a playwright will write with a particular local audience in mind, be recognized and produced by a mainstream academic or regional theatre institution largely supported by nonindigenous theatregoers, and then become anthologized by a respected commercial or university press. Eventually, she or he may find a small but important educated audience in university classrooms and theatres. Concerned less or not at all with the legality and strategizing of international law and human rights groups, Native American drama generally avoids specific political issues with its host government in favor of conflicts arising from self-identity, cultural hybridity, negative cultural images, and an eroding traditional ethos. Writing and appearing in plays about contemporary indigenous life, women have been particularly interested in theatrical presentation.

The relatively apolitical—or nonpartisan—approach of most recent Native American drama contrasts with the highly critical and argumentative essay form favored by indigenous theorists in the U.S., where, typically, specific books, films, and artists are critiqued to clarify a social condition or to correct politically based misconceptions. The Native American playwright's lack of involvement in onstage dialectic, in the "purpose, passion, discussion" approach of Shavian dialogue for socially based plays, does not imply a lack of political consciousness. Quite the contrary, drama centering around the family and its local environment is highly charged by the cultural and economic forces of the dominant culture. Stereotyping and common prejudice deeply affect these families. The hopes and dreams that guide the daily lives of family members are tied problematically to the false values and destructive centripetal forces of hegemonic cultural forms. Natural landscape is often featured in these plays, though not in the deterministic way developed by the early twentieth-century Naturalism movement in mainstream theatre. Rather, characters refer to nature and natural sites as sustaining, though endangered, features of cultural identity and spiritual insight. Native American filmmakers are more likely to engage a Shavian dialectic approach with their characters, though particular political solutions are ignored or, as in the case of *Powwow Highway*, considered only as past events.

The indirect approach to political theme in Native American drama contrasts with the drama of other indigenous movements worldwide. In Australia, for example, playwrights such as Jack Davis produce rhetorically based plays about land rights, degrees of aboriginal autonomy, and the conscious erasure of indigenous history by the dominant majority (Davis, 1982). The more issue-oriented drama of Australia attests in part to a different history of indigenous treatment. In Australia, the systematic attempt to assimilate aboriginals began under government mandate in the early twentieth century. Individuals were raised by selected white families with the intent of biological and cultural absorption. Light-skinned people were prohibited from marrying dark-skinned individuals and so on. Such practices led to an interest in cultural dislocation as it has affected indigenous identity in Australia. Moreover, after World War II, significant attention was given to the concept of "aboriginality," a theoretical activity that perhaps motivated aboriginals to create issue-based political drama. Critics such as Marcia Langton (1993) have argued against any notion of the "fixity" of aboriginal identity. Interest in the problem of self-identity for a relatively powerless minority in Australia parallels concerns for cultural integrity in U.S. indigenous writing.

While American Indian drama has recently received a degree of institutional acknowledgment within university theatre departments, regional theatres, and in off-Broadway New York, mainstream U.S. culture remains unaware of such activity, a situation lamented by critics such as Churchill (1992), who observes the dominance of white writers among the popularizers of contemporary Native American life. Inevitably, such writing, while often well-intentioned, remains at least one step removed from social and political understanding. The penchant for Europeanizing the most profound elements of indigenous American culture has long existed, as Ernst Cassirer (1946) made clear in his seminal study of language and myth. For example, white notions of "the Great Spirit" attributed to several indigenous groups throughout the continental U.S. proved to be inaccurate reifications of difficult spiritual concepts, attempts to substitute a personal, original being for what in fact was nonsubstantial notions distributable over many substances of nature (Cassirer, 1946, pp. 66–70).

Native American drama in the 1990s follows its own course, avoiding both the issue-related plays of Australian aboriginal stagecraft and the emphasis on myth and ritual apparent in Nigerian drama. In this respect, it also differs from recent Native American novels, which often incorporate ritualistic themes, structures, and symbols. While U.S. indigenous stageplays make allusion to religious concepts and practices, these remain parenthetic to the stage action and even to the expressed motivations of the characters. For the characters, present circumstances and future possibilities or dilemmas inspire, rather than an historical or cultural past per se. Typically, the action remains unresolved, the fate of particular characters ambivalent or uncertain. Still, individuals retain a degree of hope. Nihilism and social determinism are kept at a distance—a quality that parallels traditional mainstream worldviews in U.S. literature—and neither indigenous religion nor Christianity is either entirely rejected or accepted without reservation. Whether this middle view is informed by a balanced appreciation of human existence inherent in Native American life or is the result of more recent and specific social and economic influences is open to question.

Paula Gunn Allen (1986) finds ritual and mythic elements in recent Native American novels a distancing device to prevent "colonial or exploitative" mindsets (p. 79). On the other hand, Simon Ortiz (1981) sees no conflict in the use of Eurocentric literary forms. He affirms "the creative ability of Indian people to gather in many forms of the socio-political colonizing force which beset them" making "these forms meaningful in their own terms" (p. 8). Native American playwrights and screenwriters use European genres with less emphasis on mythopoeic forms, finding realism an appropriate vehicle for indigenous audiences familiar with U.S. entertainment media—film, videodrama, radio—using them to engage Indian and European cultural tensions. This approach is apparent in Terry Gomez's first full-length play.

Inter-Tribal: The Multiple-Present Moment

With roots in the Comanche Nation of Oklahoma, Terry Gomez was raised in a progressive urban American culture, San Francisco, and attended the University of New Mexico and the Institute of American Indian Arts in Santa Fe. She writes, "This play is not a pageant, although it contains scenes from a pow-wow, and one actor is wearing his Indian clothes. This play is not mythology. It is more about symbolism and finding humor in tragedy" (Perkins & Uno, 1996, p. 199). While *Inter-Tribal* (1994) celebrates the American Indian struggle and affirms the undervalued contribution of women to this history, its main focus remains intergenerational relationships, a perspective that allows for the exploration of contemporary Native American lifestyles and inner lives that confront contradictory needs and obligations. Pressing social issues remain in the foreground, but partisan political commitments are entirely absent, except as an unspoken urge toward ethnic and feminist goals. The Brechtian assumption that conventional plots and character relationships in the drama inhibit significant social critique may be applied to questions of the play's effectivity.

The women of *Inter-Tribal* inhabit a world where Western social coding combines with a traditional ethos based on the passing of wisdom between the generations. Baby, a late teenager who dresses as a typical mainstream youth, is pursued by her grandmother, Hattie, who has raised her alone. Hattie follows Baby into a pool hall filled with men who look suspiciously upon the older woman. Baby's desire to enter mainstream culture is centered on her respect for her friend Joyce, an older, more socially sophisticated Indian woman dressed glamorously in Western clothing and suffering from alcoholism. Joyce has loved Two-Step since she was a teenager, but he is married with children and will only meet Joyce at night to avoid detection. When Two-Step tells Joyce that he will never leave his wife because of the children, Joyce leaves the pool hall in despair, defiantly giving up her goal of 12-step rehabilitation. Harley, a pool-hall acquaintance, tries to seduce Joyce while she is angry; when she refuses, he rapes her. The final scene in Hattie's house reveals Baby's early loss of a child and Hattie's attempt to give her granddaughter inner strength by reminding her of the heritage of an Indian woman. The play ends on a hopeful note when Hattie allows Joyce and Baby to live with her while Joyce recovers from the rape.

Hattie and Baby function as *raisonneuse* and protégée within the argument of the play. Hattie's awareness of the negative stereotypes threatening American Indian culture is counterbalanced by her commitment to the enduring patience and strength of her traditional culture. Christian progressive as well as indigenous in her religious outlook, Hattie cautions Baby that she is far from "the wise old medicine woman who can give you the meaning of life while we sit and bead-work" (Gomez, 1996, p. 213). Rather, her life-long experiences reveal a profound hybridity that combines feminist discourse, civil rights, a repressive boarding school period that separated her from her grandparents, and an enlightened Christianity. She tells Baby that these experiences gave her a strong sense of self, rather than a compliant acceptance of dominant culture: "I was taught that the white way was the best way to live, it took me years to figure out that who I really am is all of these things" (p. 213). Hattie's experience of the white world has not prevented a prospective view of life, one where a positive hybridity becomes a seamless understanding of justice and human dignity despite economic hardship.

Gomez avoids to a degree the complacent resolution Brecht rejected in the commercial theatre by substituting a gesture of group solidarity. An unexpected reconciliation takes place between Joyce,

representing the temptations of mainstream culture and Indian vulnerability, and Hattie and Baby, who embody the continuity of
intergenerational life. When Baby angrily accuses Hattie of lacking
compassion for Joyce's victimization, Joyce appears at their home
to accept Hattie's invitation to stay for her recovery. Hattie gives
Joyce and Baby her bed, thereby substituting their generation for
her own within the Indian household. This gesture of goodwill is explained in Hattie's speech to Baby, which justifies the continuance
of Native American culture and particularly women's lives as recon-
cilers and nurturers of that tradition.

I do the best I can. I'm not perfect. . . . I'm a woman who has been brought up
learning about the woman's lib, the civl rights movement, why, we were allowed the vote just after I was born. . . . I do the best I can. I was taught that
the white way was the best way to live, it took me years to figure out that who
I really am is all of these things. The main thing I realize is that Indians survive. We have so many things against us, and we are alive! Every generation
knows more of the white way, but we old folk have to hurry and teach you all
we can. Show how to be proud of yourselves. We are beautiful people. We
don't deserve all that we have been through. (pp. 213–214)

Hattie's reaffirmation of her roots replaces the happy ending of
conventional drama, where social degradation is overcome by con-
trived endings or a dedicated public sector. Gomez retains the didactic orientation in the resolution by associating Joyce's plight with
the commonality of obstacles to self-esteem. Baby laments, "There
are things like what happened to Joyce, unemployment, drugs and
alcohol abuse, even when our own people make it they forget where
they come from" (p. 214). However, Hattie's strength offers Joyce
another chance and Baby a positive image of perseverance. Inward
endurance rather than outward circumstance offers redemption in
this play. Gomez's characters speak in the manner of William Saroyan's
lost misfits, who maintain hope despite rejection and hardship. Like
these, Gomez's people acknowledge their sorrows and express new
visions of fulfillment, despite overwhelming circumstances. While
her characters seem unconcerned with partisan movements and
particular reforms, they are highly conscious of the snares the dominant culture has presented to Native Americans and of their own
vulnerabilities and strengths. Diane Glancy's (1996) play to be discussed next offers a similar prescription for endurance, but her comic
approach adds a dimension of irony to the understanding of social
justice for Native Americans.

Weebjob: Transcending Oppositions

Choosing a variant of a traditional European comic plot allows
Glancy to present a positive and affirming social statement of Native

American life while keeping the threat of loss of identity and economic exploitation near at hand. She bypasses Brecht's contention that conventionality in the theatre prevents productive political thought by reversing the classical triangular love plot of comedy. Rather than offering two young lovers the opportunity to marry over a father's selfish wishes, *Weebjob* allows an intergenerational marriage with the father's blessing. In this way Glancy confirms Indian solidarity and maintains hope through a renewed commitment between the generations.

The father, Weebjob (the name alludes to the biblical father who suffers a legion of misfortunes) is a stubborn, impractical but amiable figure who "always seems to be at a crossroads in his life" (Glancy, 1996, p. 170). His wife Sweet Grass loves him but has taken to living with her sister because Weebjob "takes her for granted" (p. 170). His daughter Sweet Potato has left the reservation several times for other parts of New Mexico in search of herself. These problems plague Weebjob, but he is most bothered by his best friend's wish to marry his daughter. Pick Up is close to Weebjob, but is in love with Sweet Potato. These threats to the integrity of the small Mescalero Apache community are not as bad as the overreactive Weebjob imagines. Sweet Grass confesses to her daughter that being Weebjob's wife "feels right. . . . I see him as the man he wants to be, even when he falls short of it" (p. 182). This faith in her husband is paralleled by Sweet Potato's trust in Pick Up, who, though a generation older, can offer a happiness her younger suitors cannot. "Pick up makes me feel happy. He's someone to hold on to when there's nowhere for me, no place I really fit" (p. 183).

Unsure of his faith in the endurance of love, Weebjob feels adrift. His son tells him that he is "like one of the trees in the nursery truck with your roots wrapped in a bag of sand" (p. 183). Weebjob overcomes self-doubt by discerning the healing power of his wife's love. "I will watch Sweet Grass weave—making form out of all those strands of wool, then I can make sense of everything again" (p. 183). Like *Inter-Tribal*, Glancy's comedy promotes women as sustainers of community and organizers of the reality that imbues cultural identity. The family is united in the ending with the wedding ceremony of Pick Up and Sweet Potato, which harmonizes King James biblical language and native religious expression. The family's cultural hybridity becomes a seamless fabric, like the organizing and sustaining power that unifies the generations. This image of social fulfillment is traditional to European comic endings, but Glancy reverses the classic comedy love triangle where the generations are placed in opposition to one another with the father figure as "blocking character." The father prevents his daughter or son from marrying the young lover for the sake of an older friend or business associate. By resolving the comic plot with an intergenerational wedding, Glancy underscores the strength of native heritage centered on family structure.

Gomez and Glancy comprehend a vital and fulfilling culture independent but not fully distinct from the dominant order of the world's superpower. Their characters possess an astute awareness of their own vulnerability as indigenous minorities within this order and the overdetermined roles that society has forced upon them: drunken Indian, wise old squaw, wild warrior, nature sage, stoic medicine man, or noble savage. Gerald Vizenor (1998) comments upon the tendency of Native American writers to replicate these powerful stereotypes as "similatives of dominance." What Vizenor looks for is native writing that critiques such hegemonic constructions through irony and what he terms "Indian simulations of the tropes of transmotion and survivance" (p. 134). The neologisms "transmotion" and "survivance" are meant to define the capacity of Native American culture to adapt creatively and positively under the threat of mainstream centripetal forces. Vizenor's theory intends not so much to reclaim an identity obscured by loss and dislocation as to develop those existing elements of native culture that uphold a uniquely alternative way of life within a majority culture. Native Americans become not victimized minority members but upholders of the values of social justice, community solidarity, and ecological awareness. Gomez and Glancy represent such advocates in their plays.

Smoke Signals: Saving Figures

While strong father figures are absent from the families of *Inter-Tribal*, and reaffirmed in *Weebjob*, the meaning and importance of the fatherly role is intimately explored in Sherman Alexie's film *Smoke Signals* (Eyre, 1997), based on his short story collection, *The Lone Ranger and Tonto Fistfight in Heaven*. Winning two awards at the 1998 Sundance Film Festival, the film uses comic elements and a uniquely Native American sense of self-deprecation to probe the effects on two young men in a world without fathers. It became the first film written, produced, and directed by Native Americans to receive wide distribution. The film represents more than the backhanded compliment elicited from James Sterngold (1998), who reveals the ongoing stereotypical thinking directly challenged by recent Native American writing: "[*Smoke Signals*] is a step by a new generation of Indian artists toward finding an idiom for exploring their individual and cultural identities without resorting to self-pity, political correctness or Hollywood clichés" (p. 12). Just how the issues of self-pity and political correctness figure in American Indian writing and filmmaking in the U.S. Sterngold does not explain. In fact, Chris Eyre, the film's director, has created a rare verisimilitude through closely acted ensemble performances and dialogue carefully inspired by Alexie's stories. As with Gomez and Glancy, Eyre and Alexie have avoided articulating political programs and systemic social agendas, instead relying on the relationality of the characters to carry social commentary. In this respect the film is masterfully effective, chiefly because the satirical wit of the characters is rendered more incisive by their strikingly original performances, which abolish all delimited views of Native Americans.

Two young Coeur d'Alene Indian men, Thomas and Victor, grow up together without fathers. Thomas, short and bespectacled, his hair unfashionably braided and wearing an incongruous dark broadcloth suit, was rescued as an infant from his burning home by Victor's father, who could not save Thomas' parents. Victor grew up witnessing his father's violence against himself and his mother. When his mother demands that he stop drinking, his father deserts the family for Arizona. Victor's anger grows into manhood, as he remains on the reservation without meaningful work and protective of his mother. When news arrives that Victor's father has died suddenly in Arizona, Thomas offers Victor his savings if he is allowed to go along to claim his father's ashes. Victor accepts the deal, knowing that Thomas will annoy him with made-up stories of people and incidents from the past and present. On the bus, Thomas probes Victor about his feelings for his lost father, but Victor angrily rejects his queries.

In a desert trailer camp Victor and Thomas meet Suzie Song, a young Indian woman who lived with Victor's father until his heart attack. She encourages Victor to see his father's love for him, and tells him that he stopped drinking and talked about his wife and son continually. He also learns about his father's deep remorse from accidentally causing the fire while drunk that killed Thomas' parents. While returning home, Thomas and Victor witness an auto accident and Victor runs miles into town to find help. At first accused of the accident, they are released by the police when the wife of the perpetrator reveals her husband's guilt. Victor's heroic efforts to save the accident victims remind him of his father's love for him and Thomas when he rescued both from the fire years before. For the first time able to move beyond his own anger, Victor shares his father's ashes with Thomas, stating that he must let things die for life to go on. Thomas receives the ashes as a gift, feeling the loss of his own father's death. Both throw the ashes into a cascading river while a voiceover asks the question, "How do we forgive our fathers?"

While its plot involves a private quest for the lost father, in fact *Smoke Signals* presents a tapestry of Native American reservation life interwoven with stories of the moral imagination. Over Victor's objections, Thomas persistently creates stories of recent interpersonal encounters that become life-affirming reflections on the native dilemma within a wider world that has separated and forgotten reservation life. Thomas often places himself and those closest to him in situations of fulfillment or happiness. His tale of a journey to a white-water river to contemplate suicide ends when Victor's father, who becomes the fallen savior figure in the film, prevents his death by inviting him to a fast-food restaurant for breakfast. Thomas' description of their hearty breakfast together becomes a meal of redemption. Thomas is thus twice saved by Victor's father, who performs these saving acts in a land of no jobs, no futures, and broken family life.

Another Christ figure is Victor's mother, who, in Thomas' tale, has only enough frydough for 50 Indians at a meal for one hundred guests. She raises a loaf above her head and divides it in two, thus providing bread for everyone. As in Christ's miracle of the fishes and loaves, everyone is served when everyone shares. Thomas wryly notes how simple the solution is. Victor's mother is a loving and caring figure whose supportive presence throughout the film is overlooked by her son in his anger over his father's abandonment. Throughout their journey together in search of the father, Thomas' stories gently remind Victor of how much he is loved, despite his disillusionment and cynicism.

Fantasy becomes a means to manage reality on the bus journey south. When Thomas demands a story from Suzie, she asks him if he wants the truth or lies. "Both," he replies with an appreciative smile. Parentless, Thomas has learned to cherish what little life has offered him. His understanding of the importance of human relationality is apparent in his active pursuit of Victor's friendship, even when Victor turns against everyone. When Victor asks whether he does not have better things to do with his money than buy two bus tickets to find Victor's father, Thomas responds knowingly, "What do you need with money on a reservation?" The young men contrast each other, Thomas embodying wise contentment through a positive imagination, and Victor representing the restless search beyond familiar horizons.

If Thomas delves deeply into life's perplexities, constructing his own group identities and self-images, Victor remains the outward realist, challenging mainstream cultural ideals and prejudices. In the bus he berates Thomas for wearing braids, a dark suit, and especially a broad smile, which will only bring the contempt of the non-

Indian world. When Victor reminds him of the Native American male's warrior tradition, Thomas lets his hair flow freely and discards his suit. Still, Thomas reminds Victor that their ancestors were fishers, not warriors. A dialectic of defensive cynicism and imaginative openness continues throughout the journey, as Victor mocks Thomas for watching *Dances with Wolves* two hundred times, while Thomas confronts Victor about his self-destructive bitterness and apathy. Near the end of the bus ride, the good-natured Thomas uncharacteristically reproaches Victor for not believing in anything, especially the value of human relationships.

Victor backs away when Suzie presents him with the urn of his father's ashes. Thomas takes the ashes eagerly, knowing how valuable fathers are, even if only in memory. Suzie reveals to Victor that his father felt remorse because he accidentally set fire to the house of Thomas' parents. Victor begins to understand the contradictions within his father, why he embraced him and kept him at a distance. When Victor saved the life of the auto accident victim by running long distance for help, he repeats his father's role as savior. The father figure in *Smoke Signals* exists ambivalently and precariously. Tensions that drive him away from his wife and son are never fully comprehended, and his heart attack or suicide remains unexplained.

The forces separating and uniting individuals on the reservation are contradictory and illusive, but the understanding the two men find in the end reveals the continuation of Indian culture on the reservation. The river sequence of plunging white water at the end does not seek to explain human existence so much as reveal its compelling complexity. Like the river, life passes, only memory endures. Thomas' tall tales serve as a running chorus to the inexplicable in human life, providing substance and meaning to events that otherwise would leave only pain. Victor's vow to "let things die" as he shares his father's ashes with Thomas opens the possibility for a new, more promising life.

The way in which outward circumstances affect inner lives reaffirms Native American identity in *Smoke Signals*. As such, the film resists the empowered culture, which has repeatedly sought to reduce Indian ontology through oversimplification (see Churchill, 1992, p. 230). By astutely uncovering the deeper conflicts between individuals in community, Alexie and Eyre offer a lyrical example of contemporary Native American culture. Moreover, by revealing the inner struggle of their characters, they expose the political dynamic between reservation life and hegemony. Thomas and Victor are displaced from their seats on the bus by two middle-aged white men, whose arrogant self-assurance forces the young men to move to the back of the bus in silence. For once Thomas is without a tale to reaffirm the situation. The confrontation momentarily disrupts the journey of the young men towards personal realization and acceptance, just as the 400–year displacement of native culture in the U.S. has inhibited the personal quest for meaning. References are made to this displacement throughout the film. Such allusions often take the form of humorous self-deprecation—as opposed to self-effacement. Thomas remarks about the television that the only thing more pitiful than cowboys killing Indians is Indians watching movies about cowboys killing Indians. Other characters also reveal a penchant for such commentary. Victor's mother offhandedly remarks that only bad things happen when Indians sign documents. The film's political references can also convey a certain pride mixed with irony, as when the tribal radio station WREZ announces each morning, "It's a great day to be indigenous." In fact the reservation conversation is rife with references to alienation and displacement.

The film's opening sequence shows the radio announcer at the crossroads of the only highway through the reservation. He reports on who passes by in what vehicle, their arguments, and their companions. This small-town humor establishes the tightly woven community, its local eccentrics and hangers-on. Two young reservation women drive their car backwards out of necessity, a memorable trope for the Native American counterculture and its resourceful alternatives. Eyre's focus on two men without fathers includes a deep depth-of-field that encompasses the alcoholism and poverty, the intimacy and convergent values, of contemporary reservation life.

Walking Hollywood Parameters

Less introspective but no less political in theme is Jonathan Wack's *Powwow Highway* (1989), a serious exposé of reservation conditions within a not inappropriate comic form. Like *Smoke Signals*, the film involves a journey in search of identity, but its scope is wider, including the recovery of native heritage, which becomes the sought-after "medicine." Philbert, an amiable reservation Cheyenne, takes his rusty Buick to New Mexico with his activist friend Red Bow. The poor housing and bad working conditions on the reservation are shown to threaten the dignity of the community, but the high jinks of the travelers serve to overcome despair with exuberance and spirit, a cancellation that at times threatens to push the film into the Hollywood road movie formula. Still, the comic byplay and lighthearted treatment of real reservation deprivations interfere with the message only to a degree. In fact, the comedy often expresses a positive exuberance that keeps disillusionment at bay. Its main characters are likable without being two-dimensional "nonthreatening Indians." Their motivations derive from the urge to recover a lost past through a journey of discovery.

What would otherwise be taken to be antisocial behavior is so focused in the film's storyline that it works as a form of defense against the empowered culture threatening at every turn the mission of cultural recovery. The roundabout trip to New Mexico becomes a journey into a Native American past denied or undervalued by mainstream culture. The power of collective memory is a strong theme in the film. As Martha Banta (1999) observes in reference to the suppression of marginalized culture, "Memory is the agent that verifies the existence of the past, but also required for memory's crucial work are material evidence and material transmitters for that evidence" (p. 175). Although the film's resolution is not fully effective as social statement, the issue of recovering lost values while enduring the social predicament caused by such loss is particularly telling in Wack's filmmaking. *Powwow Highway* succeeds despite its Hollywood orientation and plot inconsistencies, perhaps because its theme of Native American recovery is so significant.

While *Smoke Signals* and *Powwow Highway* explore the social and moral dimensions of identity, Michael Apted's *Thunderheart* (1992) sacrifices such concerns to an incongruous commercial formula. Surprisingly, the film follows the director's probing documentary about civil disobedience at the Pine Ridge Indian Reservation in South Dakota during the 1970s. While Apted's *Incident at Oglala*, featuring the Indian activist Leonard Peltier, is an accurate and uncompromising account of federal overreaction to civil protest and of reservation exploitation, *Thunderheart* compromises such honesty with a crime/action plot wherein Native American culture is exoticized and sentimentalized. While the wry humor of the Graham Greene character to some extent offers an ironic commentary on white misconceptions of native culture, his discourse is silent on the major events of the film—the white intrusion and needless violence against the Indian protest movement. Kilmer, a young, part-Sioux FBI agent, is awakened to his heritage while on assignment, but this realization remains underdeveloped and never interferes with his institutional agenda. The complacency of the film's premise reinforces stereotypes of native violence while featuring white characters at the cost of representing two-dimensional Indian personalities, who are given only one-liner witticisms to advocate their cause.

Dances with Wolves

Robert Franklin Gish (1996) describes Kevin Costner's tremendously influential *Dances with Wolves* (1990) as "commercial slickness and rampant romanticism" (p. 80). Certainly, the celebrity-studded Hollywood blockbuster was widely criticized by both Indian and non-Indian viewers for its reliance on stereotypical views of native culture and its caricature of cavalry troopers. The expansive American prairie was stunningly represented by panoramic cinematography and a symphonic sound track, features that offered familiar conceptions of a romanticized Old West. Although Costner's voiceover descriptions of Sioux virtues are unnecessarily utopian and absolute, the film cannot be easily dismissed as frivolous and exploitative. In fact, it is in many ways a forceful expression of human commonality and a cogent argument against prejudice and exploitation. Its theme goes beyond correcting European misconceptions of Native Americans. It suggests what Gish (1996) asks later in his essay, "What else is the New History, the New Ethnicity, other than the old democracy?" (p. 85).

Sickened by the continual slaughter of the Civil War, Dunbar, a young Union officer, accepts an assignment to contact Sioux in the Dakota territory. His first encounters with a tribal scouting party present a study in intercultural communication. Sioux attitudes towards whites are shown to be as misconceived as whites' views of Indians. As Dunbar is accepted into the buffalo hunting group, his future father-in-law, Kicking Bird, befriends him. Both men learn from each other. Just as the wolf learns to accept food from Dunbar under his urging, "Come on, you can do this!", so Dunbar and Kicking Bird learn to cross forbidden boundaries. They exchange important information and gifts. Winds-in-his-Hair, initially mistrustful of all whites, learns to trust Dunbar when the officer helps the community against Pawnee rivals and federal units who seek their confinement. As Dunbar reluctantly leaves forever the Sioux camp, Winds-in-his-Hair calls to him in the most poignant moment of the film, "Do you see that I am your friend? Do you see that I am your friend always?"

Overcoming group restrictions for the sake of a wider connectivity is the main matter of *Dances with Wolves*, not the uncovering of Native American life, which the film handles unevenly, although with moments of insight and intimacy. The wide popularity of the film has attracted more negative criticism than positive, perhaps understandably, since three-dimensional glimpses of American Indian life have been practically nonexistent in American theatre and cinema. Even Arthur Kopit's celebrated play *Indians* (1969) is more about Buffalo Bill's betrayal and inner life than about Indians. While far from impoverished, Costner's message suffers from a serious structural shortcoming. Dunbar's beloved, Stands-with-Fist, is not Indian at all, but a full white woman raised by the Sioux after her own parents were killed by another tribe. Thus, a level of interracial and intercultural intimacy is prohibited. The story of a white being raised by Indians is not new to American romanticism, and Costner's counterhegemonic theme is compromised significantly. Interracial closeness is restricted to platonic friendship in the film, and the boundaries between Indian and white are maintained to a considerable extent despite a critical theme that attempts the transgression of boundaries.

The influence of *Dances with Wolves* on both Native American and mainstream cultures has been considerable. In fact, Victor scolds Thomas in *Smoke Signals* for viewing the film "two hundred times." More broadly, the intertextuality of Native American literature since the rise of the American Indian Movement (AIM) and what has often been termed the New Ethnicity has been informed by cultural integrity and preservation, but equally as much by concerns for the kind of significant intercultural dialogue expressed in *Dances with Wolves*. Dunbar's egalitarian friendship with the Sioux is by far the film's most important social contribution.

Of course, more is needed than cross-cultural dialogue to effect structural change in indigenous life. What is so far missing in Native American cinema and theatre is an expression of the kind of community-based social thinking and sustained pragmatic planning advocated by such figures as Paulo Freire, whose movement seeks to link social theory to narratives of human freedom (*Pedagogy of the Oppressed*, 1993). Native American drama has located a strong sense of tradition in the family and has narrated a search for roots in a geographical and imaginary past, but this has been undertaken by circumventing the kind of discourse necessary for effective political organization. Wack's *Powwow Highway* raises issues of social degradation and the mismanagement of corrupt Indian leaders and enterprisers, but these stories are sidelined in the film in favor of Philbert's quest for a warrior identity and "tokens" of his healing "medicine." His transformation remains an individual achievement and does not carry over into his Idaho Cheyenne community. Though Red Bow possesses the political awareness Philbert lacks, he is too consumed by personalized issues of anger to advocate grassroots organizing. Red Bow's bitterness flares into anger in scenes that have a comic rather than political import. To this extent the film plays with negative stereotypes of Indians as violent and impulsive. Though some characters allude to their involvement in the Wounded Knee protest incident, and Philbert stops his Buick to view the Fort Robinson site, where Cheyenne were forcibly detained by the government in the nineteenth century, the activist struggle remains a past event.

Philbert's journey to self-respect and Dunbar's way to greater intercultural understanding and solidarity have no immediate political consequences. Dunbar and Stands-with-Fist separate permanently from the Sioux winter encampment at the end of the film, leaving the intervention of the white power structure behind. In fact, the narrative voiceover describes the eventual confinement of the plain's Sioux with no mention of an ongoing struggle. History ends in these films with a retreat into personal lives and a mixed message of individual triumph but group enclosure. Similarly, Gomez and Glancy present families brought together under the threat of social degradation and alienating power formations, but these native triumphs remain at the familial level, with no suggestion of particular issues around which group unity can form. Missing in these narratives is the sort of oppositionality brought to bear by progressive groups that broaden the participation of individuals to control the conditions of their existence (see West, 1993, pp. 184–185). Also missing is any sense of what James Ruppert (1995) defines as "mediation": "two-voiced discourse that appropriates one audience's discourse to force its own cognitive reorientation" (pp. 20–21). For Ruppert, this approach for Native Americans becomes necessary within a culture dominated by a largely unresponsive and powerful culture with universal and exceptionalist agendas. To this end, a pointedly more critical stance towards mainstream culture can only enhance Native American narratives of identity.

Chapter 9

FABULOUS THEATRE AND EPIC THEATRE: THE POLITICAL CAST ANEW

In December 1999 President Clinton publicly admitted that the "don't ask, don't tell" policy within the U.S. military had been a failure from its inception in 1993. Referring to the beating death of a gay soldier at Fort Campbell, Kentucky, in July 1999, the President hoped the incident would "give some sobering impetus to a reexamination about how this policy is implemented" (Pear, 1999, p. 1). Government at all levels in the United States seems unwilling to move beyond either policies that encourage a closeted hypocrisy, such as President Clinton's, or overly specific legal concessions. Moreover, the ongoing refusal of the courts after the case of *Bowers vs. Hardwick* to consider lesbian and gay men a "suspect"—meaning oppressed—class, thus eligible under the provisions of the Fourteenth Amendment for protection, is indicative of the dimensions of the struggle for equal rights (Halley, 1989). However, during the same period, the movement for gay rights and recognition has expanded internally and gained more exposure within the cultural mainstream. U.S. theatre, in particular, has proved a seminal artistic form for this social justice movement, even as it has been greatly responsible for revitalizing that country's drama in the last two decades of the twentieth century. World cinema has made a contribution to this discourse as well, a circumstance that raises new questions about the capacity of political drama worldwide to influence social ideas and behavior. Finally, as Tony Kushner and others have reminded mainstream intellectuals, gay men and lesbians have always "been in the forefront of causing American society to confront sexuality" (Lowenthal, 1998, p. 153).

ALL ABOUT MY MOTHER: INTIMACY AND IDENTITY

Pedro Almodovar's humor has combined zany sophistication with a soft social criticism closer to comedy of manners than drama of partisan intent. In *All About My Mother* (1999), however, he moves one step closer to social statement while avoiding the pitfalls of "grave sincerity." For the first time, the exuberant role-playing to overcome the social restrictions of his characters crosses into explicit social statement in ways the French and U.S. films versions of *La Cage aux Folles* (1978; *The Birdcage*, 1996) manage to avoid for all their bravura. Moreover, gay and straight identities—as well as the worlds of men and women—cross one another in ways more intimate and meaningful than in those two popular films. While the hypocrisy of respectability and politicized "family values" are exposed to ridicule in the *La Cage* versions, the satire stays at the level of farce, never penetrating to deeper explorations of oppositionality. By contrast, the gays and straights in Almodovar's film at once penetrate each other's lives more significantly, developing towards states of *rapproachement* and even the deepest form of understanding. The effect is a kind of unified opposition to the "don't ask, don't tell" official hypocrisy of the 1990s closet, an alliance that crosses boundaries of both sexual orientation and gender. In the solidarity of gay and straight, the filmmaker seems to be agreeing with Hans-Georg Gadamer's general observation about human experience: "The self-preservation of what is alive takes place through its drawing into itself everything that is outside of it. Everything that is alive nourishes itself with what is alien to it. The fundamental fact of being alive is assimilation" (1982, p. 223). Such inclusive understanding seems Shakespearean in its wise tolerance. Almodovar presents through his film a coalitionist thesis that moves beyond the common divisive arguments of "everyone's homosexual" or "homosexuality is correctable."

After her 18–year-old son Esteban is killed in a Madrid car accident, Manuela reads in his notebook that he longed to meet his father. "I don't care who he is, or how he behaved with my mother. No one can take that right away from me." She never told him who his father was, only that he "died long before you were born." In fact, his father had long before changed his name from Esteban to Lola and moved to the more progressive Barcelona to begin a new life. In memory of her son, Manuela leaves Madrid for Barcelona to find her husband, with whom she is still in love. She wants to tell him that he had a son whose last words were directed at him. Her search becomes a rediscovery of her own past, as she reestablishes friendships with the gay community she knew when she and her husband were together. She meets Agrado, a transsexual and mutual friend of Lola. By reviving her life's memories, Manuela actualizes relationships and ways of being she had left behind years before.

Agrado is a male prostitute whose sense of self is affirming and even evangelizing. But unlike the widespread homophobic belief that such overtly gay personalities aim to proselytize in an aggressive manner, Agrado merely tells his story with wry humor at once self-deprecatory and self-endorsing. Through Agrado, Almodovar uses the association of gay identity and spectatorship to present a *raisonneur* who will explain the transformative nature of human identity to a mixed audience. In a theatrical scene that becomes the occasion for the mouthpiece of the director/writer, Agrado—Spanish for "liking" and "to appreciate"—recounts his series of operations that transformed his identity from male to female. Listing also the prices paid for each part of his transformed body, Agrado instructs a filled playhouse audience on the nature of identity—it is something transformable and therefore not essentialized at birth or death. His speech brings approving applause—befitting his name—from his mixed mainstream audience, and functions as a treatise for boundary crossing in the sense of Paul Ricoeur's observation that "the text"—meaning culture experience—precedes the ego: "It is the text, with its universal power of world disclosure, which gives a self to the ego" (1976, p. 95).

When Manuela finally contacts Lola, it is at the funeral of a young female social worker who dies from AIDS as a result of contact with a priest. Lola the Pioneer, as he is called by the Barcelona community that knows him well, is remorseful when he learns that he had a son who died tragically. Manuela can only feel love for Lola, despite his decision that broke their lives apart years before. Lola's feelings for Manuela are mixed with regret and profound sadness for the lost opportunity as parent and husband. Implicit in the reunion, however, is the understanding that their identities are different and their lives will continue, at least to some degree, along different paths. Nevertheless, the nature of their future relationship remains open. Disputing conventional love stories of reconciliation, Almodovar depicts profound feelings of love between a gay and straight partner, thus suggesting that the separation of love by sexual orientation is a politically based either/or fallacy. Other characters in the film also demonstrate boundary trespassing between the gay and straight worlds. Agrado flirts with a straight stage manager who wants to have oral sex but does not care whether "the girl has a penis or not."

A middle-aged actress begins a relationship with Manuela that seems platonic and professional when she offers to hire her as a companion and dresser once her long-term female lover leaves her to get married and have children in suburbia. The range of cross-overs between the hetero- and homosexual communities in the film contests the divisionisms that support the social control of identities based on gender and social orientation. As political statement, Almodovar goes beyond the *La Cage* versions and other, less well-known films featuring positive images of gay characters by incorporating a drama of mixed tone—serious and comic—for characters more fully developed, whose lives reveal an ambiguity and verisimilitude that question dominant categories. Almodovar's gay and straight characters form a community for coalition building advocated in the 1990s by such playwrights as Tony Kushner, Naomi Wallace, and Craig Lucas (Lucas, 1993).

Kushner, the leading advocate of "political drama" in the United States, has acknowledged his debt to the traditions of other political groups. Speaking in April 1993 before the March on Washington for Gay and Lesbian Rights, he defined an image of the "Black Other" and its significance to him in his own "embrace of [his] status as a pariah" (Geis & Kruger, 1997, p. 5). However, Kushner's notion of a "universalized citizenship" has been challenged by African American critics who suspect a variation on the centuries-old projection of racial anxieties and fantasies by whites onto black identities (Minwalla, 1997). Such dialogue raises long-standing issues of essentialist notions applied to identity politics, where attempts to define perceived racial, gender, ethnic, and sexual orientation groups—even particular political movements—have run aground, at times even dividing and disintegrating coalitions. Against such dilemmas, built upon moral and epistemic absolutes—whether absolute relativisms or universalisms—Almodovar's wise drama of intimacy between people with different sexual orientations and between the genders offers a safeguard, preventing political entropy. *All About My Mother* proves that association builds understanding and that ignorance breeds contempt.

STRAWBERRY AND CHOCOLATE: IGNORANCE AND PERCEPTION

Intimate association through a developing friendship is the theme of Tomas Gutierrez Alea's *Strawberry and Chocolate* (*Fresa y chocolate*, 1995), discussed in a different context in Chapter 4. When David, a young doctrinaire communist, visits the apartment of Diego, an openly gay intellectual with religious leanings, to report on his

political heterodoxy, mutual suspicion leads to tolerant understanding. Neither friend knows of the other's awareness until well
into the relationship. Although both retain their sexual orientations, they form a private coalition that eventually defeats the individuals representing official authority, who would deny Diego
certain individual rights by virtue of his sexual orientation. David
changes the most. As a young communist vigilant, his social naiveté
at first prevents him from seeing the injustice of denying the right to
practice one's sexual orientation. Diego's open acceptance of life, his
liberality and humanity impress David. Opposing Diego and the
comforts of his Epicurean, idiosyncratic apartment is the complacent arrogance of David's young communist friends, who crack
homo jokes unhesitatingly and form a male-bonding group of their
own. In fact, David's immediate superior is a young man who shows
homoerotic tendencies of his own towards David, an ironic detail
that adds to the film's gentle satirical humor.

Diego and David begin to discuss political matters openly, indi-
cating a new level of trust. Just as Agrado is able to discuss the intimacy of his reconstructed self before a diverse and mainstream
audience because the audience senses his honesty and humanity,
so David and Diego discuss political heresies openly once the initial
fear of mutual betrayal is overcome. David's homophobia at first
prevents him from establishing a meaningful dialogue with Diego,
but when Diego early on propositions David, knowing that he will refuse, he comments on the commonplace that "every homo wants a
nice straight boy." This gesture breaches the initial barriers of social
coding, allowing for self-disclosure. Thereafter, the friendship becomes the moral achievement of Alea's film. Boundaries constructed
by the dominant narrative—in this case that of Cuban communism,
itself influenced by the strictures of a prerevolutionary capitalist
and Christian culture—are not deterministic, but give way to forms
of self-actualization. David begins by learning that gay guys can be
okay, but then starts to question his wider political presuppositions. Tolerance in one field is infectious.

Specifically, David perceives for the first time the hypocrisy of the
communist vigilance movement within Cuban society. His male-
bonded comrades derogate homosexuals while watching an official
film criticizing the oppression within a U.S. client state of Central
America. Maria, the vigilance representative in Diego's building, is a
close friend of Diego and does not report the irregularities of his lifestyle and unacceptable artistic proclivities. Despite her official status as a vigilant, she herself has suicidal tendencies and has been
saved several times by the kind understanding of Diego, who forms
his own unofficial vigilance committee of one as he watches out for

her. Such ironies expose the hypocrisy and shallowness of officially sanctioned restrictions, which mistake outward personal behavior for political threat. David helps Maria in a way that Diego never could, by taking a sincere romantic interest in her. Thus his once official vigilance—unaware and intolerant—gives way to a heterosexual intimacy that contrasts ironically with the harsh machismo of his locker-room buddies at the local communist youth organization. David's decision to leave that world in favor of a long-term commitment to Maria and Diego has consequences that threaten his own future, but in this 1990s morality tale David's pilgrimage successfully moves from a City of Destruction to a City of Light. The appreciation of nonrepresentational art and the love of a heretofore despairing woman are among the possibilities open to David. In their advocacy of a tolerant and boundless humanity, Alea and Almodovar present political narratives of alternative lifestyles beyond the divisiveness of both universalism and exceptionalism.

FIRE: TRADITIONAL DUTY AND WOMEN'S FULFILLMENT

Although banned in India, Deepa Mehta's *Fire* (1996) has won international critical acclaim. Its frank depiction of the second-class nature of women in contemporary Indian society foregrounds the issue of lesbian relationships as an alternative for women who demand more than the traditional role of helpmate and homemaker. The film is more dialectic than the depiction of lush flowery meadows and the soundtrack of evocative traditional music would suggest. Mehta weaves into the fabric of the film's rich setting her theme of gay and gender liberation. The *raisonneuse* in *Fire* is not an older character who comments wisely on the *agon* of the main action, but Sita, the younger of the two women involved in the budding romance and the youngest of the featured characters. Fully aware of the cultural implications of their budding romance, Sita and Radha move into uncharted waters where words fail them. As Sita laments, "there is no word for how we feel in our language." Denied the perspective of appropriate vocabulary, the lovers hesitate only briefly before abandoning their traditional lives for the promise of a more tender and supple love. Their defiance of India's male-dominated marriage arrangements is most fully expressed by their sudden departure, an action reminiscent of Nora's escape from her husband and children in Henrik Ibsen's *A Doll's House* (1879). Their futures will be uncertain, but the promise of a more meaningful love is predicated on equality and freedom from traditional roles.

Married to a store owner whose religious piety has led him to demand from her a childless marriage of celibacy, Radha maintains a busy routine of managing the store and caring for her husband's mother. She is soon disrupted when her brother-in-law brings Sita, the bride of his arranged marriage, to live in the household. Sita's marriage is without passion, since her husband has been in love with a Chinese woman for years and continues to visit her and her cosmopolitan family. Resentful of his duty to marry Sita, he remains only civil to her, and sex with her is only obligatory. The two brothers represent opposites. The older, Radha's husband, devotes evenings to the all-male environment of his local swami, whose chief preachment is "desire causes all evil." This Hindu and Buddhist commonplace becomes a debate proposition throughout the film. The younger brother is secular, shuns rituals and fastings with contempt, and questions traditional obligations that conflict with his and his girlfriend's Western individualism. By presenting the brothers in dialectical opposition, Mehta, who also wrote the screenplay, enriches the dialogue of liberation by revealing the complexity of oppositions to dominant cultural formations. The younger brother's feelings of escape from tradition—he is obliged to have a male heir, but his Chinese girlfriend had refused to marry him—parallel Sita's. However, his resentment of the marriage and, more importantly for the main thesis of the film, his unconscious denial of Sita's identity, prevent him from discussing openly his frustrations in a culture that places "devotion" over individual fulfillment. Mehta's irony is deep here—if he had regarded his wife as an equal, they may have located mutual dissatisfactions and arrived at an understanding, and perhaps even vitalized their relationship. But Sita's husband remains a creature of the traditions he protests so bitterly, and he expects from his new wife what he himself cannot accept—conformity with the hierarchy of tradition.

When a servant informs the older brother of his wife's relationship with Sita, Radha confronts her husband with the fact that their own marriage relationship has been all one-sided and that his voluntary celibacy has been at the expense of her obligatory denial of pleasure. His enlightened piety is challenged suddenly and unexpectedly, and he at first reacts bitterly by grabbing her face and kissing it furiously. When he sees that she does not respond as she has previously, perplexity leaves him immobile. He refuses to help Radha when her dress catches fire during their argument, a response that breaks his own devotion to "aspiration" over "desire." He cannot accept the reality of what he has professed throughout the film—the equality and freedom within a marriage informed by religious piety. Mehta challenges the limitations of religious ethics by exposing the oppressive reactions of a man respected in his community for his liberality and sense of religious detachment—concepts central to

Hindu and Buddhist thought. The reality remains quite different from the preachment, Mehta is saying, and civil rights in India still have far to go.

Although Sita is the youngest marriage partner with the lowest status, it is she who initiates the love relationship with Radha and conceives the plan of leaving together to begin a new life. Her argument to Radha is the most direct and articulate expression of gender rights in the film, grounded on their mutual perception that "devotion has never been for us, always for them." The decision to abandon their husbands and households to begin life anew closely parallels Nora's choice in *A Doll's House*. For Nora, marriage to someone who does not consider her a full human being, but rather a doll to be fondled and fussed over, becomes an intolerable violation of human dignity, preventing her own self-fulfillment. For Sita and Radha, their husbands' lack of consideration and condescension also derives from a culture that prioritizes men over women. Curiously, the homosexual relationship the women discover was never mentioned directly by the men. Radha's husband reacts with shock and anger when he interrupts them in bed, but his later confrontation with Radha never mentions the nature of the relationship. In the film, the effect of the unmentionable is chilling rather than cautious. By never naming the act and feeling of lesbianism, beyond Sita's private comment to Radha that the word "for what we are" doesn't exist in their language, the film underscores the sense of denial that has accompanied this form of love in Indian culture. This repression is comprehensive, as the various of characters across the cultural spectrum react in similar ways towards the women. The three people who know of the gay relationship, Radha's husband, his enfeebled mother who cannot talk or write, and a shop assistant who reports the news, represent the secular (Westernized), traditional, and progressive religious elements of contemporary Indian society. The narrative's power as dialectic derives from the humanity of the two women, who are driven to affirm their freedom for individual fulfillment, in contrast to the obsessiveness and hypocrisy of the other characters, whose only arguments are social dominance and the tyranny of silence. Opposing Sita's liberating moment, when she speaks of the reality of her love to Radha, is the silent contempt of the mother-in-law, who spits in Radha's face after she is exposed.

Fire argues for liberation of sexuality in all its forms from, on the one hand, the rigidities of religious praxis, and, on the other, the proprietary control of love that capitalism has claimed through commercial pornography. The shop assistant, a distant family relation, represents the materialism of technological capitalism through his habitual masturbation before a pornographic video. He, together with the hedonism of Sita's husband and girlfriend, represents a threat just as great as that of traditional culture to the humanity of Sita and Radha's love. Mehta's message is affirming but hardly reassuring, since the denouement leaves disturbing questions, just as Ibsen's did a century before. Where will the two women go, what will they do without the traditional support and protection of family and local community? Such questions define the limits of sexual and gender freedom at the end of the twentieth century.

THE NORMAL HEART, ETC.: CLEAR AND TENTATIVE STEPS

In the First World, communities of substantial size now support gay values and life choices, as Almodovar's film attests and Mehta's film urges. Written early in the AIDS crisis, when the gay community in the United States was still to a large extent in denial about solutions, Larry Kramer's stage play, *The Normal Heart* (1985), presents a community in many ways distant from the world of *Fire.* The men of the play possess the vocabulary and relationality—part of which is covered by the inclusive term "camp"—that have provided gay and lesbian communities with a distinctive culture for support and security. Still, the dominant narratives of mainstream heterosexual culture remain a threat, as much to the characters' political rights as to their sense of identity and self-esteem. The AIDS epidemic was initially perceived as a threat to the civil rights of gay males, who understood that the slow response of official institutions—federal agencies, the medical establishment, New York City government— endangered their political liberties and inhibited their acceptance by the wider society. In the play, Ned tries to convince other members of the gay community that their lifestyles must change to a degree to end the epidemic. Although Ned himself is unsure of what needs to change to control the epidemic, his suggestion immediately elicits a volatile rebuttal from within the community that such views show a "blame-the-victim" mentality, which, moreover, unfairly restricts the lifestyles of its members. For fear of losing their careers, his friends prove reluctant to go public with the AIDS threat. Ned's struggle is also with the mainstream culture, which refuses to broadcast the nature and extent of the epidemic or deal with its political implications. His gay lover Felix works for the mainstream media, *The New York Times,* which, he contends, is not interested in such troubling issues. Ned's straight brother Ben represents a Manhattan law firm that reluctantly accepts his new organization on a *pro bono* basis after Ned's persistent urging. These powerful institutions represent in the play the formidable opposition to the discourse of gay rights and identity during the 1980s.

Thus, the play follows closely the Shavian tradition of presenting "problem plays" through the use of wit and humor in dialogue. However, unlike Bernard Shaw's didactic pieces, which were criticized for presenting a dramaturgy not of purpose-passion-perception, but of purpose-passion-discussion, *The Normal Heart* moves away from the camp wit and argumentation of the earlier scenes towards an increasingly tragic tone. Felix's unexpected contraction of the HIV virus contributes to the urgency of the dramatic question, which remains focused on the truthful exposition of the epidemic to the public. As Felix's condition worsens, Ned's personal crusade intensifies. He is excluded from the organization he founded just as it has begun to receive national coverage. These structural elements of the play create a crescendo effect that leads to an obligatory deathbed scene but also to the triumph of Ned's long struggle to expose the seriousness of the epidemic. Just as the medical establishment begins a belated effort to focus research funding on the virus, the death of Felix leads Ned to an overdue rapprochement with his brother, whose inability to accept Ned's identity caused their estrangement. Emma, the maverick doctor who helped expose the nature of the epidemic and struggled within the medical establishment for its recognition as a significant communicable disease, appears as well at Felix's climactic deathbed scene, which turns the play towards a melodramatic denouement. This sentimental element—and some may observe that sentimentality comes with the grain of contemporary U.S. culture and is hardly specific to Kramer's drama or the AIDS recognition movement—arguably moves the play away from an epic theatre perspective, thereby preventing the necessary rupture in the sensibilities of theatregoers and diluting the message of denial, hypocrisy, and moral myopia. The conventionally sentimental elements of the play are in fact typical of social drama in the United States, from William Saroyan and Clifford Odets through William Inge. Nonetheless, the death of Felix—unexpected and denied by nearly everyone in the play, including Ned, the most clear-sighted and morally intrepid of the characters—parallels the social nature of the disease, which strikes the young and otherwise healthy. His downward struggle gives a tragic sense of inevitability to the play, something Brecht spoke against as diversionary to the drama's social discourse. However, the inevitable death of Felix contributes thematically to a sense of the disease's mystery and degenerate deadliness. Moreover, Kramer's ample use of statistics as background exposition throughout the play is an important epic device that demonstrates there is no mystery to this virus, only lack of institutional and political recognition.

Each character in the play represents broad areas of the U.S. public: Emma, the medical establishment, Ben, the legal and political institutions, Felix, the mainstream media, Hiram, the governmental bureaucracy, Bruce, the respectable and closeted gay element, and Ned, the moral consciousness of the gay community. The association of particular characters with recognizable groups is a significant allegorical element of the play, a feature that resonates with the highly partisan drama of Odets in the Depression era. The effect is to present Ned's personal and public world as a microcosm of U.S. culture, containing representations of negative and positive consciousness during the early years of the AIDS crisis. As the plot intensifies, the dialectic becomes more explicit. Long speeches replace short argumentative conversations, a rhetorical element that serves a documentary device, since the speeches largely narrate actual developments in the struggle for public and institutional recognition. While the speeches are not specifically Brechtian in that the characters never talk directly to the audience—out of character in that sense— they instead provide the context of the characters' personal struggle by commenting caustically on the intransigence of institutions during the early 1980s.

Emma delivers the first long speech, in Scene 12, where she confronts a proprietary medical establishment in the form of her peers at the National Institutes of Health. Her attempt to wrest money for AIDS research from their four billion dollar budget is both an indictment of the tardiness and irresponsibility of the medical establishment and a rebuttal to those who have stereotyped the disease as homosexual. Ned's extended response in Scene 13 to Bruce's letter that dismisses him from the AIDS organization committee is an historical justification for the continuation of the fight for social recognition, which becomes in the play a struggle for identity and personal affirmation. Ned's plea evokes the rhetorical specificity and flair of Odets' partisan dramas of action, *Waiting for Lefty* (1933) and *Awake and Sing* (1935). While Odets' characters argued for labor solidarity, Kramer's protagonist connects political organization with the affirmation of a distinct and positive self-image: "and until we do that, until we organize ourselves block by neighborhood by city by state into a united visible community that fights back, we're doomed. That's how I want to be defined: as one of the men who fought the war" (Kramer, 1985, p. 95). *The Normal Heart*, as its inclusive title avers, pleas for both understanding from the mainstream community and organized action for change—both sexually and politically—from the gay community. As a partisan drama with a specific agenda, Kramer's problem play stands as a distinctive piece, uncompromising in its message despite occasional melodramatic lapses.

Later playwrights, most notably Tony Kushner, would build upon his use of individual characters who represent social groups and cultural institutions, his rhetorical flair and humor, and his connection of social crisis with human identity.

First World plays and films with positive gay themes have proliferated in the later years of the AIDS crisis, although few have approached Kramer's straightforward political agenda and persuasive exposition. Typical of many commercially successful fare is Paul Rudnick's *Jeffrey* (1994; film, 1995), which ran off-Broadway as an identity play with a prominent AIDS crisis theme. Lacking the argumentative force and partisan orientation of *The Normal Heart*, it fell easily into the urbane New York comedy form, which depends upon a procession of interesting but familiar types and conventional plot structure. Without much exaggeration, *Jeffrey* could be described as a same-sex modification of the boy-meets-girl formula. Sentimental and innocuous when more genuine social critique is possible, the play easily falls within the parameters of the boulevard theatre Brecht warned of. Fitting the bill for commercial drama of identity politics, where too often a mere story of an individual's life told with interpersonal honesty and a degree of self-searching substitutes for wider social analysis, the play lacks a deeper commitment.

Josiane Balasko's film *French Twist* (1994) is a witty treatment of patriarchal attitudes towards women in First World society with strong and appealing lesbian characters. The director moves a standard romantic comedy formula towards genuine social satire as it shows the appeal of the company of women in a world of thoughtless and chauvinistic men. The more emotionally disturbing implications of the confrontation between a lesbian lover and the husband is avoided through the comic turns Balasko introduces to move the plot in the direction of "everyone is a fool in love" rather than the more politically consistent "men abuse women systematically on many levels." With its light satire and generalized theme, *French Twist* received a degree of box office success. In the same category are the U.S. films *Go Fish* (1994), directed by Rose Troche, and *The Incredibly True Adventures of Two Girls in Love* (1995), by Maria Maggenti.

The first presents an urban community of young lesbian friends and lovers who collectively deserve the title "normal heart" with no irony. No overriding social or political convictions propel the characters, in fact the personal problems are no more than the search-for-the-girl-next-door variety. A forthright account of a community of women with fears and joys, its romantic plotline is political only in the sense that it documents what hegemonic narratives have long avoided. The love that dares not speak its name is not a problem in Troche's film, since the characters remain entirely within a same-sex community of a large and anonymous city. Only one scene implies that this community is an oppressed minority. When one woman has a one-night stand with a man, her friends scold her repeatedly. However, the scene's social significance is mitigated somewhat by the comic nature of the scolding and the rapid pace of the editing, which prevents a deeper exploration of social and political motives.

Girls in Love, like *Fire*, is a story of discovery, not community. Two U.S. high school girls begin a friendship that turns into romance, unknown to their families and friends. Their relationship is tested when the girls make the inevitable disclosure to their friends and parents, in that order. While the subject is politically relevant and necessary—teenagers have almost no exposure to alternative lifestyles through U.S. mainstream culture—the treatment is too insouciant to open a meaningful exploration of the social consequences of same-sex relationships. The girls approach their relationship in an offhand manner. Their reactions to the mutual exploration of forbidden love is overly casual for credibility, as if they were momentarily preoccupied with boy problems or a troublesome teacher. The effortless reactions may be a misguided attempt by the director to make their feelings seem natural, thereby furthering the implied thesis of acceptance and understanding. Or, it could be a strategy to appeal to a broader spectrum of potential audiences by transmuting the political and personal implications of their choices into a more agreeable adolescent angst. In any case, the film suffers from a comic lightheartedness. This is not the case with Kimberly Pierce's *Boys Don't Cry* (1999), a powerful exposition of permissible violence and bigotry within First World culture.

Teenage Teena Brandon has reversed her name and passes as a man in the Western redneck bars she frequents at night. While living with her cousin who is fed up with the way she draws violence to herself, Brandon meets a girl and they begin a romance that eventually leads to family upheaval and finally violence. The girl's brother and friend rape Brandon after they discover that she has a woman's body. The mother and other family members attempt a cover-up, and their attitude of denial becomes a general signifier for small-mindedness in a culture with rigidly defined gender roles. Pierce's film draws upon the details of local working-class culture to create a naturalism akin to the politically based dramas of late-nineteenth-century European naturalism—scenes of large-group interaction and careful attention to accurate local characters and dialogue to create an oppressive environment that motivates the characters. In contrast to the dialectics of Kramer's and Rudnick's plays, Pierce's statement derives less from a dialogue of persuasive exposition than from the sheer violence of the characters as they react to the central character's alterity. If the girlfriend's family—dysfunctional, violent, and co-dependent—represents repressive mainstream attitudes towards gender identity, its addictive propensities comment more widely on the causes of discontent within U.S. culture.

Representative of the numerous dramas of gay and lesbian identity in the 1990s is *Another American Asking and Telling* (1999) by Marc Wolf. Author/performer Wolf's one-person piece is a straightforward *Lehrstucke* in the dialectical tradition of Brechtian theatre. Characters argue contrasting positions on the issue of gays in the military. Wolf has carefully selected military personalities who typically shun openly gay personnel, using arguments from congressional hearings and news interviews. The advocates for gay recognition win the rebuttals morally and professionally. Wolf prefers a lightly focused thesis piece, avoiding the wider implications of the discourse. On this point Michael Feingold (1999) observes, "Unlike [Anna] Deavere Smith, Wolf has built in certain limits, both artistic and ideological. He displays a less extensive range of speakers, and tends to confine what we hear from them more strictly to the issue, where [Smith] might have looked for illumination in the atmosphere surrounding it" (p. 77). Borrowing Smith's interview-and-impersonate strategy for the theatre, Wolf's play is straightforwardly and unapologetically partisan. In contrast, Tony Kushner's celebrated two-part play, *Angels in America: A Gay Fantasia on National Themes. Part I: Millennium Approaches* (1993) and *Part Two: Perestroika* (1994), has been criticized for presenting an ambivalent dialectics with a message too complex for partisan drama.

ANGEL'S IN AMERICA: PERESTROIKA OR NYET?

Rightfully considered the seminal U.S. drama of the 1990s, Kushner introduces the issue of gay rights and recognition within a grand narrative that demonstrates the insufficiencies of both traditional religion and Marxist theory. Its dramaturgy has ambitiously combined what has been described as the theatrical spectacle of Walter Benjamin's messianic consciousness with a by then rather familiar AIDS-crisis plotline conveyed by camp humor and representative urban characters. However, while the play uses parody in interesting ways, it ultimately fails as effective drama of social justice through its thematic ambiguity and perhaps an unconscious retreat from genuine oppositionality. Kushner (1994) considers himself a political playwright, as his remarks in the Afterword of *Part Two* confirm, where a "belief" in "radical democracy" empowers the play (p. 154). However, his remarks about a close friend and collaborator in the same essay stand as an accurate description of what is missing in the *Angels* plays:

More pessimistic than I, Kimberly is much less afraid to look at the ugliness of the world. She tries to protect herself far less than I do, and consequently she sees more. . . . most people I know, myself included, would rather be spared and feel safer encircled by a measure of obliviousness. She's capable of pulling things apart, teasing out fundamental concerns from their camouflage; at the same time she uses her analysis, her learning, her emotions, her lived experience, to make imaginative leaps, to see the deeper connections between ideas and historical developments. (p. 153)

Probing analysis and an unambiguous vision of ultimate goals are missing from a drama that heralds new directions for U.S. theatre and the wider culture. Instead, *Angels* offers a plot—familiar by 1993—of individuals pained by the plight of AIDS alongside a (tentative?) rejection of traditional religious messianism and socialist theory of history. In its place is only the most vague insistence on "*More Life*" and a reductionist assumption that all current theory is of no use for the future. Throughout the play, particular issues are dismissed out of hand or raised and then ignored, as if discussion of such topics is nullified simply by the fact that there are two sides to every question. For example, Louis and Belize suddenly begin an argument over Palestinian rights in Israel near the end of *Part Two*, only to be cut off by Prior's remark, "I'm almost done" (p. 146). In fact, the character with the most "authentic pathos" and stage prominence, as even the conservative critic Harold Bloom (1998) has observed, is Roy Cohn, the chief lawyer for Joseph McCarthy of the 1950s House Un-American Activities Committee (p. 405). The narrative's concern with Cohn's earthly personality and future soul occupies several scenes. Moreover, he is continually allowed to upstage the other characters with cogent rejoinders that tend to validate theatrically his regressive opinions: "But the thing about the American Negro is, he never went Communist. Loser Jews did. But you people had Jesus so the reds never got to you. I admire that" (p. 24). Similar observations by Cohn and other characters maintain binary oppositions that reinforce traditional divisionism and defeat the holistic vision the playwright claims for the plays. *Perestroika* (social restructuring) cannot happen when *Angels* returns continually to conventional boundary maintenance against the other.

Moreover, the play's use of stereotypical commentary at the expense of marginalized groups exists within a plot structures that remains focused on the individual, the middle-class urban intellectual. Kushner avoids the ensemble effect of late nineteenth-century naturalism, the form that comes closest to his stated interest in presenting a new vision of society beyond capitalism's cultivation of the individual. The play's humor typically brings low such heavenly figures as angels with a conversational remark. But its parody lacks the sort of constructive irony needed for shattering conventional ways of seeing and opening new visions. Often, such humor is sophomoric rather than ironic in an epic theatre sense—"if [the Mormons' angel's] name was Moroni why don't they call themselves Morons?" (p. 60). The Mormon religious tradition, angels as biblical messengers of God, and other traditions are introduced to explore new visions for U.S. culture but in effect only obsess on the cultural past of Manifest Destiny—a concept that is never critiqued directly but rather taken as some sort of essential for future identity. Also, Kushner's preoccupation with "America" to the exclusion of international themes favors isolationism over pluralism. Nationalistic mindsets, which the playwright claims to have rejected, are taken as givens at the expense of the exploration of new forms of polity and relationality. While the retrograde character Cohn is given prominence to speak—some spectators may even find his eloquent villainy appealing—particular issues are avoided, and race and class are both downplayed, a fact that has prompted revealing critical analysis. Race hierarchies are reinscribed, not challenged, especially through the representation of Belise, the African American character (Minwalla, 1997).

Janelle Reinelt (1997) regrets the drift away in *Angels* from the type of wider social analysis that its multiplot construction invites. "The replacement of class analysis by other identity categories, while useful and strategic in terms of contemporary exigencies, leaves the play with no other foundation for social change than the individual subject, dependent on an atomized agency. Since this subjectivity is contradictory and collapsed, the only horizon must be transcendent." With no programmatics in the play, "the fact of liberal pluralism tinged with despair that marks America at the end of the century goes unchallenged, in fact is reinscribed" (pp. 242, 243). Offering a more fundamental challenge to the claims of *Angels*, David Savran (1997) argues that the play's intended "undecidability" is "always already resolved because the questions that appear to be ambivalent have in fact already been decided consciously or unconsciously by the text itself" (p. 15). As the title suggests, "America is in essence a utopian and theological construction, a nation with a divine mission. Politics is by no means banished insofar as it provides a crucial way in which the nation is imagined. But it is subordinated to utopian fantasies of harmony in diversity, of one nation under a derelict God" (p. 31). With a woman and African American man in roles of caretakers, cross-dressing only by women actors, and middle-class men directing the dialectics, *Angels* resolves itself to a vague—and facile?—American optimism in the tradition of William Saroyan, a sort of neoliberalism featuring identity politics and atomized individuals. In all of this there is a basic confusion between an openness towards the future, a Brechtian indeterminacy, and a misguided ambiguity. Perhaps the basic problem lies in the play's larger dialectics, which, as Art Borreca (1997) states, is "the idea of defining America" (p. 254) As a grand query, it reframes its discourse to a delimited nationalism rather than striking forth in new directions as promised in its revolutionary millennial theme.

Although overpraised, the *Angels in America* plays have succeeded more generally in reviving a general discussion of the social importance of drama for a new age, which in the post-Cold War era had threatened to be subsumed entirely by the end-of-history ideology of international corporatism. What cannot be denied is the revitalization of First World drama through the agency of the gay and lesbian rights movement, which has produced a drama of exceptional variety in a few short years. Indeed, it would not be overstating the case to say that alternative lifestyle issues, gender identity, gay and lesbian rights issues, and the fundamentals of cultural formation with respect to sexual orientation together have been the central impulse for political drama in the 1980s and 1990s. This impulse has just been opened, in fact has yet to achieve a full flowering, but is accompanied by formidable intellectual movements such as queer theory in academe, gender and cultural studies, and women's and men's studies, all of which promise to affect the wider culture in the early decades of the twenty-first century. Missing thus far is a recognizable international dimension to the field—both within First World theory and within the Third World. Though extremely nugatory at present, the international connection shows some glimmerings, as this chapter demonstrates.

Chapter 10

AFRICAN AMERICAN THEATRE: RACIAL IDENTITY AND COOPERATIVE PLURALISM

The discourse of social justice depends above all upon a cultural base that prioritizes progressive agendas and perspectives for change, rather than exceptionalist or elitist viewpoints. Accordingly, mediated views of race that revise hegemonic ways of perceiving and employing social identities can become positive agencies for human rights and democratic goals. Within this framework, reductionist equations of white equals power and black equals powerlessness need to be replaced by more nuanced and probing analyses of the relations of power, class, and race within First World contexts. Happily, recent drama in the United States presents possibilities for modeling interracial relationships that enable open-ended rather than closed agendas for positive social change. I wish to discuss plays by well-known African American playwrights that depict such open-ended interracial possibilities—rather than singular perspectives—and that demonstrate the complexities of black-white relationships where the maintenance of power remains only one possibility. I will also explore the direction of recent whiteness discourse to better understand in social context both its present limitations and its possible enlistment for projects of cultural inclusiveness.

AFRICAN AMERICAN DRAMA

With a background of political activism, Lorraine Hansberry recognized the potential of drama for political statement. Her father,

Carl A. Hansberry, had been chief counsel for the landmark fair housing case before the U.S. Supreme Court in 1943, *Hansberry vs. Lee*. *A Raisin in the Sun* (1959), her major play, deals specifically with the problem of housing discrimination in American cities, but her characters are compelling portraits of individuals struggling to maintain dignity and to preserve family integrity. The only white character, the lawyer Karl Lindner, represents a white protectionist organization, ironically called the Clybourne Park Improvement Association, that seeks to exclude the Younger family from its neighborhood. Lindner's motives fit current definitions of whiteness: the maintenance of power structures and economic exclusivity. However, the play's ending keeps open the possibility of change as the Younger family members unite to face the certain resistance of the white community. As Walter Younger tells Lindner, "We don't want to make no trouble for nobody or fight no causes, and we will try to be good neighbors" (p. 148). Hansberry keeps an open-ended outlook— not unresolved, as some critics have charged—offering an affirmation that allows the possible change of attitude of the Clybourne Park white community.

In the early 1950s, Hansberry developed a political view that emphasized the determining factor of class as much as race. Her choice of a working-class rather than a middle-class African American family for *Raisin* was motivated by the conviction that the working-class struggle is "more pertinent, more relevant, more significant . . . more *decisive* in our political history and our political future" (Terkel & Hansberry, 1984, pp. 7–8). *The Sign in Sidney Brustein's Window* (1964) centers on a white protagonist who, unlike the working-class members of Clybourne Park, possesses political awareness but also a cynicism that has prevented him from renewing the social struggle. Sidney Brustein's "whiteness," that is, his willingness to maintain exclusive power or at least his refusal to fight against it, is revealed at the beginning of the play as a moral lassitude that has driven him to callous selfishness and a kind of bohemian snobbery as a lifelong resident of Greenwich Village.

By the end of the play, Sidney's involvement in a local political campaign has rekindled his sense of social justice, and his passive cynicism gives way to a renewed commitment. Pondering the dilemma of radical change in American society—"how does one confront these thousand nameless faceless vapors that are the evil of our time?" (p. 296)—he affirms a Whitmanesque optimism for social and spiritual transformation. He is, in fact, "[a] fool who believes that death is waste and love is sweet and that the earth turns and men change every day and that rivers run and that people wanna be better than they are and that flowers smell good and that I hurt terribly today, and that hurt is desperation and desperation is—energy and energy can *move* things" (pp. 339–340). But Hansberry is careful not to render her white protagonist too naive for the disillusioning struggle that cannot be easily won: ". . . some of us will be back out in those streets today. Only this time—thanks to you—we shall be more seasoned, more cynical, tougher, harder to fool—and therefore, less likely to quit" (p. 338).

As Julius Lester remarked, "*Sidney Brustein* . . . is a call to arms to white liberals and intellectuals" (Nemiroff, 1995, p. 18). Hansberry's inclusive sense of the struggle for structural change within Western society grounded her view of whiteness. Shortly before her death, she wrote in *The New York Times*, "Few things are more natural than that the tortures of the *engage* should attract me thematically. . . . It is the climate and mood of such intellectuals, if not these particular events, which constitute the core of [*Sidney Brustein*]" (Village Intellect, 1964, Sec. 2, p. 1). At the important forum at New York Town Hall in July 1964, "The Black Revolution and the White Backlash," Hansberry expressed what was at the time an unpopular view among many African American activists. Pointing out that many who died in the civil rights struggle were white men, she commented, "I don't think we can decide ultimately on the basis of color. The passion that we express should be understood . . . in that context. We want total identification. It's not a question of leaving anybody out; it's a merger . . . but it has to be a merger on the basis of true and genuine equality" (in Nemiroff, 1995, p. 17).

Hansberry's concept of merger with equality paralleled her view that drama was a particularized expression of a universal struggle, a movement that was by necessity beyond what has since been termed "identity politics." For Hansberry, this commonality gave all races the same mandate: "only . . . when the white liberal becomes an American radical will he be prepared to come to grips with . . . the basic fabric of our society" (in Nemiroff, 1995, p. 24). Hansberry's interracial mandate may have found new expression during the 1990s through the notion in whiteness theory of race traitoring. For example, in "Toward a New Abolitionism: A *Race Traitor* Manifesto," John Garvey and Noel Ignatiev (1997) question in explicit terms traditional categorizations of racial status and political commitment (pp. 346–349). Among their suggestions is telling other white people, "I am not white," when remarks and humor are passed as safeguards of racial status. Beyond such individual acts, Hansberry also sought to enlist white people of conscience for organized political action.

Sidney Brustein includes several white characters who are at different stages of political awareness and race consciousness, ranging from the unthinkingly conventional (Mavis) to a woman (Gloria) who loves a black man (Alton) and hopes he will marry her. Gloria is rejected by Alton when he learns that she has been a street prostitute. She has felt the pain of social hypocrisy and knows its racial signification in American culture: "Do you know what some of the other girls do? They go off and sleep with a colored boy—and I mean *any* colored boy so long as he is black—because they figure that is the one bastard who can't look down on them five seconds after it's over!" (p. 326). In a long disclosure, Alton confesses to Sidney that he cannot marry a former prostitute because he learned from his family never to take anything second-hand from white people. "I don't want white man's leavings, Sidney. I couldn't *marry* her" (p. 303). Alton, however, is not another version of George Murchison, the black bourgeois character in *Raisin*, who thinks only of status and assimilation. Rather, Alton's rejection of Gloria follows from a family pride and political sensibility that rigidifies in the face of interracial commitment. In this, the politically committed Alton shows his hypocrisy, something that he is aware of intellectually but cannot bring himself to overcome. After Gloria's subsequent suicide, Sidney realizes more fully the dangers of compliance with society's false values, lamenting, "The slogans of capitulation can *kill!* Every time we say 'live and let live'—death triumphs!" (p. 338). Sidney's choice is to fight a longtime friend who has become part of the New York political machine.

The depiction of a white liberal who learns that organized commitment and interracial cooperation are the only means to progressive change received some measure of success in the New York theatre (101 performances). Continuing this trajectory, Hansberry conceived *Les Blancs* (performed 1970) as a statement of interracial cooperation on a global level. The title was an ironic glance off Jean Genet's *The Blacks*, which had received much critical attention in New York at the time. Like *Sidney Brustein*, the play focuses on the exceptions to "whiteness" as a definition of power equated to white people. A range of white characters are also represented. In *Les Blancs*, however, the races dispute with one another (and intraracially) in dramatic dialogue that revives the discursive style of Bernard Shaw. Hansberry's most astute dialectic is saved for the discourse between Charlie Morris, a white liberal journalist, and Tshembe Matoseh, an African returned to his homeland after a period of assimilation and interracial marriage in England. Their debate is resumed throughout the play, continuing the tendency of the white and black characters in *Sidney Brustein* to comment on political agendas before acting upon them.

Charlie is a common type of white liberal who easily dismisses race as a reality and wants Tshembe to accept him without the barriers of race. Tshembe, however, knows that race, though only a perception, a consequence of colonialist ideology, has nonetheless become a reality that cannot be dismissed, even in relationships of individual intimacy. Charlie can only be educated by another white, Dr. Willy DeKoven, who has spent years at the African medical mission where he has learned the truth of white attitudes towards the colonial subject. "Mr. Morris, the struggle here has not been to push the African into the twentieth century—but at all costs to keep him *away* from it! We do not look down on the black man because we really think he is lazy, we look down on him because he is wise enough to resent working for us" (p. 152). DeKoven's years in Africa have radicalized him so that he supports the local uprisings that are resuming in earnest. He tells Charlie, "I came here twelve years ago believing that I could—it seems so incredible now—help alleviate suffering by participating actively in the very institutions that help sustain it" (p. 153).

Another European who has rejected the power base of whiteness is the wife of the chief missionary doctor, Madame Neilsen, who has long realized that the patronizing approach of her husband (an unseen character whom Hansberry may have based on Albert Schweitzer) did not help Africans but instead reinforced the white power structure of colonialism. She encourages Tshembe, whom she helped raise from a small boy, to join the anticolonial forces of his country despite her knowledge that the same warriors just killed her husband and other white enforcers. In a lyrical scene, she tells Tshembe, who hesitates choosing between his European and African worlds, "I once taught you that a line goes on into infinity unless it is bisected. Our country needs *warriors*, Tshembe Matoseh. Africa needs warriors. Like your father" (p. 169). Her advice is taken, but she soon is shot in crossfire between soldiers and the warriors now led by Tshembe, dressed in his father's robe. As she dies in his arms, Tshembe gives a deep cry of mourning. Earlier, when asked by Madame if he hates whites, his response is a succinct statement of the cooperative pluralism that grounds Hansberry's understanding. Racial identity is not static and deterministic, but instead dynamic, offering the promise of change: "Madame, I have seen your mountains. Europe—in spite of all her crimes—has been a great and glorious star in the night. Other stars shone before it—and will again with it. The heavens, as *you* taught me, are broad and can afford a galaxy" (p. 168).

A gesture of interracial promise beyond categories of race occurs when Charlie and Tshembe reach a plateau of agreement and even solidarity as the government helicopters sweep down:

Charlie: I'm me—Charlie Morris—not "the White Man!"

Tshembe: (*Cupping his ears*) I'm sorry, Mr. Morris, I cannot *hear* you.

Charlie: (*As the chopper recedes somewhat*) Then try, Matoseh. Because I've heard you.

Tshembe then shakes Charlie's hand and lifts their united hands "towards the sky" as the helicopters of the colonial police circle above (p. 164). The theatrical image is powerful in the context of the struggle between the boundary-breaking solidarity of interracial understanding, on the one side, and the forces of oppression and divisionism, represented by the white Major George Rice, on the other.

To achieve the "merger on the basis of true and genuine equality" that Hansberry urged in the last year of her life at the New York Town Hall forum, white people—such as Charlie Morris, Willy Dekoven, and Madame Neilsen—need to begin a journey of understanding and self-critical exploration. Their goal, however, cannot be separatism, which Hansberry recognized to be compliant with the current culture of dominance. Rather, white people must attempt to break the boundaries of the social structures that confirm racial identity.

Critical reception of the original production of *Les Blancs* was predictably polarized, with mainstream reviewers either reacting defensively by seeing the play as an attack of blacks on whites or defending it as an exposé of racism and colonialist repression (see, for example, Barnes, 1970, and Watts, 1970). Mainstream critics left unmentioned Hansberry's documentation of interracial cooperation beyond definitions of power. Madame Neilsen encourages the hesitant Tshembe to take up arms against European colonialists; Charlie undergoes a political education and affirms Tshembe's position as a detribalized revolutionary; and DeKoven declares his allegiance to the African cause. They are all "race traitors," as prescribed by Garvey and Ignatiev, willing to forego their status in a colonialist society for a commonality beyond racial boundaries. Tshembe also accepts the hybridity of his identity, his European life and "mixed-race" family no longer presenting a barrier to his acceptance of the revolutionary cause and the "coat" of his father. While Hansberry's sympathetic reviewers defended her challenge to American and global racism, they ignored her efforts to transcend determinist definitions of race. Tshembe becomes the play's *raisonneur*, explaining to Charlie that, while race is an illusion, it is a fantasy the horrible consequences of which cannot be ignored.

Alice Childress: Intimacy and Social Cooperation

Alice Childress pioneered a drama of social realism that exposed the forbidden in American culture. She won critical acclaim for *Trouble in Mind* (1955 Obie Award), but perhaps her most complex and moving drama was *Wedding Band* (finally produced for television in 1973). Its depiction of an interracial relationship was ahead of its time in its expressions of intimacy and the penetration of cultural forces in such relationships. Herman and Julia live in the black section of a Southern city where Herman is tolerated as a white, but looked upon with suspicion. Julia is the subject of gossip by her neighbors and resentment by the men of the community, but she struggles for dignity when confronting the suspicion of blacks and the rancor and hypocrisy of whites.

Childress's depiction of strong individuals who successfully overcome social opprobrium and isolation promotes her theme of nonconformity and boundary crossing. Herman's illness exposes the interracial relationship to his family members. His sister's shock gives way to hostility, even though she herself wants to leave with a sailor whom her family has looked down upon. The play's paralleling of classism and racism expands the theme of boundary crossing, just as the representation of the white characters breaks new ground in American literature. Herman's mother responds contemptuously to his domestic arrangement and immediately attempts to cover over the relationship, announcing to Julia's black landlady, Fanny, that her son was delivering baked goods when his illness struck. Fanny knows to agree without comment, and the complicity of both women demonstrates the cooperative nature of cultural segregation. Their mutual hypocrisy succeeds in the cover-up, but Herman dies with Julia at his bedside in a final scene of isolated interracial understanding.

The poignancy of Julia and Herman's last moments together remains a unique expression of interracial bonding in American, and world, literature. The playwright describes Julia's final rejection of the pillars of her own community—Fanny and Lula—in a revealing stage direction: "She is going through that rising process wherein she must reject them as the molders and dictators of her life" (p. 132). The "rising process" of the play brings about a final reconciliation between the interracial partners, since, unknown to the outside world of black and white, they have undergone a struggle for acceptance and understanding within the relationship. As Herman dies, Julia offers him an image of their escape from the narrow limits of the world that has harmed each of them profoundly. Her image of their departure on a passenger liner bound for New York presents the realization of their freedom to love without limits, a freedom that has been prevented as much by their own struggle to love across racial lines as by the prejudices of their society: "out to sea . . . on our way . . . yes . . . yes . . . yes" (p. 133). Julia's endeavor to accept Herman's unconscious prejudices throughout the years of their relationship leads to his realization that he has internalized the very cultural values that have denied his freedom to love.

The communities of black and white threaten to force their way into Julia's house—Herman's family, through the police power that they control, and Fanny, by her right as the owner of their house. Meanwhile, Julia seeks a final closeness with Herman by pressing the issue of his contradictory allegiances. His father was a member of a KKK organization, and Herman has been unable to recognize the false values his father affirmed: "HERMAN: He never hurt anybody. JULIA: He hurts me. There's no room for you to love him and me too. . . . it can't be done" (p. 129). Julia then presses Herman to admit that he never condemned white oppression after hearing news of lynchings and discrimination. His response—that he was not personally responsible—was not the point for Julia: "Whenever somebody was lynched . . . you and me would eat a very silent supper. It hurt me not to talk . . . what you don't say you swallow down." Herman's response, "I was just glad to close the door 'gainst what's out there. You did all the givin' . . . I failed you in every way" (p. 130), reveals a long-standing denial that their relationship could not exclude social reality, no matter how much their love revealed the basic lie of that reality. Herman and Julia achieve a new-found closeness as Herman confronts the negativities of his white identity, a recognition that allows him to accept Julia's love unconditionally.

Revealing the intimacy of an interracial relation, where power is more evenly based and discourse between the partners more negotiable than in the social sphere, allows Childress to explore white perspectives in an alternative space. Significantly, Annabelle, Herman's sister, secretly listens from the outside window during the deathbed conversation between Julia and Herman. Her interest in interracial contact foreshadows the enlistment of great numbers of whites into the civil rights movement of the late 1950s and 1960s. Annabelle is struggling to break free from social propriety, represented by her mother's refusal to allow her to marry outside their social sphere. The possibility remains for her to follow Herman in crossing boundaries of power, an activity she is somewhat envious of, despite her initial shock over his disobedience of racial coding. Childress presents a white family in various stages of moral and political awareness who are challenged by a situation that demands the surrender of their presumptions of power and status. Herman's realization that his own tribal allegiances have hurt the person he loves the most associates with Charlie Morris' understanding that race is an illusion that nonetheless matters. His acceptance of the inevitability of Tshembe's struggle allows both men to begin a new partnership. Herman's full acceptance of Julia comes only when their relationship is revealed to his family, a circumstance that forces his choice between the ethics of white power and his own sense of inclusiveness.

Hansberry and Childress wished to explore territories of race beyond the stereotypical, which they regarded as overly determined and counterproductive for the new era of civil rights activism. Hansberry was aware of the limitations of *Raisin* soon after its New York opening. For her, the play, though powerful and popular, relied too much upon conventional representations of race to brings its audiences into a new era of social consciousness. Ben Keppel (1995) has observed that what Hansberry called her audience's "prior attitudes" were not overcome by the play: "In seeing through these screens, uncomfortable audiences could ignore representations too far afield from well-worn stereotypes, and instead fasten onto a superficially familiar theme or plot device, elevating it to the play's center" (p. 181). By the early 1960s, Hansberry was ready for a more focused exploration beyond socially coded racial identities. Accordingly, her later plays focus on white identities and the dialectic between black and white, as she realized that whites themselves must change their preconceptions—hence their identities—for the new era of social transformation. "I hope that in the next ten years we will begin to recognize the void that racism has left in the character of white Americans. The sorry absence of courage on the race question presents terrifying implications for our culture" (in Keppel, 1995, p. 203).

By the early 1960s, Hansberry may have been familiar with Brecht's Epic Theatre technique. Her disappointment with *Raisin*'s reception confirmed Brecht's own disappointment with the popular theatre of his day. Brecht also wished to overcome Hansberry's dilemma, the "prior attitudes" of her audience. Only drama that could "make strange" through an "alienation effect" (*Verfremdungseffekt*) would force the audience to look at overly determined social codes in a new light, exposing the invisible of collective denial. Although Brecht had class consciousness foremost in mind, his theatre technique applies most penetratingly to racial categories in twentieth-century America. Only by presenting the unmentionable, the denied, the covered up in a new way—a "strange" way—could audiences critique their most basic issues. That meant above all racial identity for Hansberry and Childress. Whites need to be shown how their own identities prevent progressive change. Even more, both playwrights assume that racial identities have the capacity to change from within. For James Baldwin, whites must first be presented with the inconsistencies and pathologies of their own racial identities before such identities can be changed. But Baldwin's devastating drama, *Blues for Mister Charlie* (1971) also presented a model, however flawed, for white consciousness in the character of Parnell.

James Baldwin: Beyond Categorization

Baldwin's view of race in the 1960s challenged deterministic categories for the sake of a transformative consciousness. Thus, he shared the political optimism of Hansberry and Childress. In Baldwin's preface to *Blues*, "Notes for Blues," a cohesive view of human development ("the American people") is presented, an understanding of race, which, while hardly denying the negative effects of racial divisionism in American culture, spoke of a commonality of commitment transcending race identities: "But if it is true, and I believe it is, that all men are brothers, then we have the duty to try to understand this wretched man; and while we probably cannot hope to liberate him, begin working toward the liberation of his children" (p. 243). Baldwin's irenic language here is surprising when considering his often pathological treatment of the play's characters and dialogue. More startling still is his suggestion of a shared responsibility—but not collective guilt—for the ethos of the "white man." In 1964 the play was attacked not only for the frank depiction of white bigotry and hypocritical respectability but also for Baldwin's inclusive commentary on the play. This apparent contradiction derived from his insistence that white identity had within it the capacity to change. As with Hansberry and Childress, white identity was not absolutely determined by power arrangements, but was subject to historical development.

Juanita, the black friend of Richard, murdered by Lyle, a white store owner, describes Parnell as the dragon slayer of the town. Son of a wealthy businessman, Parnell edits a progressive and nonconformist newspaper that takes risks for causes. He dreads his compromising position in a community where his peers are white and his friends are black. He tells Juanita, who questions him on his success in prosecuting Lyle, "I am not a good man, but I have my little ways" (Baldwin, 1971, p. 247). As events unfold, however, he becomes less certain of his ability to bring justice for Richard's murder. To Meridian, Richard's father and the chief black minister in town, Parnell describes the ambivalence of being white and having a conscience: "please try to understand that it is not so easy to leap over fences, to give things up—all right, to surrender privilege! But if you were among the privileged you would know what I mean. It's not a matter of trying to hold on; the things, the privilege—are part of you, are who you are. It's in the *gut*" (p. 267). Faced with Lyle's assertions of innocence and pressure from the white community, Parnell's modest sense of having "his little ways" around the boundaries of black and white has given way to a retreat into "whiteness." When on the stand during the trial scene, Parnell expresses less certainty of the guilt of Lyle, choosing instead to stress the doubt of circumstances, the Blacktown court audience reacts with dismay. For the black citizens, suspicions are confirmed that all whites in the end close ranks around the maintenance of power.

However, Baldwin refuses to categorize Parnell so simply. He remains a victim of racial segregation through his unfulfilled love of a local black woman. Parnell's soliloquy explores the ambivalence of white people toward the racial divide they have created. For Parnell, this perplexity combines the ratiocination of an intellectual with overwhelming libidinal imagery: "All your life you've been made sick, stunned, dizzy, oh, Lord! driven half mad by blackness. Blackness in front of your eyes. Boys and girls, men and women—you've bowed down in front of them all! And then hated yourself. Hated yourself for debasing yourself" (p. 304). Parnell's personal attempts to probe the deeper feelings of race leave him confused and despairing.

After the trial scene, Parnell is given another chance to recover the healing side of his identity when, in the closing dialogue of the play, he approaches Juanita to be included in the organized protest: "Can I join you on the march, Juanita? Can I walk with you? JUANITA: Well, we can walk in the same direction, Parnell. Come. Don't look like that. Let's go on" (p. 313). Juanita becomes the reconciler in the play, taking up Parnell's job of civil protest when he has failed the cause of justice in his court testimony. Her willingness to trust her white friend once again—there is an indication in their dialogue that they once had a nascent romantic relationship—parallels Baldwin's own inclusive language in the "Notes for *Blues*." While whites have failed once again to bring justice and abolish segregation, their misgivings qualify them for a second chance. Here white people are not monolithically reactive, but are willing to continue the struggle despite their (Parnell's) own failures. By joining the march of protest over the court ruling, Parnell reaffirms his commitment to the cause of racial justice, a position that is incompatible with the maintenance of white power.

Charles Fuller: Institutional Justice and Racial Understanding

Charles Fuller's *A Soldier's Play* (1981), while less ideologically based than the dramas of Childress, Hansberry, and Baldwin, nevertheless also presents a spectrum of white intentionality rather than a single motivation of white hegemony. The responses of the white officers to the murder of a black sergeant in the American South during the 1940s range from the predictably indifferent to the regretful. Fuller chooses as a major character a white officer with the capacity for change. Capt. Charles Taylor is not the most progressive white officer on the base—Jed Harris, mentioned by name twice but never appearing in the play, is the only officer who argues for integrated officers' quarters. Taylor views the murder case, in which suspicion has fallen on two white officers, as a matter of military fairness for the sake of unit morale. He tells Davenport, the black military police officer sent from Washington to investigate the case, that "people around here don't respect the colored" (Fuller, 1981, p. 889). His remark to Davenport is more self-disclosure than warning—"So I frankly wasn't sure how I'd feel—until right now—and—(*struggles*) I don't want to offend you, but I just cannot get used to it—the bars, the uniform—being in charge just doesn't look right on Negroes" (p. 889).

Although their first encounter ends in *"cold stares,"* at their next meeting Taylor shows more motivation to find the murderers. Like Parnell, Taylor regards himself as a maverick among whites: "I'll never be more than a Captain, Davenport, because I won't let them get away with dismissing things like Water's death. I've been the commanding officer of three outfits! I raised hell in all of them, so threatening me won't change my request [to be in charge of the case]" (p. 897). To Davenport's suspicion of cover-up, Taylor asserts his impartiality in the racial incident. He confides that he has requested an investigation every day since the murder and sees Davenport's color as a signal from headquarters of their lack of seriousness, knowing that a black investigator will have no credibility in the South.

Taylor's concern for justice balances a decided lack of sensitivity toward the black men he commands. He nervously halts a conversation with them when it becomes too personal—an incident that Sergeant Waters and the other black enlisted men immediately comment on once Taylor leaves (p. 896); he can describe only the most external behavior of black soldiers—something Davenport notices at once (p. 905); and he confesses to Davenport a general lack of knowledge of the personal lives of his black men (p. 905). Still, his insistence that he is "not some red-neck cracker!" (p. 907) is sincere, and, in the play's final scene, he reveals a new respect for black officers: "I was wrong, Davenport—about the bars—the uniform—about Negroes being in charge. [*Slight pause*] I guess I'll *have* to get used to it" (p. 911). Although the white characters offer no deep confessions of the heart, unlike the white characters of the other plays discussed, the white officers and the black enlisted men of the unit achieve a final unity when it is revealed that the entire unit was killed during the Ruhr Valley campaign in Germany. Fuller's drama of straight realism does not attempt the lyrical levels of Childress, Hansberry, and Baldwin. He moves beyond ideology, at least in overt ways. Water's murderers are found to be black soldiers, not the suspected white officers. Moreover, Davenport and Taylor achieve a kind of respect for one another that does not necessarily include affection or identification. In this respect, Taylor differs markedly from the other white "race traitors," Parnell, Herman, and the positive white characters of *Les Blancs*. Although lacking Parnell's passionate regard for African Americans, Taylor can be depended upon in his identity as a maverick, refusing to let racial injustice slip by. Fuller allows room in the end for a more inclusive understanding of race, as Taylor's increasingly confessional remarks to Davenport demonstrate.

NEW REGIONS OF RELATIONALITY

Richard Dyer's seminal analysis of whiteness found that "white power secures its dominance by seeming not to be anything in particular" (1993, p. 44; see also Henry Giroux, 1992, p. 15; and Nakayama & Krizek, 1995, pp. 292–94). Whiteness most often appears as invisible, entailing universalizing notions to which other cultures and races are negatively compared, their difference denied. Whiteness functions as a kind of white noise of unnoticed background that critical whiteness theory has sought to identify and hence interrogate. But the increased emphasis on whiteness and other racialized identities in critical theory, and in much of applied discourse, has once again fixed racial identity, giving support to deterministic notions of human development and relationality. Examples of language encouraging essentializing conceptions of whiteness abound. Often theorists slip into such language even when they attempt to move beyond it, as for example Ronald L. Jackson (1999): "nor would [white people] imagine that their mere existence has somehow been calculated as the factor which declines privileges to Others" (p. 40). AnnLouise Keating (1995) has expressed grave "misgivings" about such tendencies, and she places the noun whiteness in quotation marks (p. 913). For her, recent definitions of whiteness that

attempt to deconstruct 'race' often inadvertently reconstruct it by reinforcing the belief in permanent, separate racial categories. Although they emphasize the artificial, politically and economically motivated nature of all racial classifications, their continual analysis of racialized identities undercuts their belief that 'race' is a constantly changing sociohistorical concept, not a biological fact" (p. 902)

Other theorists have emphasized the impermanence of racial identity, also pointing out the dangers of essentializing characteristics of
race: "Whatever 'whiteness' really means is constituted only
through the rhetoric of whiteness. There is no 'true essence' to
'whiteness'; there are only historically contingent constructions of
that social location" (Nakayama & Krizek, 1995, p. 293). Hence,
whiteness can only be understood as particular historically determined "discursive strategies that map the field of whiteness"
(p. 303). Keating (1995) points out the ease with which her students
conflate "whiteness" with "white people," some unable to see beyond
highly negative explorations of the latter (p. 908).

One by-product of fixing identity is fixing difference. Universal
standards of human rights, social justice norms, and intercultural
cooperation towards progressive goals are all inhibited by rigidifying
boundaries of difference. Unhappily, the valorization of difference
has already appeared in other areas of social and political theory in
the post-Cold War period. In such discourse an ideology of difference can be retrogressive and supportive of the geopolitical status
quo. For example, in "Culture, communication, and control: A quest
for order and social harmony," the prominent communication theorist John C. Merrill (1999) finds that "As the third world sees it, order
and discipline are preferable to freedom and competition" (p. 1).

George Lipsitz (1995) has called for commensurate articulations
of human identity that overcome the essentialization of whiteness
and other racial rigidities. But Henry Louis Taylor's (1995) response
to Lipsitz's prescription is a reminder of the power basis of whiteness: "[U]nity across the color line has foundered. This happens because the ideology of whites derive from racial exploitation and
oppression" (p. 404). His solution, however, is not to retreat to the
simplistic binary oppositions Keating's students so quickly fall into.
Rather, interracial cooperation and black-white unity can be
achieved through social planning, which "promotes the interests of
both blacks and whites. This will require stimulating public discourse on the 'real' economic, social, and political issues affecting
blacks, whites, and the entire nation" (pp. 404–405). Taylor returns
to the bottom line of all race theory, which is the power base as revealed in social structures; however, he affirms the capability of
white people to move beyond the current pathology of whiteness defined in whiteness theory.

African American drama has not accepted unchanging binary
oppositions; instead, it has proposed the importance of interracial
communication and the commonality of black and white identities
despite the political realities of oppression and exclusivity. George
C. Wolfe's critique of racial stereotypes, the play *The Colored Mu-*

seum (1991), opened the door for new conceptions of racial identity. But the 1990s American theatre had not progressed further than hermetic monologues that question fixations on race and all-encompassing definitions. *Fires in The Mirror* (1996), by Anna Deavere Smith, includes such a monologue by Wolfe himself. Speaking directly to the interracial audience, he cautions,

But I am—not—going to place myself *(pause)* in relationship to our whiteness, I will talk about your whiteness if we want to talk about that. . . . My Blackness does not resis-ex-re-exist in relationship to your whiteness. (p. 494)

However, what Hansberry and Baldwin envisioned, and what Henry Louis Taylor called for again in the 1990s, is more than a realization that definitions of difference cannot restrict human identity—interpreted by most of Smith's characters in individualistic terms. More than that, the new theatre without stereotypes must construct new regions of relationality beyond dominant racial definitions. This work can build upon the perceptions of earlier African American playwrights as they sought to engage white and black characters in dialectic that explored deeper understandings of themselves. The American theatre needs to pick up where Lorraine Hansberry's *Les Blancs* left her characters—with raised hands of unity attempting greater understanding and intimacy in cooperative efforts.

Stuart Hall (1996) has called for a new understanding of racial identity that avoids essentializing trajectories. His placement of "ethnicity" within an historical, and therefore developmental, context, avoids determinist, transhistorical definitions of race. He terms this new approach "the new ethnicity." It understands "the place of history, language, and culture in the construction of subjectivity and identity, as well as the fact that all discourse is placed, positioned, situated, and all knowledge is contextual" (p. 29). As such, the new ethnicity perceives racial identities as complex instead of one-dimensional and changeless, as permeable instead of deterministic.

To historicize whiteness keeps open the possibility of change over time within race identities while at the same time allowing for a synchronic understanding of levels of identity within the individual. In the latter sense, white individuals can perceive their identities as multifaceted, comprised of positive aspects that may be enlisted to overcome dominant structures of thought and practice within the Western construct. Such openness was not usually apparent to first-wave whiteness theorists, who uplifted the abstraction "whiteness " in part as an effectual replacement for "white racism," a phrase possessing too much emotional resonance in American culture to withstand the new levels of discourse hoped for by the incipient movement.

We have only to note the substitution of "racial events" for "racism" among prominent Clinton Administration officials and speech writers to find confirmation of this judgment. However, as we have seen, the choice "whiteness" has come with baggage of its own, not so much emotional as reifying and totalizing.

Definitions of whiteness have usually centered around social and political formulas that present a rhetorical position. Thus, whiteness is short for "the discourse of whiteness," which is perceived in terms of the perpetuation of power. Daniel Bernardi's definition is drawn from recent scholarship: "The discourse of whiteness refers to the persistence of racial hierarchies that, in the United States, have systematically privileged those who count as white—generally European Americans—at the expense of those who do not count as white—generally non-European Americans" (1996, p. 104). In this passage, whiteness seems to be for Bernardi a sustained position of dominance within society. In the same article, however, his definition shifts to embody cultural attributes: "a representational and narrative construction with identifiable properties and a specific history" (p. 107). Bernardi's shifting definition of whiteness is typical of its nonspecific usage in current theory, creating problems when such a floating term is reified into actual human beings. Fred Pfeil (1997) laments the recent equation of the hegemonic goal of whiteness with white people, citing examples by journalists after the Oklahoma City bombing, which, according to *Washington Post* writer Juan Williams, was committed by "white men in their natural state" (in Pfeil, 1997, p. 22). To this, Pfeil replies, "such a broad-brush portrait of American white men, or, for that matter, of any gender and/or racial-coded group, is bound to occlude more than it reveals. . . ." (p. 22).

Pfeil rejects the reductionist equations of whiteness with white people as a group, finding instead a wider ground upon which white men in particular can begin to construct new modes of relationality beyond exclusivity:

to be men 'for something; for equality, for feelings' and against a business culture inimical to both—they would have to join with those both spiritually and materially alienated from its code of hyperrationality and repressive selfishness and to work with them to construct an alternative and oppositional culture in both the public and the private spheres. (p. 31)

Such perspectives seek to redefine universal definitions of the human so as not to exclude any group: a "universal extention of the universal, a universal without a remainder, without an outside," as Warren Montag (1997) has put it (p. 289). These new openings may prevent once and for all attempts to exclude any group from the hu-

man, while appreciating the commonality of human rights standards and social justice issues around the world. Culture is here
seen as primarily educational and progressive, not static and determined, much as Matthew Arnold envisioned it in *Culture and Anarchy* (1960). For Arnold, culture remained an exploratory tool for
progressive change, not an ontology defining particular originative
peoples. A similar outlook appears in African American drama,
where black and white characters probe pragmatic rather than defi-
nitional views of race. Far from essentializing race into groups with
power and groups without power, these playwrights recognize the
efficacy of open definitions of race wherein interracial cooperation
and tolerance are primarily transformative.

Chapter 11

CONCLUSION: COMMON PLACES
FOR WORLD DRAMA

CYNICAL SURVIVAL, UNSPECIFIC LIBERATION, AND POLITICAL MOMENTUM

Social justice drama looks towards innovative means of locating areas of human living heretofore untouched by the theatrical and cinematic forms of dominant cultures. However, it must also explore, as Brecht and others urged, new structural forms that enable an oppositional alternative to those same self-perpetuating dominant representational traditions. Furthermore, dramatic and cinematic forms that expose structural injustices need to include themes that endorse the unifying potentials of heretofore separate disenfranchised groups, stressing the commonality of exploited majorities. To these ends, alienation techniques become shock therapy against the conformist forces of transnational monoculture—wakeup calls against the complacency of corporatism's "one world." Ever new possibilities for solidarity and coalition building need to be explored through the drama and its audience development experimentation.

Retreat into the Individual

Recognition of the fundamental but elusive unity of the masses—who by the early nineteenth century were no longer commonly referred to as "the mob"—came early in the industrial era among certain romanticist writers. Wordsworth in *The Prelude* envisioned the potential for unity, rather than alienation, among the urban populace:

> among the multitudes
> Of that huge city, oftentimes was seen
> Affectingly set forth, more than elsewhere
> Is possible, the unity of men. (1966, p. 286)

Later, Dickens and Engels offered glimpses of human solidarity, as the organizational capabilities of the urban working classes became more apparent when their concentrated numbers grew throughout the nineteenth century. In the early twentieth century, Erwin Piscator, founder of the Proletarian Theatre in Germany, proclaimed that "No longer is the individual with his private, personal fate the heroic factor of the new drama, but Time itself, the fate of the masses" (in Ewen, 1970, p. 74). For Piscator, committed organizations of citizens, not lone individuals, would advance the cause of social justice, a reality that has on the whole been overlooked in the dramas of the new millennium's advent years. Group protagonists no longer seem the preferred choice of contemporary political drama, as we have seen in the works of such diverse writers as Kushner in the First World and Alea in the Third World. For these and other important practitioners, social solidarity seems unattainable for the disaffected bourgeois intellectual, who remains preoccupied with either the individual pursuit of a rapidly disintegrating national culture (Kushner), or a self-centered, but elusive desire than cannot be fulfilled (Alea).

Much of current political drama is dissatisfied with the inevitable partisan nature of the task, preferring instead to document the subjectivity of individuals who attempt social change rather than the dynamics of social change itself as it is undertaken through group interaction. The straightforward exploration of class solidarity evident in Hauptmann's *The Weavers* (1892) often has been replaced by the angst of solitary individuals under social oppression, whose cry expresses a world-weary defeatism. Other writers, among them Terry Gomez, Diane Glancy, and Sherman Alexie, present characters who compellingly represent the negative effects of social neglect and discrimination, but stop short of representing the positive forms of relatedness that foster progressive change. Dramatic forms that represent group solidarity within the project of social transformation are seldom produced, while films that reveal internal dissension or the ubiquity of a globalized transnational culture prevail. What may be lacking among political dramatists and filmmakers today is not creativity, motivation, or even conviction, but rather a clear vision of the pathways toward positive change.

The general turn away from socially committed partisan drama should not come as a surprise, since the general tendency has been accurately predicted by Raymond Williams (1989a), among others:

The often successful attempt to de-politicize Brecht, by bringing up the elements of cynical survival and unspecific liberation and playing down the firm attachments to a common condition and common struggle, is characteristic of that phrase of accommodation and incorporation of the avant-garde which happened so widely, in the West, after 1950. (p. 91)

In recent forms, it seems that the political momentum of social justice drama has given way to a vague or pseudo-liberation, akin to Williams' prophetic summary of postmodern popular culture and its New York Pop Art predecessor: that it only confirmed "the pattern of the settlement: old orders and young pseudo-freedoms" (1989b, p. 68). To be sure, Brecht's seminal theatre of alienation was not without its shortcomings. His plays typically present an isolated individual against the total system. As such, they fall short of integrating group protagonists in conscious and focused class struggle onto his dramas of social analysis, a representation that would reveal a means towards the goal of progressive change. Brecht's best plays represent the failures of individual characters within social systems. While this trajectory focuses on outward rather than inward obstacles to human freedom, it remains negative, with no positive diagnosis for change.

Williams has called for a new appreciation of naturalism, the form Brecht and other innovators had initially rebelled against by turning to nonrepresentational forms such as expressionism and surrealism. Williams (1989b) believed that naturalism, especially in its cinematic and theatrical forms, could provide the exposition needed in a world increasingly enthralled by late capitalism's globalizing cultural monoliths: "there are social realities that cry out for [naturalism's] kind of serious, detailed recording and diagnostic attention" (p. 115). By and large, Williams found existing cinematic and theatrical fare lacking in such expositions: "there are still vast areas of the lives of our own people which have scarcely been looked at in a serious way" (p. 116). To this drama of social exposition must be added a political drama of some momentum—that includes plots and characters in social contexts that construct positive means of social change. In fact, such representations may be beyond the capacity of existing dramatic forms. One of the best recent expositions of human rights, David Riker's *The City* (1999), stops short just as the factory workers of the final vignette begin an unplanned work stoppage. The dramatic depiction of positive, cooperative social change has remained elusive throughout the twentieth century. What early playwrights of naturalism like Hauptmann began has not been pursued with any significant results. Why is it that there has not been a single significant stage or screen drama about the civil rights movement of the mid-century, surely the most positive social mobilization of the century in the United States? The few attempts by Hollywood have produced only tepid, even retrograde formula films. The most popular instance is Allan Parker's *Mississippi Burning* (1988), which has the FBI—a politically retrograde institution at the time (!)—single-handedly bringing justice to the deep south. Incredibly, the film entirely excludes the social protesters whose organizations abolished legal segregation through sustained, heroic actions of civil disobedience.

Clearly, however, corporate power structures and their not-so-alternative "independent" film and off-Broadway theatre systems can be held only partially responsible for the dearth of positive forms of social drama. More recently, postmodernist relativism—a complex of ideas by no means confined to intellectuals and academics—and establishment-oriented identity politics have helped steer socially conscious writers towards the kinds of "cynical survival" and "unspecific liberation" subject matter Williams observed in late twentieth-century political drama. To achieve the level of political momentum Williams envisioned, dramatic structures that feature group protagonists must reemerge. In this regard, it is not reductive to claim simply that group protagonists are necessary—but not sufficient—for plays that move beyond the mere documentation of social oppression and its symptoms to the articulation of positive means for social change. Such dramas must include other qualities as well—motivated characters, a focused dialectic, a relevant context presented with specificity and verisimilitude—goals seldom, if ever, achieved by the current commercial fare.

This is not to say that political drama that stops at the representation of social inequities, dominant structures, and political corruption has not served the cause of social change in important ways. It continues to reveal what is hidden and denied by dominant social structures, thereby informing the public significantly. What is missing are narratives that move one step further, into transitional realms where political movements become effective through sustained action. Recent political playwrights worldwide continue to profess a commitment to pragmatic social consciousness but fall into the familiar pattern of avoiding the presentation of actual group interaction that is deliberate and positive. For example, the Nigerian playwright Tess Akaeke Onwueme (1993) writes expressly to build political awareness within her Nigerian audiences: "I feel that history is made, not by accepting history as it is, but by people rewriting it. . . . I consider writing to be a dialogue between the writer and the society. . . . People create social conditions and people can change social conditions for the better" (p. 11). In Onwueme's *The Reign of Wazobia* (1993), the promise of a wise women's rule that will overcome traditional feudal structures is clearly and forcefully articulated by the characters. Although Wazobia, a disaffected resister, would undertake a program grounded on the positive premise that social structures can be fundamentally improved through grass-roots solidarity movements, her viewpoint remains only a vision, followed by no effective cooperative action. Like Brecht's major works, Onwueme's dramas compellingly present the negativities of social protest and nonconformity without programmatic representation and group agendas. Their dramas, often set in a distant or legendary past, are in this respect prolegomena to narratives of social solidarity, articulating the pitfalls and impediments to effective social mobilization and democratic resistance, but stopping short of representing momentous group actions with all their dynamic intrigue and heroic commitment. Also in ways similar to Brechtian stagecraft, Onwueme avoids the actions of group leaders in political movements, focusing instead on individuals in isolated struggle against a repressive establishment.

Return to the Group Protagonist?

Clearly, new possibilities of solidarity and coalition building for receptive audiences need to be explored through stage and screen. The late-nineteenth-century example of Hauptmann's plays, particularly *The Weavers*, broke new ground in naturalism by attempting to explore the community, as opposed to individuals and families. Further, it presented class divisions with unprecedented power and probity. Moving beyond accepted conventions of late-Victorian plot structure, *The Weavers*, for Raymond Williams, "is a deliberate chronicle, without surprise, without uncertainty, without complication, except insofar as these are generated by the collective action of the weavers." What replaces the romantic nineteenth-century plot is "the determinism of the operation of a class . . . the revolt of the body of weavers, springing from their poverty" (1952, p. 176). Williams saw that this new subject matter transformed the dramatic form profoundly. The dramatic power of *The Weavers* lies in the event as stage action, hence, traditional structural elements such as situation, plot, spokespeople and *raisonneur* characters are abandoned in favor of what Williams terms the play's 'choral' element. This is represented mainly through typical, everyday group activities: "the interaction of the group *as a whole*" through ongoing bargaining and brinkmanship with management—the employers and their corporate bureaucracy (p. 177). Williams compares this dramatic method with the novel, insofar as Hauptmann focuses on the sort of broad descriptions of context (scene) and persons with a commentary (choral) form of dialogue. Although Williams qualifies his praise of Hauptmann's innovative method by acknowledging the novel's superior capacity for such environmental descriptions, he nonetheless finds distinct possibilities in Hauptmann's power of expression. Williams also recognizes alternative forms of social drama, notably in the expressionism of August Strindberg and Ernst Toller, but he finds their attempts to report class antagonism limited either by too narrow a focus on isolated individuals (Strindberg), or by oversimplified sloganeering (Toller). In the case of Toller, however, he rejects the particular plays but applauds the method, that is, Toller's use of direct commentary and class focus in such plays as *Hoopla!* (1927) and *Masses and Man* (1921).

While political drama throughout the twentieth century has refused to follow in the direction of Hauptmann towards an exposition of progressive change on the social level, screen and stage plays have melded environment into the social lives of their characters to such an extent that group protagonists often have made accommodations with their environments, at times initiating significant social transformations. In Peng Xiaolian's *The Women's Story* (1989), as we have seen, the three women return to their village empowered with knowledge of the new freedoms available to them in the city. At the film's end, they have learned how to stand up to the local thugs who enforce traditional dominant structures in rural China. The final scene is no static denouement but instead represents the women as they advance as one towards their would-be oppressors. Although lacking the complexity and scope of *The Weavers*, Xiaolian's film offers portraits of three diverse women who unite at the street level through their political education. In this regard, the cityscape, rather than the more typical rural landscape, becomes the chief iconographic motif throughout the film. The city not only represents for the women their political education but also offers possibilities for greater personal and group freedom through economic and social self-actualization. The simple naturalism of the film's cinematography and acting style confirms Raymond Williams' view, referring to early twentieth-century expressionistic drama, that "a set of techniques" alone is not enough to create coherent drama of social justice (1977, p. 223). In Xiaolian's film, nonrealistic elements and direct commentary prove unnecessary for its social message.

Although recent political drama generally lacks the self-assurance and discernment evident in Hauptmann's exposition of social mobilization, it is not incapable of presenting group protagonists in effective dramatic narratives. A case in point is Manuel Octavio Gomez's *Now It's up to You* (*Ustedes tienen la palabra*, 1974), which presents characters immersed in the daily life of social transformation under Cuban communist policy. While the film is an effective and wise analysis of popular justice, concluding that traditions of justice that assume individualistic, property-oriented mentalities linger even in revolutionary practice, it remains primarily negative in its approach. Put more positively, Gomez admonishes vigilance in the pursuit of new social structures, reminding his largely Cuban audience that there is no clear demarcation between political apathy, social hypocrisy, and counterrevolutionary thinking. While the practice of popular justice in the film is a difficult undertaking, rife with pitfalls and backsliding, the proleptic title, *Now It's up to You*, suggests a revolution largely gone astray from its originative ideals, but one that is redeemable, with a positive future. Its revolutionary praxis lacks the affirming assumptions of the factory workers in *The Weavers*, who remain in charge of their own destinies, despite the suffering that goes with the struggle. Still, Gomez's citizenry are not without an enduring commitment to egalitarian social goals, no matter how latent such ideals may appear. The basic presupposition of the film involves a progressive evolutionary outlook and so qualifies as an effective drama of social justice.

Despite the present commitment to partisan theatre and film in several Third World societies, no single formula for success has been discovered and developed. The New Cinema movement throughout Latin America shows perhaps the clearest commitment to the development of an international drama of social justice, as recent national film traditions have consciously crossfertilized filmic images and themes that expose systemic oppression and class struggle. Brazilian *cinema novo*, Cuban state films, Mexican alternative expressions, and at least a half dozen other national film traditions across Latin America and the Caribbean share audiences and filmmakers with political commitment. The future is promising but always in doubt as to whether such traditions will continue to flourish when they remain underfunded and subject to various degrees of international and local pressure to offer a more conformist product congruent with the exigencies of global capital.

Considering the General and Specific

Two approaches to politically based drama have been rearticulated in recent decades. The more ambitious one, held by Brecht, searches for dramatic forms in varied contexts that go beyond the

mere critical analysis of human oppression to somehow enable social transformation by representing, or suggesting, the means to
such ends. However, Brecht was more poetic than concrete about
the specific features of drama and performance that would allow
such goals, and later in his career he became less doctrinaire and
more open to changing possibilities in new cultural contexts: "How
can the shackled, ignorant, freedom-and-knowledge-seeking human being of our century, the tormented and heroic, abused and ingenious, the changeable and the world-changing human being of
this frightful and important century achieve his own theatre which
will help him to master not only himself but also the world?" (in
Calderwood & Toliver, 1968, p. 275). Nonetheless, Brecht never gave
sufficient attention to the diversity of world cultures nor to their innumerable performance traditions, which have become more apparent to artists and writers in recent decades, in part through the
technological channels of the global village. Brecht's lack of attention to multicultural concerns is perhaps beside the point, since his
argument was to back away from the prescriptive approach of his
earlier career to allow each society to finds its own way and "achieve
his own theatre."

The second approach to political drama is less ambitious of concrete goals for change but just as clear about exposing the forms of
systemic injustice routinely denied by the communicative channels
of dominant culture. Martha Nussbaum's emphasis on the dramatic imagination as it explores the social particularities of oppression stops short of offering the how and the why of such actions, as
Brecht would want. Instead, her drama values the extended hypo-
thetical example to place the spectator in the shoes of the disenfranchised. Her imagination cares not to distinguish between forms of
emotional response—whether empathic or distanced, for example.
Rather, she seeks educational value in the imagination, which can
enable, say, a young man to experience how it must feel to face concerns particular to women in most societies. Accordingly, Nussbaum
is more confident than Brecht that the spectator can transcend the
drama's individualistic bias to question the dominant values of her
or his society. Acknowledging second-wave feminism's connection
of the personal with the political, she does not find problematic the
audience's interest in the details of the characters' individual lives.
Rather, she would make connections to universal human rights
standards through the concrete and particular of character, action,
and scene. For Nussbaum, Greek comedy presented classical Greek
audiences with the means to apply abstract notions of justice and
social wellness to the particularities of the power structures within

the *polis*. However, Nussbaum (1997) questions whether drama by itself can become a socially transforming activity:

Literature does not transform society single-handed. . . . Certain ideas about others may be grasped for a time and yet not be acted upon, so powerful are the forces of habit and the entrenched structures of privilege and convention. Nonetheless, the artistic form makes its spectator perceive, for a time, the invisible people of their world—at least a beginning of social justice. (p. 94)

Throughout these chapters we have seen dramas that expose the hidden and give substance and voice to the disempowered, achieving the minimum goal of Nussbaum's vision. But is exposure, as Nussbaum suggests and Brecht's plays for the most part aim for, all that political drama can and should achieve? Moreover, is the mere exposure of repressive actions and institutions enough, given the powerful centripetal force of globalization? Is there an uncertainty principle of sorts at work when "authentic" dramatic forms at local levels achieve international recognition? Can such works retain their original political identity under the powerful spotlight of the international public sphere, or will they fall apart beyond recognition like so many subatomic particles? Here there is reason for greater hope. While it has been proven again and again that local political criticism is often mitigated or even entirely removed when reproduced for global consumption, as, for instance, we have seen in certain films and plays about Native Americans, it is also true that the international public sphere remains a rapidly expanding channel for human rights consciousness.

Growing awareness of the universality of human rights standards can only continue as computer and other telecommunications technologies develop. This may only mean that there will be more avenues through which dominant ideologies can travel, but it also means that there will be more pathways for alternative voices, pathways that enter the home itself and are thus harder to control through government and corporate regulation. World opinion does affect matters of social justice, and the multiplicity of private and public organizations have already used high technology to expose otherwise hidden social repression (Lengel, 1999). In drama, the movement to internationalize cinema has created a human rights community that communicates through such technologically related avenues as film festivals and televised awards recognition. One such Cinderella story has been the global recognition given the Iranian film industry, which, like the Cuban film industry, focuses on developing international discourses—both artistic and political—through its products. Such successes counter the notion that globalization will be dominated by the most powerful and predatory actions of corporatism and militarism.

A related problem raised by Michael Etherton (1982) is the exploitation of alternative forms of drama by local elites. Observing recent developments in Africa's postcolonial countries, he dismissed many attempts to create political drama, finding such works too "intellectual" and unable to touch the mass of the people despite their purported concern with them (p. 318). In some instances he finds that local repressive regimes have simply co-opted social justice drama for their own narrow purposes. Such local threat to popular freedom of expression demonstrates the need to examine the necessary conditions that make political drama culturally authentic. In this regard Wole Soyinka's approach directly answers Etherton's charge that grassroots arts movements are doomed to local co-optation, and Jameson's contention that alternative political forms will end in globalized oblivion (1990, 1991).

For Soyinka, only a conscientious program of clear national goals for political equality is capable of overcoming the penchant in colonial and postcolonial Africa for the surrender of democratic aims to local political elites and transnational corporate interests. In fact, Nigeria's abundant oil reserves have made the country a geopolitical target for economic and military control over the decades following independence (Drilling and Killing, 1998). Nigeria's alternative forms of political expression have centered on the universities since the vibrant early years of postcolonial formation. At first the newly independent government supported a national theatre movement in the interest of uniting an ethnically diverse nation, whose borders were, from the perspective of African cultures, arbitrarily imposed by colonialist powers. However, Northern groups, favored by the British from the incipient years of colonial rule, controlled the government and military, and soon sought dominance and self-aggrandizement (Cohen, 1998a). Complicating the task of developing a drama reflective of the new nation's ideals were the undemocratic and repressive practices of these controlling local elites, who were negatively depicted by Nigerian playwrights. Moreover, the awkward nature of the dramatic form itself, which depends for its inspiration on local cultural expression but was derivative of Western artistic structures— plot, character, setting, and so on. Yet another complicating element was the postcolonial intellectual's dependence upon Western concepts of democratic practice and organizational methods for populist mobilization. Thus self-determination was for Soyinka and other Nigerian playwrights of his and later generations both a banner of change and a limitation, since all intellectuals recognized the value of Western political methods in the shrinking world of the twentieth century.

Soyinka realized that only broad-based education programs, organized and supported by a national movement, would produce the sort of political drama for social change envisioned by the Brechtian method. He soon realized that a national movement could be augmented by a regional movement of postcolonial nations with geographical and economic ties, and a similar history of colonial occupation. Therefore, Soyinka along with other Nigerians have valued the opinions and forms of expression offered by South Africa's newly formed democratic government and its internationally renowned leader, the recently retired Nelson Mandela. They recognized that a strong regional movement with cultural and political dimensions could help mitigate the formidable influence of geopolitical power. Whereas one postcolonial country alone would struggle with forming its own cultural and economic future, several countries together, including two or three populous states, could create a secure space for voices of independence and integrity.

The move from national cultural self-determination to regional and even global alternative formations remains a possibility for the Third World, in Latin America as well as sub-Saharan Africa. Other cultural spheres where this may occur include the Arab-speaking world, where fictional forms and cinema remain strong points of contact across nation states, and in the Muslim world in general, which is only beginning to develop an independent international marketplace of ideas. The Iranian film industry is perhaps the most recent success story in Islam. Within only a few years it has managed to create a highly sophisticated and complex response both to the geopolitical threat of dominance and to the undemocratic pressures within Iranian society. It is important to remember that the self-determination advocated by these recent successful alternative movements did not develop in a vacuum. Rather, they were greatly enhanced by international recognition through Western-style cultural organizations. Thus the international film festival movement—always growing in number and diversity—as well as the increasing importance of international awards and the publicity derived from them, have fostered film movements in Latin America and Iran, often directly inspiring local filmmakers. Films, as well as stage plays, are much more readily available in educational and public settings than they were only a few years ago, a circumstance also contributing to the influence of future film development.

China's nascent but highly creative film movement has been inspired significantly by the importation of foreign films, which have been viewed eagerly and studiously by Chinese intellectuals and artists as well as the general public. Although most of these films are mainstream commercial formulas, this has not prevented "fifth-generation" Chinese filmmakers from using their film techniques to create alternatives to those same products. Chinese filmmakers, perhaps not unlike most filmmakers everywhere, are testing the boundaries of cultural and political expression imposed upon them by their government. Perhaps understandably, this frontier remains fickle and its bureaucratic justifications ambivalent, as China as a whole struggles with its centuries-old dilemma of how much West to let into the East. Compared to Western alternative standards, the filmmakers of the "fifth generation" have been rather indirect in their approach to social justice. They generally prefer a cultural analysis of timely issues—such as the adjustments women must make to break free from the restrictions of village and family, and the debilitating isolation of traditional rural life—to the more confrontational approaches found in many Western political forms. However, this reluctance to engage in direct criticism of existing institutions cannot be attributed to China's "culture of consensus," since China has demonstrated a great capacity for direct political confrontation during the Cultural Revolution of the 1960s, albeit in a highly repressive manner. Rather, young Chinese filmmakers realize that their art form has the potential to enlist positive government support, but only if they pursue an artistic and thematic policy of cautious gradualism.

In the case of Nigeria, the generation of playwrights following Soyinka have moved beyond the aim of creating a national culture of unification through the incorporation of local ritual and myth into a social dialectic, as Soyinka himself accomplished. What Andrew Gurr (1980) describes as the "quietist wisdom, resignation, and acceptance of one's fate," characteristic of Soyinka's use of the Ogun mysteries in his play, *The Strong Breed*, has been discarded in favor of a more directly confrontational approach in the plays of Femi Osofisan. As a member of the second generation of postcolonial dramatists in Nigeria, Osofisan has sought to overcome what Herbert Marcuse (1970) called the co-optation of "negative thinking" by advanced capitalist society. Instead, Osofisan's plays present the positive and utopian attributes of Jurgen Habermas' "life world," which is capable of overcoming its "colonization" by postmodern commodification and bureaucratic rationality (Habermas, 1992, p. 266). He has answered Marcuse's call for a dialectic that would "risk defining freedom in such a way that people become conscious of and recognize it as something that is nowhere already in existence" (1970, p. 68). If Osofisan's dramatic characters embody Marcuse's "happy consciousness" of the citizenry under advanced capitalism, they are also aware of their own unhappiness and resent the false values they live by. By raising the issue of the middle-class intellectual's co-optation in his plays, Osofisan avoids the charge, made by some Marxists against much of Third World drama, of offering a narcissistic consciousness, a preoccupation with middle-class modes of thinking and behavior at the expense of the exposition of working-class issues. Rather, his characters are haunted by their own inability to avoid the seductions of local political elites and transnational corporate influence.

In Osofisan's *No More the Wasted Breed*, *Birthdays Are Not for Dying*, and *The Oriki of a Grasshopper*, isolated individuals of conscience are shown as incapable of resisting what Marcuse describes as "the fate of being absorbed by what they refute" (1964, p. 70). But the playwright is comprehensive in his critical analysis of postcolonial globalization. These plays boldly reject Nigeria's cultural past for the sake of a redesigned future of social justice, but they just as clearly attack Western ideology with its profit motive and double dealings. The reconciliation of the two young lovers in *Oriki*, Moni and Imaro, transforms their self-pity into a reaffirmation of the social struggle for their nation's liberation. Osofisan seems to be saying that only organized resistance of a sustained and uncorrupted kind can defeat the structural evils of this world. Faith in either traditional religion or the culture of geopolitical power will not bring about positive social change. The dramatization of this viewpoint is as close as any dramatist or filmmaker in the twentieth century has come to Brecht's mandate for a revitalized political theatre. Moreover, Osofisan's use in his plays of parody, ritual, and intense self-reflective analysis—the probing self-examination of the middle-class intellectual—lowers the chances of their eventual co-optation by existing commercial entertainment forms. His uncompromising probity cannot easily be circumvented or redefined, but instead offers a positive life world in the sense Habermas envisions.

AUDIENCE PERCEPTION AND CROSS-CULTURAL SOLUTIONS

Considering the various degrees of success of political drama throughout the world and the increased dependence upon intergovernmental and nongovernmental organizations for progressive change, Michael Etherton's assessment of the efficacy of drama presented in the introduction to this book needs to be reconsidered: "The theatre, and even its 'revolutionary' drama, remains inaccessible to the mass of people. The socially committed theatre contributes to the process of social change only insofar as the intellectuals themselves acquire political consciousness" (1982, p. 318). The oft-repeated binary of intellectual versus popular theatre needs to be probed more thoughtfully as to the nature of social change. History has shown that progressive change begins almost always not with a general uprising among an awakened oppressed populace, but through persistent middle-class agitation, education, and organization. The broad-based advantage comes only at a certain point, with the wide participation of coalitions within middle-class and working-class associations, professional organizations, private member societies, guilds, unions, and so on (Williams, 1982). From this perspective, the capacity of partisan dramatic forms to reach "the mass of the people" remains only one indicator of social effectiveness. Thoughtful ideas must first affect thoughtful people, those either endowed with the advantages of formal education or enlightened through the experience of direct social struggle. Thus, postcolonial Nigeria's early recognition of the value of its own university system offered the locus of political expression for a highly articulate and knowledgeable element of its populace.

Still, political drama needs to be clear and unambiguous—without losing artistic nuance—if it is to persuade any group within the society. Here the decades-old conflict in Hollywood between profit and political statement has presented a product that is typically ambivalent towards—even counterproductive of—progressive change. Tim Robbins' anxiety over the reception of his film about political people (as opposed to a political film), *Cradle Will Rock*, quoted at length in the introduction, is governed by the same fecklessness. Robbins avoids direct political discourse in the film because he finds that, first, most people involved in the social struggle at the time of the film, the 1930s, were not politically aware, and second, by showing his characters' "hunger" rather than their ideas, the point is made. Both arguments seem weak. While it is true that most people affected by the Great Depression were not schooled in political ideology, it is reductive to believe that political ideas did not pervade the ordinary lives of most people struggling with unemployment and underemployment. Robbins' second argument, that the depiction of suffering rather than verbal dialectic is sufficient to make a political statement, can be answered by Brecht, who knew that the documentation of suffering alone is not efficacious. To inform, political drama must use critical analysis of the structural harms within the society, since the implications of social suffering are not always—usually not—apparent in mediated forms. Moreover, education for Brecht always assumed a clear ideological framework, which he increasingly perceived as approachable to the general populace.

The Brechtian vision today remains among the most effective politically based stage and screen traditions, simply because it leaves the particulars of dramatic form to the specific cultural situation while emphasizing the need for clear analysis and critical dialectic. The latter is achieved either through the dialogue of the characters themselves or by others means—plot development, choral commentary, scenography. Most essential to Brecht (1964) are the implications of the social documentation from any given period: "in order to put living reality in the hands of living people in such way that it can be mastered. . . . Our conception of *realism* needs to be broad and political, free from aesthetic restrictions and independent of convention" (p. 109). Thus the form itself of Epic Theatre matters less than the discovery of the reality of oppression revealed through the drama. To achieve this, a critical dialectic must accompany the dramatic exposition, either overtly or indirectly. This is what is achieved in the most effective films and plays examined in these chapters. In David Riker's *The City* (*La ciudad*, 1999), for instance, the characters in the four stories seldom express verbally a critical discourse about their oppression, yet the plot structures, socioeconomic situations, and character behavior reveal a clear critical stance towards the economic repression of Third World immigrant labor in First World settings. Unlike *Cradle Will Rock*, Riker's film does not inhibit the political message for the sake of commercial formula. Such elements in Robbins' film, such as the use of popular screen actors, glamorous celebrity characters, the heavy use of 1930s nostalgia in the *mise-en-scène* and musical score, and certain scenes of pure entertainment, prevent serious analysis of the structural dilemmas of the era. On the contrary, clarity and consistent political analysis prove the most important prescription for the drama of social justice.

The question raised in the introduction, whether disenfranchised audiences need a Brechtian distancing device, must be reconsidered in light of the globalizing effects of advanced capitalism. It is true that in many Third World settings, audiences may be prepared to connect the dramatic action with social themes without theatrical distancing devices, since they have been made keenly aware of the contradictions between official words and actions, and since they often are already alienated from the values propagated by the institutions of power within their own countries. On the other hand, the global reach of dominant ideologies is such that even communities within the broad populace who experience official lies daily nonetheless can still be influenced by the culture that inhibits basic human rights. Under such circumstances, the alienation effect of Epic Theatre may have validity. Making strange what even the oppressed have come to accept unquestioningly can open windows to new perspectives. As we have seen, Brecht came to leave open the specificity of Epic stagecraft, realizing that all distancing techniques in drama were relative cultural formations and therefore not effective under all circumstances.

The question of whether all audiences need distancing devices to see the reality of oppression in their lives moves beyond either/or solutions. Yes, certain audiences under certain circumstances already comprehend the irony of official ideology, often in subtle and profound ways, but on the other hand all audiences have at least the potential of being cajoled, enticed, seduced, intimidated, confused, or simply deceived into accepting the values that support their own oppression. Levels of education and distance from dominant institutions have little to do with the ability of dominant ideologies to reach even the most remotely excluded groups today. Still, for audiences made aware of their own oppression by the reality of daily living, empathic response to dramatic characters may not prevent a critical distance that reveals the social causes of oppression. Under such circumstances, Brecht's alienation devices are unnecessary. For these spectators, empathy may actually enhance political analysis. On such theatrical occasions, direct political solutions may even be possible, as in the plays of *teatro campesino*. This goes beyond Brecht and the American political dramas of the 1930s in the degree to which programmatic solutions are possible within the performance occasion. If Brecht typically stopped at level two of Alan Monroe's Motivation Sequence: (1) Attention; (2) Need, some highly focused political drama has followed Monroe through all five steps, including (3) Satisfaction; (4) Visualization; and finally (5) Action. Brecht commonly stopped after revealing to audiences the underlying systemic causes of social oppression without offering specific solutions and the means to bring them about. Thus Suzanne Langer's view that ideology and entertainment are exclusive in drama, that "sociological abstraction has no meaning in the theatre," needs to be rejected in favor of a more open understanding of the educational possibilities of drama (see Langer, 1968, p. 257).

What threatens all forms of alternative drama, however, is their assimilation to widespread commercial forms. Fredric Jameson (1990) cautions that expressions of solidarity such as various forms of political drama have remained efficacious by keeping independent of the market and commodity system. Moreover, authentic political art does not emerge merely by infusing the art work with political slogans and class-identifying signals. Rather, "class struggle, and the slow and intermittent development of genuine class consciousness, are themselves the process whereby a new and organic group constitutes itself, whereby the collective breaks through the reified atomization . . . of capitalist social life" (p. 24). Jameson's point is that political awareness develops across broad areas of hu-

man living and within communities, not within one area—drama—
for one individual alone. Thus time and social space are needed to
nurture political education. Postcolonial Nigerian playwrighting has
profited immensely from its locus within communities of struggle
that have undergone just such a developing class consciousness.
Unfortunately, the sort of university communities that have fostered the creative production of Nigerian drama are not commonly
available, especially in Third World settings.

Moving beyond the dominant dichotomy of local versus global
culture, of the postcolonial versus the geopolitical, Homi Bhabha
(1994), citing Wilson Harris, offers the most affirmative new paradigm for social justice drama (more fully presented in this volume's
introduction). They call for a positive "assimilation of contraries"
and a "Third Space," which "may open the way to conceptualizing an
*inter*national culture, based not on the exoticism of multiculturalism or the *diversity* of cultures, but on the inscription and articulation of culture's *hybridity*" (p. 38). Bhabha's experience of the
ideology of difference makes him wary of the geopolitical uses of relativism. This particular co-optation is "the demand that, in analytical terms, [the 'other' culture] be always the good object of knowledge, the docile body of difference, that reproduces a relation of
domination and is the most serious indictment of the institutional
powers of critical theory" (p. 31). To counteract this tendency, Bhabha
sees cultural hybridity as a positive remedy, becoming "the cutting
edge of translation and negotiation" that successfully eludes the
politics of polarity. Less suspicious of cultural hybridity in the international public sphere, Bhabha, along with Aijaz Ahmad (1996),
views the First World translation of Third World social justice drama
as a potential cosmopolitan good, creating the necessary "*in-between*
space" for social progress. Accordingly, Bhabha would welcome
cross-cultural art forms that expose the underlying hegemonic motivations of geopolitical forces as well as the "differentialism" of repugnant creeds and ethnic exclusivity. This commonplace approach
may in the end prove the most productive for raising political consciousness through the changing idioms of social justice drama.

REFERENCES

Adedeji, A. (1993). Marginalization and marginality: Context, issues and viewpoints. In A. Adedeji (Ed.), *Africa within the world: Beyond dispossession and dependence* (pp. 1–14). London: Zed Books.

Ahmad, A. (1996). The politics of literary postcoloniality. In P. Mongia (Ed.), *Contemporary postcolonial theory* (pp. 276–293). London and New York: Arnold.

Alea, T.G. (Director), Cuban Film Institute (ICAIC). (Producer). (1966). *Death of a bureaucrat (Muerte de un burocrata)* [Film]. Center for Cuban Studies (Distributor).

———. (Director), Cuban Film Institute (ICAIC) (Producer). (1968). *Memories of underdevelopment (Memorias del subdesarollo)*. [Film].

——— (Director), Cuban Film Institute (ICAIC) (Producer). (1971). *A Cuban struggle against the demons (Unda a pelea cubana contra los demonios)* [Film].

———. (Director), Cuban Film Institute (ICAIC) (Producer). (1976). The Last Supper *(La ultima cena)* [Film].

———. (Director), Cuban Film Institute (ICAIC) Producer. (1994). *Guantanamera.* [Film]. New Yorker Films (Distributor).

———. (Director), (1995). Cuban Film Institute (ICAIC) (Producer). *Strawberry and chocolate (Fresa y chocolate)* [Film]. Robert Redford and Miramax. (Distributor).

Allen, P.G. (1986). *The sacred hoop: Recovering the feminine in American Indian traditions.* Boston: Beacon Press.

Alston, J.B. (1989). *Yoruba drama in English: Interpretation and production.* Lewiston, NY, Queenston, Ontario: Edwin Mellen Press.

Althusser, L. (1971). Ideology and ideological state apparatuses. In B. Brewster, (Trans.), *Lenin and philosophy and other essays*. New York: Monthly Review Press.

Almodovar, P. (Director), Sony Pictures Classics (Distributor). (1999). *All about my mother*. [Film].

Amado, J. (1971). *Tent of miracles*. New York: Avon Books.

An-Na'im, A.A. (1987). Religious minorities under Islamic law and the limits of cultural relativism. *Human Rights Quarterly*, 9,1–18.

———. (Ed.). (1992). *Human rights in cross-cultural perspectives: A quest for consensus*. Philadelphia: University of Pennsylvania Press.

Apted, M. (Director), (1992). *Thunderheart* [Film].

Ards, A. (1999, July 26/August 2). Organizing the hip-hop generation. *The Nation*, pp. 11–20.

Arnold, M. (1960). D. Wilson (Introduction). *Culture and anarchy*. Cambridge, Eng.: Cambridge University Press.

Attenborough, R. (Director). RCA/ Columbia Pictures (Distributor). (1982). *Ghandi* [Film].

Attridge, D. (1999, January). Innovation, literature, ethics: Relating to the other. *PMLA*, 114, 1, 20–31.

Babenco, H. (Director), New Yorker Films (Distributor). (1981). *Pixote: The survival of the weakest*. (*Pixote: Alei do mais fraco*) [Film].

Balasko, J. (Director), Miramax Zoe (Distributor). (1994) *French twist* [Film].

Baldwin, J. (1971). *Blues for mister Charlie*. In C.F. Oliver & S. Sills (Eds.), *Contemporary black drama* (pp. 250–331). New York: Scribner's.

Banta, M. (1999, March). If I forget thee, oh Jerusalem. *PMLA*, 114, 2, 175–183.

Barnes, C. (1970, November 16). Theatre: *Les blancs. The New York Times*, p. D28.

Bernardi, D. (1996). Introduction: Race and the emergence of U.S. cinema. In D. Bernardi (Ed.), *The birth of whiteness: Race and the emergence of U.S. cinema*. New Brunswick, NJ: Rutgers University Press.

Bhabha, H. (1994). *The location of culture*. London and New York: Routledge.

Biskind, P. (1999, April 5/12). On movies, money & politics: Beatty, Baldwin, Glover, Robbins, Stone and Lear. *The Nation*, pp.13–20.

Bloom, H. (1998). *Shakespeare: The invention of the human*. New York: Riverhead Books.

Bonhoeffer, D. (1967). *Letters and papers from prison*. E. Bethge, (Ed.). New York: Macmillan.

Borreca, A. (1997). "Dramaturg" the dialectic: Brecht, Benjamin, and Declan Donnellan's production of *Angels in America*. In D.R. Geis & S.F. Kruger (Eds.), *Approaching the millennium: Essays on "Angel in America."* (pp. 245–260). Ann Arbor: University of Michigan Press.

Borter, B. (1997). Moving to thought: The inspired reflective cinema of Fernando Perez. In A.M. Stock, (Ed.), *Framing Latin American cinema: Contemporary critical perspectives* (pp. 141–161). Minneapolis and London: University of Minnesota Press.

Brecht, B. (1964). *Brecht on theatre* (J. Willett, Trans.). New York: Hill and Wang.

Bronner, S.E. (1994). *Of critical theory and its theorists.* Oxford, Eng. and Cambridge, MA: Blackwell.

Calderwood, J.L., & Toliver, H.E. (eds.). (1968). *Perspectives on drama.* New York, London: Oxford University Press.

Cassirer, E. (1946). *Language and myth* (S.K. Langer, Trans.). New York: Dover Books.

Chaim, D. Ben. (1984). *Distance in the theatre: The aesthetics of audience response.* Ann Arbor: UMI Research Press.

Chanan, M. (1985). *The Cuban image: Cinema and cultural politics in Cuba.* Bloomington: Indiana University Press.

———. (1996). New cinemas in Latin America. In G. Nowell-Smith (Ed.), *The Oxford history of world cinema* (pp. 240–249.) Oxford, New York: Oxford University Press.

Cheshire, G. (1998, November 8). Revealing an Iran where the chadors are most chic. *The New York Times,* Sec. 2, p. 28.

Childress, A. (1986). *Wedding band.* In M.B. Wilkerson (Ed.), *9 plays by black women* (pp. 210–279). New York: New American Library.

Chow, R. (1996). Where have all the natives gone? In P. Mongia (Ed.), *Contemporary postcolonial theory: A reader* (pp. 122–146). London and New York: Arnold.

Churchill, W. (1992). *Fantasies of the master race: Literature, cinema and the colonization of American Indians.* Monroe, ME: Common Courage Press.

Clark, J. (1999, April 5/12). Primary colors: Green. Why the studios won't make political movies. *The Nation,* 31–33.

Clarke, G. (1980). Beyond realism: Recent black fiction and the language of "The real thing." In R.A. Lee, (Ed.), *Black fiction: New studies* in the Afro-American novel since 1945 (pp. 199–212). London: Vision Press.

Clough, M. (1999, February 22). Reflections on civil society. *The Nation,* pp. 16–18.

Cohen, R. (1998a, July 25). A Nigerian revisits his place in history. *New York Times,* p. A4.

———. (1998b, July 27). A book party promotes Nigerian elite's hold on power. *The New York Times,* p. A4.

———. (1998c, July 30). Marble mogul caters to the Nigerian capital's elite. *The New York Times,* p. 5.

Cooper, M. (1999, April 5/12). Postcards from the left: Under the cloud of Clintonism. *The Nation,* pp. 21–26.

Cornelius, W.A., Martin, P.L., & Hollifield, J.F. (Eds.). (1994), Introduction. *Controlling immigration: A global perspective.* Stanford, CA: Stanford University Press.

Corntassel, J.J. & Primeau, T.H. (1995). Indigenous "sovereignty" and international law: Revised strategies for pursuing "self-determination." *Human Rights Quarterly,* 17, 343–365.

Costner, K. (Director), Orion (Distributor), (1990). *Dances with wolves* [Film].

Craft, P.A., Clark, R., & Rowe, A. (1998, November 21). *Performing whiteness critiquing identities.* Paper presented at the National Communication Association Convention, New York.

Crow, B., & Banfield, C. (1996). *An introduction to post-colonial theatre.* Cambridge, Eng. and New York: Cambridge UP.

Davis, J. (1982). *Kullark and the dreamers.* Sydney, Australia: Currency Press.

Dewey, J. (1958). *Art as experience.* New York: Capricorn Books.

Dos Santos, N.P. (Director), New Yorker Films. (Distributor). (1977). *Tent of miracles (Tenda dos milagres).* [Film].

Drilling and killing. (1998, November 16), Editorial (No author). *The Nation,* pp. 6–7.

Dyer, R. (1993). White. In R. Dyer (Ed.), *The mother of images: Essays on representations* (pp. 256–278). New York: Routledge.

Eagleton, T. (1992). The ideology of the aesthetic. In S. Regan (Ed.), *The politics of pleasure: Aesthetic and cultural theory* (pp. 17–31). Buckingham, Eng.: Open University Press.

Ebrahimian, G. (Director and Writer), American Film Institute (Distributor). (1988). *The suitors* [Film].

Eltit, D. (1989). *El padre mio.* Santiago, Chile: Zegers.

Etherton, M. (1982). *The development of African drama.* New York: Africana Publishing.

Euba, F. (1972). *Abiku.* In C. Pieterse, (Ed.), *Five African plays* (pp. 1–29). London and Ibadan: Heinemann.

Ewen, F. (1967). *Bertolt Brecht, his life, his art, and his times.* New York: Citadel Press.

Eyre, C. (Director). Alexie, S. (Screenplay and novel). (1997). *Smoke signals* [Film].

Fanon, F. (1986). *Black skin, white masks.* London: Pluto.

Feingold, M. (1999, December 28). The soldier's music. *The Village Voice,* p. 77.

Ferris, E.G. (1993). *Beyond borders: Refugees, migrants and human rights in the post-cold war era.* Geneva: WCC Publications.

First, R. (1970). *The Barrel of a gun.* London: Allen Lane, The Penguin Press.

Foster, D.W. (1994). *Cultural diversity in Latin American literature.* Albuquerque: University of New Mexico press.

Frankenberg, R. (1993). *The social construction of whiteness.* Minneapolis: University of Minnesota Press.

Fraser, N., & Nicholson, L. (1988). Social criticism without philosophy: An encounter between feminism and postmodernism. In A. Ross, (Ed.), *Universal abandon? The politics of postmodernism* (pp. 83–104). Minneapolis: University of Minnesota Press.

Frears, S. (Director). H. Kureishi (Writer), Warner Home Videos (Distributor). (1985). *My beautiful laundrette.* [Film].

Freire, P. (1993). *Pedagogy of the oppressed.* New York: Continuum.

French, W.H. (1998, July 8). An awkward ally: Diplomats, in promoting democracy, seemed to shun the prime democrat. *The New York Times*, p. A10.

Fukuyama, F. (1992). *The end of history and the last man*. New York: Free Press.

Fuller, C. (1981). *A soldier's play: A drama*. New York: Samuel French.

Gadamer, H.-G. (1982). *Truth and method*. New York: Crossroads.

Garvey, J. & Ignatiev, N. (1997). Toward a new abolitionism: A race traitor manifesto. In M. Hall (Ed.), *Whiteness: A critical reader* (pp. 346–349). New York and London: New York University Press.

Gates, L.S. (1975, August). An interview with Wole Soyinka. *Black World*, 24, 20–48.

Geis, D.R., & Kruger, S.F. (Eds.). (1997). Introduction. *Approaching the millennium: Essays on "Angel in America"* (pp. 3–28). Ann Arbor: University of Michigan Press.

Giroux, H.A. (1992). Post-colonial ruptures and democratic possibilities: Multiculturalism as anti-racist pedagogy. *Cultural Critique*, 21, 5–39.

———. (1997). Racial politics and the pedagogy of whiteness. In M. Hall (Ed.), *Whiteness: A critical reader* (pp. 121–143). New York and London: New York University Press.

Gish, R.F. (1996). *Beyond bounds: Cross-cultural essays on Anglo, American Indian, and Chicano literature*. Albuquerque: University of New Mexico Press.

Glancy, D. (1996). *Weebjob*. In K.A. Perkins, and R. Uno, (Eds.), *Contemporary plays by women of color: An anthology* (pp. 168–190). London and New York: Routledge.

Gomez, M.O. (Director), Cuban Film Institute (ICAIC) (Distributor). (1974). *Now it's up to you (Ustedes tienen la palabra)* [Film].

Gomez, T. (1996). *Inter-tribal*. In K.A. Perkins & R. Uno (Eds.), *Contemporary plays by women of color: An anthology* (pp. 199–214.) London and New York: Routledge.

Grotowski, J. (1968). Preface. In P. Brook (Ed.), *Towards a poor theatre*. New York: Simon and Schuster.

Gurr, A. (1980). Third-world drama: Soyinka and tragedy. In J. Gobbs (Ed.), *Critical perspectives on Wole Soyinka* (pp. 139–146.) Washington, DC: Three Continents Press.

Habermas, J. (1992). P. Dews (Ed.). *Anatomy and solidarity: Interviews*. London: Verso

Hall, S. (1990). Cultural identity and diaspora. In J. Rutherford (Ed.), *Identity, community, culture, difference*. London: Lawrence & Wishart (pp. 86–111).

———. (1991). The local and the global: Globalization and ethnicity. In A.D. King (Ed.), *Culture, globalization and the world-system: Contemporary conditions for the representation of identity* (pp. 19–40). London: Macmillan.

———. (1996). New ethnicities. In D. Morley & K.-H. Chen (Eds.), *Stuart Hall: Critical dialogues in cultural studies*. New York: Routledge.

Halley, J. (1989, June). The politics of the closet: Towards equal protection for gay, lesbian, and bisexual identity. *UCLA Law Review*, 41, 915–976.

Hammar, T. (1990). *Democracy and the nation state*. Brookfield, VT: Avebury.

Hammond, J. (1999, April 10). *Popular education and guerrilla war in El Salvador*. Paper presented at the Socialist Scholars Convention, New York.

Haney, D.P. (1999, January). Aesthetics and ethics in Gadamer, Levinas, and Romanticism: Problems of Phronesis and Techne. *PMLA*, 114, 1. 32–45.

Hansberry, L. (1972). R. Nemiroff (Ed.). J. Lester (Intro.). *Les blancs: The collected last plays of Lorraine Hansberry*. New York: Random House.

———. (1994, October 11). Village intellect revealed. *The New York Times*, Sec. 2, pp. 1, 3.

———. (1995). R. Nemiroff (Intro. and Ed.). *A raisin in the sun and The sign in Sidney Brustein's window*. New York: Vintage Books.

Hauptmann, G. (1965). *The weavers*. Trans. C.R. Mueller. San Francisco: Chandler.

Herman, E. (1988). *Manufacturing consent*. New York: Pantheon.

Hitchcock, P. (1999, May 2). *Yellow earth*. J. Carlson. (Interviewer). City Cinemateque. New York: CUNYtv.

Holden, S. (1999, October 22). Citizens of poverty yearning to be free. *New York Times*, p. E12.

Ibsen, H. (1879). *A doll's house*. Boston: Walter H. Baker.

Irele, A. (1995). Introduction. In A. Irele (Ed.), *"The oriki of a grasshopper" and other plays* (pp. i–xxxviii). Washington, DC: Howard University Press.

Jackson, R.L. (1999, February). White space, white privilege: Mapping discursive inquiry into the self. *Quarterly Journal of Speech*, 85, 38–54.

Jameson, F. (1990). *Signatures of the visible*. New York and London: Routledge.

———. (1991). *Postmodernism: The cultural logic of late capitalism*. Durham, NC: Duke University Press.

Jeyifo, B. (1985). *The truthful lie: Essays in a sociology of African drama*. London: New Beacon Books.

Johnson, R. (1987). *The film industry of Brazil: Culture and the state*. Pittsburgh: University of Pittsburgh Press.

Johnson, R., & Stam, R. (1982). *Brazilian cinema*. Rutherford, NJ: Fairleigh Dickinson University Press.

Kaige, C. (Director), Shanghai Film Studio. (1984). *Yellow earth* [Film].

Katrak, K.H. (1986). *Wole Soyinka and modern tragedy: A Study of dramatic theory and practice*. New York: Greenwood Press.

Keating, A. (1995, December). Interrogating "whiteness," (de)constructing "race." *College English*, 57, 901–918.

Keppel, B. (1995). *The work of democracy: Ralph Bunche, Kenneth B. Clark, Lorraine Hansberry, and the cultural politics of race*. Cambridge, MA and London: Harvard University Press.

Kernaghan, C. (1996). Behind closed doors. In National Labor Committee (Ed.), *The U.S. in Haiti.* New York: National Labor Committee Education Fund.

Kiarostami, A. (Director), Facets Multi-Media (Distributor). (1992). *Where is the friend's house?* [Film].

Kline, G.L. (1989). The use and abuse of Hegel by Nietzsche and Marx. In W. Desmond (Ed.), *Hegel and his critics: Philosophy in the aftermath of Hegel* (pp. 1–34). Albany: State University of New York Press.

Koller, X. (Director and Writer), Miramax Films (Distributor). (1991). *Journey of hope* [Film].

Kopit, A. (1969). *Indians: A play.* New York: Hill & Wang.

Kraidy, M. (1999). The global, the local, and the hybrid: A native ethnography of glocalization. *Critical Studies in Mass Communication,* 16, 4, 456–476.

Kramer, L. (1985). J. Papp (Foreword). *The normal heart.* New York: Samuel French.

Kushner, T. (1993, 1994). *Angels in America: A gay fantasia on national themes. Part I: Millenium approaches, and Part two: Perestroika.* New York: Theatre Communications Group.

Lampert, L. (1986). *Nietzsche's teaching: An interpretation of Thus spoke Zarathustra.* New Haven and London: Yale University Press.

Langer, S. (1968). The dramatic illusion. In J.L. Calderwood & H.E. Toliver (Eds.), *Perspectives on drama* (pp. 251–269). New York, London: Oxford University Press.

Langton, M. (1993). *When I heard it on the radio, and I saw it on the television.* North Sydney: Australian Film Commission.

Ledbetter, J. (1997). *Made possible by . . . : The death of public broadcasting in the United States.* New York: Verso.

Le Goff, J. (1992). *History and memory.* New York: Columbia University Press.

Lengel, L.B. (1999). *Culture and technology in the new Europe: Civic discourse in transformation in post-socialist nations.* Stamford, CT: Ablex Publishing.

Levin, L. (1981). *Human rights: Questions and answers.* Paris: UNESCO Publishing.

Levinson, M. (1999, December 6). Global is as global does? *The Nation,* pp. 42–44).

Lindfors, B. (1976). Wole Soyinka, when are you coming home? *Yale French Studies,* 53, 195–210.

Lindholm, T. (1992). Prospects for research on the cultural legitimacy of human rights: The cases of liberalism and Marxism. In A.A. An-Na'im (Ed.), *Human rights in cross-cultural perspective: A quest for consensus* (pp. 387–426). Philadelphia: University of Pennsylvania Press.

Linfield, S. (1999, December 13). Why, the beloved country. *The Nation,* pp. 26– 35.

Lipsitz, G. (1995, September). The possessive investment in whiteness: Racialized social democracy and the 'White' problem in American studies. *American Quarterly,* 47, 369–87.

Love, N.S. (1986). *Marx, Nietzsche, and modernity*. New York: Columbia University Press.

Lowenthal, M. (1998). On art, angels, and "postmodern fascism." In R. Vorlicky (Ed.), *Tony Kushner in conversation* (pp. 31–58). Ann Arbor: University of Michigan Press.

Lucas, C. (1993, Spring). The eye of the storm. *BOMB*, 43, 30–35.

Lucas, S.E. (1998). *The art of public speaking* (6th ed.). Boston, MA: McGraw-Hill.

Lukacs, G. (1983). *The historical novel*. (H. Mitchell and S. Mitchell, Trans.) Lincoln and London: University of Nebraska Press.

Madison, K.J. (1999). Legitimation crisis and containment: The "anti-racist-white-hero" film. *Critical Studies in Mass Communication*, 16, 4, 399–416.

Maduakor, O. (1986). Wole Soyinka: An introduction to his writing. New York: Garland.

Maggenti, M. (Director), Samuel Goldwyn Films (Distributor). (1995). *The incredibly true adventures of two girls in love*. [Film].

Magome, P.V. (1996). The cinemas of sub-Saharan Africa. In G. Nowell-Smith (Ed.), *The Oxford history of world cinema* (pp. 663–672.) Oxford and New York: Oxford University Press.

Majidi, M. (Director and Writer). Miramax Video (Distributor). (1998). *Children of paradise*, [Film].

Makhmalbaf, M. (Director and Writer). New Yorker Films (Distributor). (1996). *A moment of innocence* [Film].

———, (Director and Writer). New Yorker Films (Distributor). (1996). *Gabbeh* [Film].

Marcuse, H. (1964). *One-dimensional man: Studies in the ideology of advanced industrial society*. Boston: Beacon Press.

———. (1970). The end of utopia. In *Five lectures: Psychoanalysis, politics, utopia*. Boston: Beacon Press.

Marin, C. (Director and Writer). MCA Home Video (Distributor). (1987). *Born in east L.A.* [Film].

Mayne, J. (1993). *Cinema and spectatorship*. London and New York: Routledge.

Mehrjui, D. (Director), New Yorker Films (Distributor). (1997). *Leila* [Film].

Mehta, D. (Director and writer). (1996). New Yorker Films (Distributor). *Fire* [Film].

Merrill, J.C. (1999, February 5). *Culture, communication, and control: A quest for order and social harmony*. Paper presented at the Sixteenth Intercultural Communication Conference, Coral Gables, Florida.

Minwalla, F. (1997). When girls collide: Considering race in *Angels in America*. In D.R. Geis & S.F. Kruger (Eds.), *Approaching the millennium: Essays on "Angels in America"* (pp. 221–240). Ann Arbor: University of Michigan Press.

Molinaro, E. (Director). Song Pictures Classics (Distributor). (1978). *La cage aux folles*. [Film].

Mongia, P. (1992). Introduction. In P. Mongia (Ed.), *Contemporary postcolonial theory: A reader* (pp. 3–26). London and New York: Arnold.

Montag, M. (1997). The universalization of whiteness: Racism and enlightenment. In M. Hill (Ed.), *Whiteness: A critical reader* (pp. 281–293). New York: New York University Press.

Moreiras, A. (1996). The aura of Testimonio. In G.M. Gugelberger (Ed.), *The real thing: Testimonial discourse and Latin America* (pp. 192–224). Durham: Duke University Pess.

Morell, K.L. (Ed.). (1975). *In person: Achebe, Awoonor and Soyinka.* Seattle: University of Washington Press.

Naficy, H. (1996). Iranian cinema. In G. Nowell-Smith (Ed.), *The Oxford history of world cinema* (pp. 672–678). Oxford, Eng.: Oxford University Press.

Nakayama, T.K. & Krizek, R.L. (1995). Whiteness: A strategic rhetoric. *Quarterly Journal of Speech*, 81, 201–309.

Nava, G. (Director/Writer). (1983). *El norte* [Film]. A. Thomas (Cowriter/Producer).

Nemiroff, R. (1995). The 101 "final performances" of *Sidney Brustein*. In R. Nemiroff (Ed.), *A raisin in the sun and The sign in Sidney Brustein's window* (pp. 78–94). New York: Vintage Books.

Nicholes, M. (Director), Miramax (Distributor). (1996). *The birdcage* [Film].

Nkosi, L. (1981). Tasks and masks: Themes and styles of African Literature. Harlow, England: Longman.

Nussbaum, M.C. (1986). *The fragility of goodness: Luck and ethics in Greek tragedy and philosophy.* Cambridge, Eng.: Cambridge University Press.

———. (1997) *Cultivating humanity: A classical defense of reform in liberal education.* Cambridge, MA: Harvard University Press.

Odets, C. (1935). *Three plays: Awake and sing; Waiting for Lefty; The day I die.* New York: Covici-Friede.

Omotoso, K. (1996). *Achebe or Soyinka? A study in contrasts.* London and Munich: Hans Zell Publishers.

Onishi, N. (1998, August 22). Mandella says Congo's neighbors will hold talks on revolt. *The New York Times*, p. A5.

Onwueme, T.A. (1993). *Three plays: The broken calabash, Parables for a season, The reign of Wazobia.* Detroit, MI: Wayne State University Press.

Ortiz, S. (1981). Toward a national Indian literature: Cultural authenticity in nationalism. *MELUS*, 8, 2, 7–12.

Orwell, G. (1953). Marrakech. In G. Orwell (Ed.), *Such, such were the joys* (pp. 143–154). New York: Harcourt Brace.

Osofisan, F. (1982). *No More the Wasted Breed.* In *The oriki of a grasshopper and other plays.* Washington, D.C.: Howard University Press.

———. (1990). *Birthdays are not for dying.* Lagos, Nigeria: Malthouse Press.

———. (1995). *The oriki of a grasshopper.* Ed. A. Irele. Washington, D.C.: Howard University Press.

Over, W. (1999). *Human rights in the international public sphere: Civic discourse for the 21st century.* Stamford, CT: Ablex Publishing.

Panahi, J. (Director). (1996). Evergreen (Distributor). *White balloon* [Film].

Pear, R. (1999, December 12). President Clinton admits "don't ask" policy has been a failure. *The New York Times*, pp. A1, 44.

Perego, E. (1998). Intimate moments and secret gardens: The artist as amateur photographer. In M. Frizot (Ed.), *A new history of photography* (pp. 219–245). Cologne, Ger.: Koenemann.

Perkins, K.A., & Uno, R. (Eds.). (1996). *Contemporary plays by women of color: An anthology*. London and New York: Routledge.

Pfeil, F. (1997). Sympathy for the devils: Notes on some white guys in the ridiculous class war. In M. Hill (Ed.), *Whiteness: A critical reader* (pp. 21– 34). New York: New York University Press.

Pierce, K. (Director), Miramax Films (Distributor). (1999). *Boys don't cry* [Film].

Redmond, E.B. (1993). Introduction: Tess Onwueme's soular system. *Three plays* (pp. 4–28). Detroit, MI: Wayne State University Press.

Reinelt, J. (1997). Notes on *Angels in America* as American epic theatre. In D.R. Geis & S.F. Kruger (Eds.), *Approaching the millennium: Essays on Angels in America.* (pp. 234–244). Ann Arbor: University of Michigan Press.

Reuters, Ltd. (1998, July 1). U.N. chief holds talks with ruler of Nigeria. *The New York Times*, p. 3.

Richards, S. (1987, May). Nigerian independence onstage: Responses from "Second Generation" playwrights. *Theatre Journal*, 39, 2, 215–227.

———. (1992). Brecht in Nigeria: A consideration of plays by Wole Soyinka and Femi Osofisan. In E. Schild, (Ed.), *On stage: Proceedings of the Fifth International Janheinz Jahn Symposium on theatre in Africa* (pp. 178–199). Goettingen: Editions RE.

Rickman, H.P. (1961). Introduction. In H.P. Rickman (Ed.), *Wilhelm Dilthey: Pattern and meaning in history* (pp. 4–35). New York: Harper.

Ricoeur, P. (1976). *Interpretation theory: Discourse and the surplus of meaning*. Fort Worth: Texas Christian University Press.

Rieff, D. (1999, February 22). The false dawn of civil society. *The Nation*, pp. 11– 16.

Riker, D. (Director), Zeitgeist Films (Distributor). (1999). *The city (La ciudad)* [Film].

———. (1999, November 25). Interview. Democracy now. Pacifica Radio (WBAI, New York). [Radio].

Rocha, G. (1982). Ema estetica da fome. In R. Johnson & R. Stam (Eds.), *Brazilian cinema* (pp. 68–71). Rutherford, NJ: Fairleigh Dickinson University Press.

Rudnick, P. (1994; film 1995). *Jeffrey*. Samuel French.

Ruppert, J. (1995). *Mediation in contemporary Native American fiction*. Norman, OK: University of Oklahoma Press.

Rushdie, S. (1987). *The jaguar smile: A Nicaraguan journey*. New York and London: Penguin Books.

Said, E. (1990). Yeats and decolonization. In D. Walder (Ed.), *Literature in the modern world* (pp.191–212). Oxford: Oxford University Press.

Salles, W. (Director), Sony Pictures Classics (Distributor). (1998). *Central station* [Film].

——. (1998), February/March). Interview. *Angelika Filmbill.* New York: Sony Pictures Entertainment.

Sanders, B. (1998, July). Who does the IMF represent? *The Progressive,* pp. 34–35.

Savran, D. (1997). Ambivalence, utopia, and a queer sort of materialism: How *Angels in America* reconstructs the nation. In D.R. Geis & S.F. Kruger (Eds.), *Approaching the millennium: Essays on Angels in America* (pp. 79–91). Ann Arbor: University of Michigan Press.

Sayles, J. (Director), Sony Pictures Classics (Distributor). (1998). *Men with guns* [Film].

Sayles, John. (1998, February/March). Interview. *Angelika Filmbill,* 12–18.

Schatz, T. (1999, 5/12 April). Show me the money: In search of hits, the industry may go broke. *The Nation,* pp. 26–31.

Sembene, O. (Director). (1966). *Black girl (La noire de . . .)* [Film].

——. (Director). (1992). *Guelwaar* [Film].

Shelley, P.B. (1965). *A defense of poetry.* Indianapolis: Bobbs-Merrill.

Smith, A.D. (1996). *Fires in the mirror.* In J.V. Hatch & T. Shine (Eds.), *Black theatre USA: Plays by African Americans.* (pp. 87–195). New York: The Free Press.

Soyinka, W. (1971). *Madmen and specialists.* New York and London: Hill and Wang.

——. (1972). *The man died: Prison notes of Wole Soyinka.* London: Rex Collings.

——. (1973). *The Strong breed.* In *Collected plays.* Oxford and New York: Oxford University Press.

——. (1976). *Ogun abibiman.* London: Rex Collings.

——. (1988). The writer in a modern African state. In *Art dialogue and outrage.* (pp. 15–20). Ibadan, Nigeria: New Horn Press.

——. (1999). *The burden of memory: The muse of forgiveness.* New York and Oxford: Oxford University Press.

Stagebill. (1999a, February). (No author given, no title given). New York: The Film Society of Lincoln Center, p. 4.

——. (1999, November). (No author given). Two masterpieces by Mohsen Makhmalbak. New York: The Film Society of Lincoln Center, pp. 7–8.

Sterngold, J. (1998, June 21). Able to laugh at their people, not just cry for them. *The New York Times,* Sec. 4, pp.12–14.

Tapper, R. (1997). *Frontier nomads of Iran: A political and social history of the Shahsevan.* Cambridge, Eng.: Cambridge University Press.

Taylor, H.L., Jr. (1995, September). The hidden face of racism. *American Quarterly,* 47, 395–408.

Terkel, S. & Hansberry, L. (1984, November). Make new sounds: Studs Terkel interviews Lorraine Hansberry. *American Theatre,* 7–15.

Thompson, R.F. (1999, June 20). (Interview). City Cinematique. New York: City University of New York Television (CUNYtv).

Tierney-Tello, M.B. (1999, January). Testimony, ethics, and the aesthetic in Diamela Eltit. *PMLA,* 114,1, 78–96.

Toer, P.A. (1999, April 18). The book that killed colonialism. *The New York Times Magazine,* pp. 112–114.

Troche, R. (Director and Writer), Samuel Goldwyn Films (Distributor) (1994). *Go fish* [Film].

Vizenor, G. (1998). *Fugitive poses: Native American Indian scenes of absence and presence*. Lincoln and London: University of Nebraska Press.

Wack, J. (Director), Miramax (Distributor). (1989). *Powwow Highway* [Film].

Wallace, N. (1996). One flea spore. In D. Dromgoole (ed.), *Bush theatre play* (pp. 284–341). London: Faber & Faber.

Wang, R.-Yu. (1999, January 9). (Lecture). *A random life: New visions, new voices*. New York: American Museum of Natural History.

Watts, R. (1970, November 16). Grim fruits of colonialism. *The New York Post*, p. 32.

West, C. (1993). *Prophetic thought in modern times*. Monroe, ME: Common Courage Press.

Wilkinson, N. (1978). Literary incomprehension: Wole Soyinka's own way with a mode. *Theatre Research International*, 1, 1, 44–53.

Williams, R. (1952). *Drama, from Ibsen to Eliot*. London: Chatto & Windus.

———. (1963). *Culture and society, 1780–1950*. Edinburgh: Chatto & Windus.

———. (1977). Social environment and theatrical environment: The case of English naturalism. In M. Axton and R. Williams (Eds.), *English drama: Forms and development* (pp. 203–223). Cambridge and London: Cambridge University Press.

———. (1982). *The sociology of culture*. New York: Schocken Books.

———. (1989a). *The politics of modernism: Against the new conformists*. T. Pinkney (Ed. and Introduction). London and New York: Verso.

———. (1989b). *Raymond Williams on television: Selected writings*. A. O'Connor (Ed). London: Routledge.

Wilmer, F. (1993). *The indigenous voice in world politics: Since time immemorial*. Newbury Park, CA: Sage.

Wise, R. & Robbins, G. (Directors). (1961). *West side story* [Film].

Wolf, M. (1999). *Another American asking and telling* [Videotape]. New York Public Library.

Wolfe, G.C. (1996). *The colored museum*. In J.V. Hatch & T. Shine (Eds.), *Black theatre USA: Plays by African Americans* (pp. 173–231). New York: The Free Press.

Wordsworth, W. (1966). The prelude. In E. De Selincourt & H. Darbishire (Eds.), *Poetical works of William Wordsworth* (pp. 381–523). Oxford: Clarendon Press.

Wright, D. (1993). *Wole Soyinka revisited*. New York: Twayne Publishers.

Xiaolian, C. (Director). (1989). *The women's story* [Film].

Yudice, G. (1988). Marginality and the ethics of survival. In A. Ross (Ed.), *Universal abandon? The politics of postmodernism* (pp. 214–236). Minneapolis: University of Minnesota Press.

Zavala, I. M. (1992). *Colonialism and culture: Hispanic modernism and the social imaginary*. Bloomington and Indianapolis: Indiana University Press.

Zelizer, B. (1995). Reading the past against the grain: The shape of memory studies. *Critical Studies in Mass Communication*, 12, 2, 214–239.

Zinn, H. (1999). *The future of history*. Monroe, ME: Common Courage Press.

AUTHOR INDEX

SUBJECT INDEX

About the Author

WILLIAM OVER is Associate Professor of English and Speech at St. John's University, New York. He is the author of *Human Rights in the International Public Sphere* (Ablex, 1999), which won the Best Book Award in 1999 from the International and Intercultural Communication Division of the National Communication Association.